About the author

I was born in 1957 in Lusaka, which was the capital of what was then known as Northern Rhodesia, now Zambia. I was sent to boarding school in Southern Rhodesia, now Zimbabwe, at the age of seven and then on to school in Cape Town, South Africa. Dad was English, as far as I knew, and my mother was Swedish. A strange mix one would think. In 1972 all of us left South Africa and journeyed by ship to England where, on arrival, my two brothers and I were dispatched off to boarding school once more. I have remained in England all my life and am the father of three beautiful daughters. I now live in the Kent countryside with my wife and our retriever dog.

HARRY'S BOYS

Richard Barker

HARRY'S BOYS

Vanguard Press

A CIP catalogue record for this title is
available from the British Library.

ISBN 978 1 78465 210 4

*Vanguard Press is an imprint of
Pegasus Elliot MacKenzie Publishers Ltd.*
www.pegasuspublishers.com

First Published in 2017

**Vanguard Press
Sheraton House Castle Park
Cambridge England**

Printed & Bound in Great Britain

Dedication

For my father
Paul Derrick Barker

PROLOGUE

It was dawn on the morning of 16th June 1940 in a tiny fishing village on the southern Brittany coastline, only twelve days since the last of the Allied soldiers had been evacuated from the beaches of Dunkirk. The German military machine was sweeping through northern France. They had arrived in Vannes, only a few miles from their hiding place.

The sun had not yet risen and a damp mist swirled around the small harbour. The tiny fishing boat, which was to be their last chance of escape, gently bobbed and nudged against the stone harbour wall. The cobbled quayside glistened in the moonlight, reflecting rays of light from the shiny surface of the dark grey pebbles. A lone seagull dipped towards the calm dock water, playing on the breeze. The reflection of the moon cast a streak of light across the gentle sway of the ocean's surface beyond.

Englishman, Harry, stood before his sons in his knee length coat, hat and black shoes. The two young boys wore grey coats, falling to just below the knee, brown leather shoes with laces done up tightly, grey socks up to their knees and woolly hats covering their ears. Beside them, their small leather suitcases with heavy straps and large brass buckles, contained all they had. They stood behind their father, their hearts filled with anticipation.

Before them stood the burly French fisherman with whom Harry had struck the deal the previous evening. He wore a tatty flat cap, which hung to the side, and a thick green coat scarred with stains from years of fighting the power of the ocean and living the life of a fisherman. Beside the boat stood three

Polish soldiers in battle-worn and torn uniforms looking towards them with desperation and fear in their expression.

"Monsieur," said the Frenchman through his heavy dark beard, holding out his hands the size of plates. "I can take you but... I am sorry, I cannot take the children. I must take the soldiers. My boat is small and fully loaded. There is no room for the children."

Harry gazed from beneath the rim of his felt hat, over the shoulder of the fisherman, towards the scene of the soldiers beyond, his heart aching. He looked up to the sky for help as the torment of being faced with this decision tore through his body.

"Do I leave the boys behind and take this last chance to escape back to England or do I stay and face the Nazi machine?"

CHAPTER ONE

Twenty-two years earlier…

It's cold and wet. I have been on this front-line stint for six days so far. Another three to go and then I will be back behind the lines for two days of respite. The weather has been bloody miserable. Grey and damp every day. You can smell the odour of rotting flesh from torn and dismembered bodies of our friends, drifting into the trench. It sticks to the back of my throat, making me want to retch. The stretcher-bearers have been out several times to scour for the living after the last bombardment, which was followed by a rush over the top and then back again. It took three days before the screaming and groaning finally stopped. If you had been hit whilst out there and not been killed outright or rescued by the men with the white armbands, you were most likely to be dead by now.

But today there's just the splatter of rain on mud and puddles. It's still grim and wretched.

And then:

'Take cover! Take cover! Incoming shells! Incoming shells!'

Boom! Boom! Boom! Artillery shells pound into the damp earth around us, followed by a shower of lumps of earth falling onto the waterlogged ground. The acrid stench of sulphur drifts across the ceiling of our trench. Another explosion, followed by another. We know they're getting closer as showers of mud begin to splatter on our tin helmets. The sound of the explosions varies, depending on whether the shell lands in a pool of water, on firm ground or in a crater. And when they land in a trench the sound differs again. The explosions are followed by the spray of dirt coming back to earth and then, after a short delay, the screaming begins.

Boom! Another shell lands – nearer. We all duck down low with our heads buried in our chests, praying that the next doesn't land in our trench. It's been going on for several hours. When will it stop? In some bizarre way we wish it wouldn't stop because, when it does, the silence will be pierced by the screams and groans of our friends in pain. Whilst the bombardment goes on we cannot hear the begging pleas of our injured and dying men. These sounds are much more painful and frightening than the thumping of bombs in the earth. Will the cessation of the bombardment be followed by orders to move forward towards the trenches we have spent several weeks staring at, or will we stay put this time? They are only a stone's throw from ours. No more than fifty yards. We just wait. We can hear the bullets flying around above us, whistling over our heads as we crouch in this muddy trench. A peek over the parapet and we see the enemy running and shouting through the drifts of smoke. Where are they going? What are they going to do next? It's all so confusing. Put your trust in the commander. He knows what is happening. He will tell us what to do and when. No point speculating or guessing. Just wait for orders. Just wait.

It is dark, cold and damp. We've been hiding in this trench for what seems like forever. It's an extreme contrast, leaving the comforts of home to come and live like a wild animal in a sewer. Food stocks are low and the tinned meats are far from appetising. We huddle together in this dark and treacherous hole in the ground, waiting for someone to shout orders. No one seems to know what's going on, but we sit and wait for orders. We believe that there's a reason for what's happening, but no one tells us anything. Our lives are held in a ditch of dirty brown mud.

Ten feet out, protruding from the earth like the handle of a dagger, stands the remnants of a signpost reading "Abbeville 72kms". I have been looking at this bloody sign for days. I wonder which way Abbeville might be. The sign is mounted on the torn stump of a wooden post, the rest of the timber nowhere to be seen, most likely having been blown to bits by a shell. The sign may have travelled some distance as there is no clear evidence of a road. It may be a little further to Abbeville than the sign says. Or maybe a little closer. Who knows? I'm not going to venture out to retrieve the dagger, so it just stands there looking at me as I hide in my muddy hole.

Boom! A searing pain rushes through my ears. Lumps of mud and warm flesh hit my face and chest, followed by a heat wave of wind which throws me off my feet and sideways down the trench. The young lad beside me has disintegrated. I did not know him. I had not even asked his name. He had only arrived yesterday and taken up the space alongside me; a boy of no more than eighteen years, with a soft white, pale face and blue eyes. I had glanced at him and smiled. Now he was no more.

I have been blown down the line of the trench by the shock wave of the blast. The lad's shredded torso litters the trench walls. It is difficult to distinguish between the parts of his uniform, the bits of his body and the reddened mud. I can see, but I can't hear anything. My body is completely numb. For what seems like forever I still have no hearing or sensation, but I can see the mayhem and panic of soldiers running over bodies and bumping into one another. Some fall, a limb missing, but try to stand and run. Some lie in dislocated forms. Part of our trench has become a crater.

'Harry! Harry! Can you hear me, mate?'

'Yeh,' I mumble. I close my eyes. No pain, no feeling at all. I am tired. So tired.

I hear muffled shouting. I am being jostled about on a canvas stretcher. I look to my left and see soldiers running in regimented lines. To my right I see another stretcher. An arm hangs from the side, prevented from falling to the ground only by a few sinews of flesh and fabric. The air is clean and the light is bright. I can see the red cross on the front of the helmet of the man by my feet. He is walking briskly but not running. He looks down at me and says, 'You'll be all right, mate. No serious damage. We'll have you in the medical tent in no time. You'll be all right, mate. Don't worry.' I feel wet and cold and there is a jabbing pain in my right foot.

I don't have a sense of time, but I am awake in a tent with rows of beds closely aligned. Above are dim domed lights stretching the length of the canvas. The tent is dark green and v-shaped, like a loft conversion with shallow sides before the angle of the roof line heads upward to the pitch. The beds are snap-out x-frames made from wood, with a canvas mattresses. Some folded fabric for a pillow, dark brown in colour. An aching pain travels up my leg, reminding me of why I am here in a field hospital. To my left and right are green beds occupied by fellow soldiers with various bandages and strapping. No one is talking. It is quiet, with only the occasional groan. On the opposite side of the tent is another row of beds, all occupied by soldiers with more bandages and strappings. It is difficult to tell if it is night or day. There are no windows to give any signs of daylight. I am not sure whether the lights are on because it is night or because there is so little light in the tent.

I sit up and look from left to right in search of someone who can tell me where I am and what is wrong with me. Suddenly there is a loud shout from immediately opposite my bed:

'Jack! Jack! Oh, God, I don't want to die! I can't see. Help, Jack, please. I can't see you, mate! Oh, God! Jack. Mate. Where are you?'

Coughing interrupts the calling out. From the far left of the tent two figures burst through the canvas doorway. One a doctor in a bloodstained knee-length coat and the other a nurse in a pristine, pale blue dress and white bonnet with a red cross in the centre. They both walk at a brisk pace towards the soldier, who is still coughing and now struggling for breath, heaving gulps for air, followed by a deep, gurgling retch. The nurse arrives first and pulls back the bedclothes. The doctor moves round to the far side of the bed and pushes the patient on to his side. The coughing resumes, followed by a rush of thick liquid hitting the floor. The breathing eases and the two medical personnel look at each other and exchange quiet words. A gentle shaking of the head by the doctor indicates that it is just a matter of time. The nurse makes her way back towards the canvas doorway. Moments later, another, younger nurse comes through, carrying a bucket and cloths. She makes her way directly to the bedside of the soldier, who is now moaning gently. Words are said, but they are impossible to decipher.

The nurse is about five foot six and carries her head high. Elegant and stylish. She has dark hair, as far as I can tell from the wisps peeping out beneath her cap. And dark brown eyes – but it is difficult to say just how dark in the dimness of the tent. Her slim profile glides the length of the ward, as if on skates, and stops beside the bed opposite. A cloth is drawn from the bucket and her next movement makes my heart miss a beat. She crouches down on her heels, leaning slightly, and whisks the cloth from left to right. Her back remains straight and her head tilts forward. It is not a task that many would wish to perform, mopping up the fleshy blood of a dying man, but the nurse carries it out with the most amazing dignity and grace.

I lie on my bed with my head tilted forward, watching events unfold before me. A soldier, scared and alone. Confused and in pain. Lost and dying. Having completed the clearing-up task, the young nurse sits quietly on the bed beside the man. With her left hand, she takes his, and cups it with her right. She leans forward and whispers something to him. His groaning stops for a few moments. He tilts his head towards hers. I see him clench her hand. He lies still and calm. It is the most beautiful thing. With bandages covering the top half of the soldier's head, he cannot see the nurse. But what she has to offer gives him an inner strength and he warms to her presence. His agitation eases and he is able to receive her comfort. His breathing calms and he settles, gently sliding into a light sleep, away from the noise of gunfire, explosions and stench of damp mud. Away from Jack.

I wake from a deep sleep and at first I am confused as to my whereabouts. I am hungry. Then I recall the events that occurred before I slept, but I still don't know whether it is day or night. I guess that I have slept for several hours. The pain in my foot is now a dull ache. I realise that the whole place now seems lighter. Perhaps the previous day had been overcast and grey, but now the tent has a bright glow about it.

Once again I see the nurse, walking slowly towards me from the far end. She is glancing from left to right as she passes each bed. I look across to the one opposite as my mind runs through what took place there before I fell asleep. There is no one there.

I look back down the ward. The young nurse is still gliding towards me. I am transfixed by her elegance, and my head is swimming. Perhaps I have spent too long in the trenches and away from the female form. Maybe I am suffering from a head injury? Whatever it is, it feels like something beyond my control. Her gentle sway from side to side is magical to my eyes. I have never experienced this before. What is wrong with me, that for no reason I can fathom, I seem to be enchanted by a total stranger? A serene, lonely young figure wandering between rows of quietly moaning men, who are littered with dreadful injuries and bandages, has turned me into an emotional wreck. I am totally unable to control my emotions towards this complete stranger. I simply cannot take my eyes off her.

As she moves closer, I cannot resist the urge to raise my hand to attract her attention. She catches sight of my movement and quickens her pace as she moves towards me. A beautiful smile lights her face as she makes eye contact. I have not seen anything so beautiful in months.

Before my injuries were sustained, I had been home on leave several times and had gone out with friends and family. We had been to the theatre, to dances and shows, to pubs and dinner parties. I have laughed and cried with them all, but none of them have ever had this bizarre emotional impact on me. It is a feeling I have never had about anyone I have ever met.

She closes in on my bedside, and she seems to be smiling not just with her mouth but with her eyes too, now.

'Hello,' she whispers. 'You're awake. How are you feeling, Monsieur?'

My God, that smile, together with that sweet French accent. I am blown away. For several moments I cannot speak. I must look like a dumbstruck baby, gawking up at her. I try to say something, but my mouth refuses to respond to my brain. It feels like an age, but is probably only a few seconds. She is simply magnificent. She has obviously had experience in greeting soldiers who have been brought into the field hospital with all kinds of injuries. Some who perhaps could not speak. Some who just gazed into space. She offers time and space to respond. I have no excuse – I am just struck dumb by her soft and gentle smile. I am embarrassed. I hope she has not seen the uncontrollable affection and admiration written on my face. I turn to one side and, unexpectedly stammering slightly, I say:

'Hello, nurse. Could you tell me what happened to the soldier who was in the bed opposite?'

'I am sorry, but he passed away in the night,' she replies.

I have lost my train of thought and do not know what to say. I really want to ask where I am and what the state of play is with my foot, but these seem stupid questions. And why have I developed a stammer? What is happening to me?

The next day I am transported by ambulance out to a casualty clearing station a few miles behind the lines. The place is buzzing with trucks and ambulances. A small town of tents and wooden huts has grown up in the countryside.

Soldiers are huddled in groups. Some sit on wooden benches chatting, some are smoking, and others march out of the base in rows. Between the various structures, medics run, with their familiar white armbands, carrying stretchers. The purpose of the white armbands is to offer these brave men some protection when collecting wounded soldiers from the trenches, craters and mud pools on the front line. Unbelievably, the Germans do not shoot at soldiers wearing white armbands. They are, however, unprotected from shells and shrapnel. The trenches are so close to one another that men with these armbands can easily be identified and generally they escape when coming into the cross hairs of the telescopic sights of a German sniper.

I am carried into a tent and placed on another canvas snap-out x-frame bed and left there. I sit up. And then, taking a deep breath, I swing my legs out over the side of the bed. The pain has subsided. I am feeling almost human again. A dull ache from my foot, but nothing too uncomfortable. I wonder whether I will see that girl again.

It is only a few days before I am back on my feet. The injury has not been too bad, but I am still not going to get my foot into a boot for a few weeks. Three days after my arrival at the casualty clearing station I am taken by truck, along with ten other injured soldiers, further behind the front line to the South Midland Casualty Clearing Station at Amiens.

The centre is made up of a collection of what seem like derelict buildings. Walls and windows are missing and most of the structures are surrounded by heaps of bricks and rubble. Between the mounds of masonry and the broken houses, camp beds have been set up in rows, both inside and out. There are hundreds of soldiers hobbling around on crutches and in wheelchairs. Many seem to have limb injuries and are here for recovery before returning to their units on the front line. Nurses in pale blue dresses meander between the soldiers, offering conversation and a little cheer. The atmosphere is much brighter than at the centre where I spent the previous three days.

The ten of us are unloaded from the truck and instructed to report to the enrolment centre.

During the following two weeks, I make some good friends and we are to remain here together for three weeks before I am declared fit for service.

The course of the war, though, has changed dramatically during my recuperation. While making my way back to my regiment on 11th November 1918, the hostilities are declared over.

Everywhere you look, there is jubilation!

Together with two of the friends I made in the casualty clearing centre, we abandon our plans to return to our regiment and decide instead to make for Brussels, from where we will travel to the coast.

The roads are packed full of soldiers, horses and vehicles of various sizes. There is mud everywhere as winter has begun to bring rain and cold.

Within two days we have found our way to Brussels and are welcomed by hordes of civilians lining the streets, waving flags and throwing confetti. I am one of six on a small military pick-up truck driving through the city streets, surrounded by ecstatic crowds shouting and singing. It is an unbelievable experience. Cheering women are running up to total strangers, kissing and hugging them. Children are being carried by mothers and elderly folk are hanging out of windows. Men brandish bottles of wine, brandy and champagne. The atmosphere is electric. In amongst the crowd I spot a familiar face. A girl I know. Oh my God! Is it her? Yes – it's the nurse from the medical centre! I jump off the back of the truck, falling into the crowd of people. I lose her just for a moment but, jumping as high as I can to see over the mass of heads, I catch sight of her again. I push and barge my way through as the cheering crowds hug and manhandle me. I finally break through into a small, quieter area and, dead ahead, I see her. It really is her. I feel my stomach tighten. I catch her glance and smile. Astonished to see me, she smiles back. I walk towards her, our eyes fixed upon each other. My heart pounds heavier and I feel the emotion rise within me. She smiles. I can no longer hear all the cheering and shouting around me. I am lost in her eyes.

CHAPTER TWO

I was not the only member of our family who had been fighting in this war. I was one of ten children, with six brothers and three sisters. We had lost one boy at an early age and my father would say, 'Had we not lost Lionel, we could have put out our own cricket side!'

My youngest brother, George, had been killed near Dernancourt in the last few months of the war, but the rest of us were alive and well. I was not the youngest. Kate and Frank were younger and all my other siblings older.

We were a close and tightly knit family, headed by my father Walter and mother Alice. My father had been running the family business in market gardening since he had taken it over from his father. Every one of my brothers and sisters had been born here in Barnes, southwest London, and our family had lived in the area for as long as I knew. My grandfather, Charles, was born in Essex, but moved to Barnes long before my father was born. He was one of five children, with one brother and three sisters. He, too, had grown vegetables and had acquired a Royal Charter as supplier to the King. My father had continued to run and develop the business when his father retired and all of us children were involved throughout our formative years, working in the fields, driving tractors, packing and planting. It was a good life.

We moved to a larger house in Barnes, known as Tangier Lodge, in 1896, when I was about eight years old. My mother and father remained until they passed away in the early 1930s, whilst my sister Beatrice stayed on. The rest of my brothers and sisters gradually moved away from the family home, but

Beatrice never did. She was the linchpin and held the family together throughout. Father was a traditionalist through and through and we lived a Victorian-style existence with all the hierarchical structures and procedures strongly adhered to in our day-to-day lives. Beatrice followed his methodology and, as Mother and Father grew elderly, she took control and ensured things remained as they had always been.

Tangier Lodge was a classic Victorian house: big and double-fronted, with several chimneystacks dominating the roofline. The front door was large and heavy, of singular hardwood with wonderful double-breasted stained-glass panels. The true effect was not really appreciable from outside, but was witnessed in late spring when the sun rose directly outside the front door and the entrance hall was lit up with a colourful display of filtered and tinted light. On entering the hall, to the left there was a morning room adjacent to a spacious dining room with a huge wooden sideboard. Behind that was the lounge with French doors opening onto the large garden. There were coal fires everywhere and a spacious hallway featured a wooden staircase that led to several bedrooms. The servants' quarters, on the top floor, were accessed from a separate stairway in the kitchen. Alongside the stairs, a passageway led through to a typical Victorian kitchen with a substantial range, another open coal fire, and then on into the scullery. Beyond the scullery there were store rooms, coal cellars and a cellar below that. All in all, it was a substantial family home.

The driveway was made of hard-packed pale brown gravel with a neatly cut-grass edge on both sides. The garden was mostly laid to lawn, as Mother and Father were not keen gardeners – somewhat ironic, given that their trade was market gardening. Some established trees were dotted around the lawned areas, with a large oak shrouding the centre green, around which the driveway circled. This was not a U-shaped drive with two entrances, which would have been considered decadent and wasteful, but a single drive with a roundabout in front of the house. There was adequate set-down and parking for several carriages. It was only in the early 1920s that the horse-drawn carriages slowly began to be replaced by motor vehicles. It was a grand Victorian house of a kind generally owned by more successful landowners, although it would be true to say that my father had worked hard to reach his standing. I grew up at Tangier Lodge and I was still there when I joined up and headed off to France.

On my return from France, I made my way home, to be greeted by Mother and Father and welcomed back into the family home. It was a good feeling. We had always had an organised and structured way of life and the farms were doing brisk business.

For several years after the war, the demand for food and fresh produce continued. The farms had been growing everything possible to support the war effort and there was to be no let-up now that it had ended. The business had grown and more land had been purchased and rented to maximise output. Machinery had increasingly replaced manual methods, but nevertheless, the number of workers had almost doubled while I was away. There were now many women working the land and involved in the administration of the business. However, family traditions had not changed. True to form, my father had ensured that everything ran like clockwork – from the management of the farms, right through to church on Sunday, followed by lunch, which all family members were expected to attend. My mother always ensured that a hearty meal was prepared and we all sat around the dining table in allocated seats, with her at one end and father at the other. We were tended to by servants, but Alice was a hands-on mother and, although she may not have actually cooked the food, she decided what we were to be given and how it was to be prepared. Sunday lunch was a formal affair and was an opportunity for the family to be together. We lived in a bubble: strict manners, formalities and behaviour. No one sat before Mother and Father had been seated. Grace was said before every meal and the King was toasted. The family had not changed the way it did things for many years. It was a ritual and as far as my parents were concerned, it was the correct way things were to be done, and that was that.

The end of the war brought much suffering to Europe. Tens of thousands of people had been displaced. Refugees were everywhere. Many homeless and lost. There were shortages of almost everything. Soldiers returned to unemployment and many families had lost their father-figure. Towns and villages around the conflict zone in Belgium and northern France had been levelled. There was no work and very little food. Men were in short supply and as the Allied soldiers returned home, the ratio of men to women increased. Europe was poor and suffering.

The defeated Germans faced terrible retribution. The French, in particular, had cause to want vengeance. Tens of thousands had been lost, and for what? Europe plunged into despair, starvation, endless vicious vengeance killings and homelessness. Europe was a desolate place.

In England and America, however, the end of the war saw the beginning of the Roaring Twenties, when both economies began to boom. Whilst Britain danced, continental Europe suffered on.

My courtship of Abbi began in earnest. At first, she would spend a week or so with us at Tangier Lodge and I would accompany her back to Brussels and take the opportunity to stay a few days. Over the next few years, she became a regular visitor and a friendship grew between her and my younger sister Kate. While I was busy running the farm, she would pass the days with Kate enjoying lunches in London and attending the odd business meeting with some hotels and hospitality venues we supplied. My older brothers had left farming to become stockbrokers in the city, but were nevertheless still actively involved with the family. Business was brisk as the era of the Flappers and jazz clubs blossomed into full bloom. It was fashionable for women to be out enjoying the nightlife. The old tradition of females not to be seen alone in a bar or club had passed and Abbi joined my sisters, brothers and myself in the evenings at dance halls all over London. With their connections in the city, my stockbroker brothers led the way for the rest of us to join in the eccentricities of the early twenties. Beatrice remained at home, disapproving of our socialising and partying.

The economic boom was a huge boost for us on the farms. Dad was now considering retirement and Alexander and I took more control of the business. I was in charge of the men on the farms and Alexander was the chief salesman, with everything carefully eyeballed by Dad.

Work provided plenty of opportunities for socialising and hospitality functions and we wasted no time in enjoying ourselves, but I was now well into my thirties. It was time to face reality. I was ready to settle down. Enough of the trips back and forth to Brussels. With Abbi's regular visits and longer stays, she had more or less become part of the family. The dancing and entertainment was beginning to wear thin. I just wanted to have her to myself. We had discussed the subject of marriage on occasions, but with so much work and play it was never discussed seriously. There was also an undercurrent of concern among some family members about a marriage between us – perhaps fostered by her mastering of the Charleston and her rather more continental spirit. After all, my brothers (and I for that matter) were very 'English' by nature, having been brought up in a lifestyle of strict regime and traditions by my father. Kate, on the other hand, was far more open and fun-loving and had convinced Abbi that her life was her own and she should follow her heart. Their relationship had become close and they had shared a great deal of time and laughter together. Beatrice, on the other hand, disapproved of the frivolity, along with mother and father. I could sense an atmosphere building within the family. Slowly but surely, the relationship between Beatrice and Abbi became increasingly spiky. As Kate and Abbi were endlessly out and about with friends and attending social gatherings, Beatrice, together with Mother and Father, began to openly display a sense of disapproval. It all came to a head in early July 1924.

'Abbi!' called out Kate. 'I have been offered some tickets to the ladies' semi-finals at Wimbledon tomorrow. We must go! It will be so much fun.'

'I have never been to a tennis tournament,' said Abbi.

'Oh golly! You will love it! Kitty McKane is playing Suzanne Lenglen. The English versus the French. It should be a wonderful match. Come on. Do come along with me!'

'Who are these players? I don't know anything about tennis.'

'Oh. These players are amongst the best in the world. Kitty is ranked as the world number two. She is also the Olympic champion and the finest of tennis players. Suzanne is such a star! She is known as "La Divine" in France and has won many, many championships. It should be the most wonderful match. You must come along. Oh please do!'

This brief conversation was to spark the first public argument between Beatrice and Kate.

'I don't think it would be appropriate for Abbi to go to Wimbledon,' said Beatrice to Kate.

'Oh. And why not?' quizzed Kate.

'Well, she has been out and about almost every day and perhaps it would be nice if one of us could go out and enjoy ourselves for a change!'

Kate was taken aback by the comment. Beatrice rarely showed any emotion and this sudden outburst came as quite a shock.

'I thought you wouldn't be interested,' said Kate. 'You have never indicated that you might like to go to any of the events we are invited to.'

'Well, I think it is about time that changed. Abbi is a guest here in this house and we never see her as she is out with you all the time. It is all very well for her to stay, but this is not a hotel!'

'I beg your pardon, Beatrice. A hotel? What are you talking about? Now that is enough,' piped up Mother. 'I will not have my family arguing in this house. Not about and in front of our guest. Beatrice, you may be right but this is not the time or place. You two go to the tennis tomorrow and we will forget that this argument ever happened. Please go into the parlour, Beatrice. I would like to talk to you.'

Abbi was shocked by this outburst – and confused about the discussion. She was not sure exactly how to interpret it. Was she out of line? Had she overstayed her welcome, taking advantage of the kindness and not being receptive to the feelings of the senior members of the household? The relationship had changed.

'Now listen, Beatrice,' said Mother. 'That was not the right thing to say, my dear.'

'I know, Mother, but over these past few years Harry and Abbi have taken over. I don't like the way she just comes and goes as she pleases. Harry never says anything and behaves as if Tangier Lodge is their home.'

'Well, it is their home!'

'Yes, I know, but you know what I mean. Abbi may be Harry's companion but she is not part of our family. She is a guest and I mean that in the nicest possible way. More than a guest, but not family. It is different.'

'I do know what you mean and in a way I agree with you. I like her very much and she and Harry are so very close, but it is different having her here so much. I am not sure if they are meant to be together. Her father is a plumber, I believe, and she comes from a completely different way of life. Are they compatible? I just don't know. For now it seems she is here to stay, for the time being anyway, and we must try to continue to make her feel welcome. Stiff upper lip! Okay?'

'All right, Mother, but things will have to change and Harry needs to sort this out.'

When I got back from the farm warehouse, I was quickly captured by Abbi and ushered into the garden.

'I need to talk to you, Harry. Earlier today Kate told me she had been given tickets to the ladies' semi-finals at Wimbledon tomorrow and asked me to accompany her. Beatrice was not happy and there was a bit of an argument. Some things were said and I feel like I am not welcome. I just don't know where I stand any more.'

'Oh, Abbi. I am sure she did not mean that you are not welcome here.'

'I'm not so sure, Harry. Your mother stepped in just in time before it blew up into a full-scale row. She said that she agreed with Beatrice. That really upset me. I think they are both of the view that my presence here is becoming uncomfortable for them.'

'Don't be silly. I am sure they don't feel like that.'

'Well, whatever they really feel may be unclear but there is definitely an atmosphere now. I am not sure I want to be here as a guest any more. Things have improved back in Brussels, so maybe I should go home.'

'That's a bit extreme, Abbi. Just because there have been a few words doesn't mean you need to run away back to Brussels. I love you. I don't want you to just leave.'

This argument had brought things to the forefront. Perhaps Beatrice and Mother felt that we were not facing reality. Just going out and having fun, regardless of how it might be impacting on everyone else. Abbi and I had been courting for getting on four years. The time seemed to have flown by and I had not really noticed. I was buried in work and when I was not in the office we were out almost every evening.

Over the summer we talked a great deal, undoubtedly prompted by the argument over tickets to Wimbledon. The irony of all this was that, although Kate and Abbi did go to the match, Suzanne Lenglen had to withdraw and the match was a walkover for Kitty, who went on to beat the American, Helen Moody, in the final.

I decided that I had to move out of Tangier Lodge and make a life of my own. I was thirty-six years old, after all – and still living at home. They were right. It was time to move on. In the autumn of 1924 an opportunity arose and I made the decision to buy a farm in Worplesdon, near Guildford in Surrey. Burdenshott Farm became my home.

Abbi spent Christmas with her family and I went to stay with Mother and Father at Tangier Lodge. She had decided that after Christmas she would travel from Brussels to see in the New Year with me. In Piccadilly the new Café de Paris had recently opened and had quickly become one of the premier nightspots in London. It had been reported that the Prince of Wales had become a frequent visitor, taking with him some of the most well-known celebrities from Europe. I decided that I would take Abbi to the New Year's Eve performance, where we could experience some of the fabulous cabaret and enjoy the fine dining and entertainment.

I travelled up to London by train from Guildford and took a cab from Waterloo Station across to Charing Cross. It was a chilly evening and I could feel the cold air prickle on my face as I stepped from the cab on to the cobbled concourse at the entrance to Charing Cross. The familiar Eleanor Cross Memorial spire, which stands just outside the station, reached high up into the clear darkening sky. King Edward I placed this memorial to his wife Eleanor of Castile in 1290 on this site. It was destroyed in 1647, but a replica was built to replace it and has become a well-known landmark.

I made my way into the station. The train was due in at 5.25 p.m. I had arrived in good time, with only an hour or so to wait. As night fell the lights in the station replaced the daylight. Evening came early at this time of year. I meandered round the station, looking in the few shop windows to pass the time. It became busier as 5 p.m. passed and men in suits and hats began to fill the platforms. More and more trains arrived. Whistles blew and doors slammed as they were sent on their way again. Great steam engines hissed and shunted as they arrived and departed. I made my way to platform three at which the train from Dover Priory always arrived. The platform was dark, apart from a few dim lights providing adequate illumination to just make out the posts and wooden benches which stretched the length of the platform. I stood in my long dark coat, collar turned up to help shelter my neck from the cold, hat on head and small weekend bag in my right hand, soft leather gloves protecting my hands. I gazed down the darkened platform, looking to see if the great black steam engine would suddenly appear from the darkness. I checked my watch. The train was late. As the minute hand moved on to the number six of my wristwatch, the dark circular frontage of the powerful steam engine pulling the wooden coaches appeared from the dimness. Great puffs of steam wafted around the engine and the steel brakes were gently applied and screeched alongside the platform. Hissing and clunking, the train slowly filled the void of the tracks and, finally, with a loud crunch as the carriages bumped into one another, the great monster came to a halt.

Faces peering from the windows of the carriages lined the length of the train. Doors were flung open and slowly people began to fall out of the carriages, filling the platform. I moved from side to side, searching between the travellers for the familiar face of Abbi. Finally, amongst the crowds she appeared. Wearing a knee-length skirt, black shoes with a small heel and laces to the ankle, a cream blouse and fur coat with black-trimmed hat sporting a feather, she moved in that elegant glide down the platform towards me. I remembered that movement from the first time I had laid eyes on her in that gloomy medical tent in France. She had not yet spotted me. Being a mere five foot eight inches tall, I had been lost in the crowd. I watched her as she moved. I was besotted. She was the most lovely creature. I was lost in the moment – just watching. Oblivious to everyone else. Just seeing her made my heart beat faster. I wanted to wrap her up in my arms. To feel her warm body close to mine. To hold her tight. To keep her close. To be with her.

She suddenly picked me out from the crowd and her face lit up with that smile. My heart missed another beat. She moved towards me and I stepped forward to catch her in my embrace. It felt amazing to have her back in my arms. Close and secure. I took her bag and we turned and moved away together out of the station, into a cab and a short journey down the Strand to the Waldorf Hotel, situated on the Aldwych in the heart of London's theatre district.

At seven we left the hotel, having decided to walk to the Café de Paris. As we passed a jewellery shop I glanced into the window display. Diamond rings, necklaces and tiaras filled the display. A light shone within. Few people were inside. I was caught in the moment. I stopped and turned to face Abbi who was slightly surprised by the sudden pause. Looking into her eyes as she looked into mine, slightly confused. I said:

'Abbi. Will you marry me?'

Still looking deeply into my eyes, the most gentle smile came across her face. Her white pearl-like teeth shone brightly, surrounded by a rich red lipstick, and she said:

'Of course, Harry. I would love to marry you. As soon as possible, please.'

I drew her to me tightly and kissed her gently on her soft red lips. I was so in love. I turned and led her into the jewellery shop. Fifteen minutes later we exited with a beautiful diamond engagement ring shining from her finger.

We went on to the Café de Paris and had the most wonderful evening, singing in the New Year. It was an emotional time for us both, but finally, as we welcomed in 1925, we were on the road to a life together.

I accompanied Abbi home to Brussels after the New Year to ask her father for his daughter's hand in marriage. He gave his blessing. I was warmly welcomed into their family. A few days later we returned to England together and invited ourselves to Sunday lunch at Tangier Lodge. This was my chance to announce our engagement to the family.

It was a sunny Sunday. We had attended church as a whole family, including Abbi, and had taken our places around the large shiny dining table. Places had been laid in the usual order, with father at the head and the brothers and sisters, starting with the eldest sons (Charles on his right and Frederick on his left), descending down the length of the table, five on each side. My sisters occupied the far end, flanking mother. Since George had no longer been with us, there had been an imbalance, but the five-a-side format returned as our special guest filled the absent family member chair.

Before the war, as one of the youngest, I had always had a brother to my right and a sister to my left, but since Abbi had become a regular guest, she had sat beside me instead. All my sisters had moved round one place to accommodate our visitor.

Shiny silver cutlery reflected off the highly polished maple table, all in perfect alignment with the white table napkins, each wearing a silver clip with our names engraved. Glasses glinted in the sunlight, spilling in from the tall dining-room windows. It was an elegant scene and one we had become used to. To many it would seem very formal but to us it was normal. From a young age, my father had insisted we dine together on Sundays and he still wanted it this way. Presentation and tradition were imperative. In recent years the atmosphere had become a little more relaxed and informal and much debate and discussion would fill the room. It was even acceptable to place one's elbows on the table.

We all entered the dining room, stood behind our respective chairs and waited for Mother and Father to each reach the end of the table. There was gentle chatter, but no one took to their seats until Mother was seated. Once she was comfortably enthroned, the room burst into noise as the remaining eleven chairs were dragged along the wooden floor and we took to our seats. It had been normal practice for the boys to draw the chairs for the girls and this remained the case, with the exception of my drawing the chair for Abbi. Once all were seated, a hush fell over the room as Dad said grace. He always thanked God for blessing us with food and shelter, but since the loss of George a short addition had been made so as not to forget all those who gave their lives in the Great War, and to remember our youngest brother. This was followed by a toast to the King.

Formalities over, the waiting staff began to enter the room with trays and plates. It was the usual relaxed atmosphere as brothers and sisters turned towards one another, asking questions and delivering stories. As usual, Kate immediately began talking to Abbi, who now had an almost fluent command of English. Despite her ability, though, when spoken to at speed in a room full of others, it was not easy for her. How was your journey this time? Nice to have you back with us again. How long do you hope to stay?

To my right sat John, who was quick to turn and say, 'You're a lucky chap to have found that gem, Harry.' It was nice of him and I knew he was sincere. As a family, we had not been too good at finding partners and I really felt that he meant what he said. It settled me quite a bit as I was a little anxious, to say the least. I suspected that all the family knew there was something afoot. Although it was accepted that Abbi used to stay with us partly because things were extremely difficult in Belgium, they all knew that she was more than just a good friend. In fact, they knew that I was mad about her. What they did not know, though, was that today I was going to announce our engagement. Abbi was obviously well aware, but was under orders not to say anything or behave in a way which might let the cat out of the bag.

Lunch continued unabated, with much conversation and jollity. The main course was lamb, so tender it melted in my mouth. If there was one thing our extraordinary cook could do, it was roast lamb. Potatoes and parsnips (roasted, of course), green beans and cabbage, accompanied by a green salad – all fresh from the farm. With crates piled high with fresh vegetables and salad in our yard, we were able to enjoy dining – and so we did.

As luncheon drew towards its close and the time approached for us to leave the table and make our way to the drawing room, my moment was upon me. With my left hand I gently touched Abbi on the forearm. She turned to look at me and I glanced into her dark brown eyes. We both knew what was coming, but neither of us knew what the reaction was going to be. It was time. I reached for a remaining spoon that lay on the table, picked it up and gently clinked my glass. The chattering stopped almost immediately and all eyes turned towards me. I rose from my chair, looking round at all the familiar faces. Silence fell over the room.

'I have an announcement to make,' I said. 'Father, Mother, brothers and sisters. We are together here today again, as a family, as it always has been, but today is a unique day because I would like you to know that our special guest is more than just a special guest. She is my life and, because of that, I have asked Abbi to be my wife. She has kindly agreed to my request and we are soon to be married.'

Eyes widened and mouths dropped open. Smiles broke out among my sisters. My brothers turned and looked at one another – I'm not sure whether in disbelief or bewilderment. Charles aside, none of my siblings were married or even in a steady relationship. It seemed alien to them, but the romance was obviously felt by my sisters. My father looked at me, then moved his gaze to Abbi. I turned to look at Mother, who sat in silence, looking straight down the table at Father.

Abbi was not a strong woman, but she had the grace of a princess. She had a soft voice and was conscientious and caring. Since that day in November 1918 on the crowded streets of Brussels, she had set her mind to learning English. In these past few years she had become almost fluent, which was a great deal more than could be said about me and my French. In truth, I had barely learned a word. I was completely dependent upon the efforts of Abbi to master my language. She had succeeded beyond belief. Not only had she mastered the spoken word, but she had also attended night school to study how to write. Had she not spoken with a wonderfully soft French accent, you would not know that she was a foreigner. Although we had not lived together as a couple at any time, we had spent many weeks together here in England and at her home in St Gilles on the outskirts of Brussels.

Abbi was one of three children. She had a half-brother and half-sister from her father's first marriage. Their mother had died and her father Leon had married again. Leon, who was a plumber, and her stepmother Stephanie had lived in St Gilles for their whole married life. Abbi, Clotilde and Louis had all been born and grown up in that very house. It was a close family and they all spent time together regularly. For Abbi to up sticks and emigrate took great courage.

As a young child, Abbi was never a strong, sturdy creature. Slight and elegant was her structure. She was not interested in sports or any type of physical activity, but rather preferred to bury her head in a book or spend time with her mother in the daily duties of running a busy household. She was not too interested in the opposite sex and found men a little intimidating. Although confident in nature and certainly bright, she seldom came to the forefront, preferring to keep her opinions and thoughts to herself. She could be described as a slightly meek personality, matching her slim, slight figure. She seemed vulnerable to almost any bug or germ that came within striking distance and regularly caught a cold during the winter months.

In many ways, I found these features endearing. I, too, was one of the quieter members of my family and these characteristics attracted me, although in these past few years we had both come out of our shells and opened up quite a bit. Nevertheless, I felt that Abbi needed me and I was able to bring her the strengths that she lacked – although she would never acknowledge that she lacked any. She was probably right in this, but it was the way I felt and it was important to me. We gelled together and our relationship worked. We rarely argued, but we did talk endlessly. It was a happy partnership.

Unfortunately, it seemed that my family were not of the same opinion about its future. Our family, although close, was much more regimented. Father did not suffer fools gladly and was the master of his ship. My brothers, in particular, were typically English, polite and official. Do everything by the book and follow tradition – apart from Kate, who was wild and adventurous by comparison. As a successful family, it was important to uphold our reputation and be seen to be proper and correct. It irritated me somewhat, as I was not always in support of the general way of doing things. It seemed to me that Father, and Beatrice for that matter, were a little stuck in the past and that times were changing. It was difficult to approach him and discuss things like this. In order to maintain the peace, we all generally went along with him.

The idea of a Barker marrying a foreigner was difficult enough, but the health of a future daughter-in-law was very important. All the family knew of Abbi's vulnerability to illness. Rarely was anything said, but I was aware of a certain restlessness over the issue. They naturally always expressed their best wishes and hopes that she would get well soon, but I could sense the underlying atmosphere of discomfort about the fact that she was not a strong woman. No one ever asked for any details when Abbi was ill, but since the announcement of our marriage the subject would undoubtedly surface at some point.

Two weeks after we had informed the family of our engagement, my father called to arrange a visit to my farm in Worplesdon. It was not uncommon for him to drive down to Burdenshott Farm, as we worked closely on the production and distribution of the produce grown here. Abbi had returned to Brussels and I was busy with the day-to-day responsibilities of running the farm. I thought nothing of his impromptu call. It did go through my mind that he might wish to discuss plans for the wedding, but that was expected, as I had planned for it to be a traditional and family affair.

From the narrow lane of Burdenshott Hill, he turned into the farm's forecourt at about 3 p.m. I was expecting him and went out to greet him. He stepped out of the car and we met midway between the house and his shiny green Daimler.

'Welcome, Father,' I said.

'Thank you, Harry,' he replied. 'Good to see you.'

'Come on in,' I said. 'I have some tea and your favourite cakes. How was the journey?'

'Much the same as usual. No real problems. With the sun out today the scenery is spectacular, particularly from Burdenshott Hill. You are lucky to live in such a beautiful spot, Harry.'

'I know, Dad. Come on in,' I said.

We entered via the old oak front door and made our way through the entrance lobby into the main sitting room. This was a large room with a low ceiling; various landscapes and the odd family portrait hung from the walls. The centrepiece was a brick inglenook fireplace with a thick, dark-oak lintel, gnarled and twisted from age. Behind was an open hearth with a cast-iron basket featuring two moulded pine cones standing proudly at each corner. Only a partly burned log and some shiny grey ash lay in the basket, flanked by a small pile of logs ready for the next fire.

I had never been fond of central heating and this old house was ideal. I preferred my sleeping rooms to be fresh and I usually slept with the window open. No doubt this would not be conducive to Abbi after our wedding. We moved towards the sitting room chairs, which all pointed towards the inglenook. During the winter the furniture was positioned accordingly.

We sat down in two large leather chairs. A low-level wooden coffee table with two cups, a teapot, silver sugar bowl, small jug of milk and a plate of cupcakes separated us.

'So how is Mother?' I asked.

'Oh, she's absolutely fine, Harry. She's busy, but now the winter has set in, things aren't quite so hectic. We are all so pleased with your announcement. Abbi is such a lovely girl and, as you can imagine, your engagement has dominated much of the conversation in Tangier Lodge over the past two weeks. How is she by the way?'

'She's fine too, Father. She managed to get back home safely. I received a telegram only yesterday saying the journey had been uneventful and that she was back in St Gilles safe and sound.'

'That's good to hear. The Channel crossing can be so frightening at this time of year. It's good to know that she is home safe. Actually, the reason I came was to have a talk with you about your decision to marry. I hope you don't mind. I am only doing the fatherly thing.'

'No, that's fine, Father. I completely understand. None of us have taken the plunge so it's not surprising to hear that I'm the number one subject of discussion.'

'You know that we all love Abbi dearly and she is such a lovely girl. She is so kind and gentle and we can see that you are both deeply in love. That being said, I am concerned for her health. The life of a farmer's wife is no pushover and it worries me that she may not be able to cope. Your farm here is very important to the family and the family business. Have you given this serious thought?'

'I did think that this issue would come to the fore at some point, Father. It has occupied my thoughts for some time. I know that she is not strong and this lifestyle will be a challenge. To be honest, I don't really know whether she will wish to be heavily involved in the running of the farm. It's not really important to me because I love her dearly and I want to spend the rest of my life with her.'

'But your livelihood is paramount, Harry. We have spent many years building this business together as a family.'

'I know, Father,. but there comes a time in everyone's life where something comes along which changes things. I don't know for sure if my current lifestyle will be in perfect harmony with Abbi. I know I love her dearly, but the future will show which direction our lives will travel.'

'Please don't misunderstand me, Harry. We do understand that you are committed to Abbi, but we – that is, all the family – have concerns and we don't want you to make a big mistake.'

'Oh, please, Father. I'm old enough to make decisions on my own. I know what you have done for me and I am very grateful, but you must try to allow me to decide how I wish to live my life. We will do all we can to keep the Barker ship afloat and sailing in the right direction. You know that, but ultimately it is my life.'

'You're right, Harry. It is your life and you must make your own way. We all pray that Abbi will be happy here, and you can take it from me – on behalf of all the family – that we wish you both happiness and prosperity.'

'Thank you, Father. I appreciate your concerns.'

The remainder of Father's visit was spent chatting about the family and going over the arrangements for the impending wedding. I knew that the family was not in full support, but there was nothing any of them could do to change my mind.

Over the next two months preparations were made for the wedding. Abbi travelled back and forth from Brussels and a meeting was convened for the parents and other family members from both sides. It took place in a fine hotel near the Pollyn family home. It was a beautiful day and, despite the linguistic limitations, Abbi hosted a wonderful lunch. Everyone was happy. On Saturday 7th March 1925, in Barnes, I married the love of my life. Abbi duly moved into Burdenshott Farm and we began our life together as husband and wife.

The following three years saw our farm grow and we settled into a rural lifestyle. For Abbi, health issues persisted through the first few years of our marriage and she continued to suffer. Nevertheless, production on the farm carried on unhindered, with regular trips to Barnes.

In 1926 Father decided to retire. He had been master of his ship for many years, however, and he did not take well to a life of leisure. He missed the affairs of the farms and struggled to adapt to a life of retirement. Now, at the ripe old age of seventy-six, he was not really able to cope with the physical side and technology had moved on. He became increasingly frustrated and irritated by not being hands-on. The traditional Sunday lunch drifted away and the importance of Mother and Father in our day-to-day lives seemed to fade into the background.

Two years later, having not suffered any serious illness, and rather unexpectedly, in mid-May, Father passed away quietly in his own bed. It came as a shock to us all. Bee and Alexander remained at Tangier Lodge and took care of Mother.

It had become increasingly tough for Abbi on the farm and Father had been right to be concerned. She had not taken well to farm life and, with her vulnerability to almost every germ that drifted into our lives, she suffered greatly. Business had continued to grow and after Father died we had invested heavily in the development of our farms. It had become a sizeable business. Abbi and I talked much about the future and how we might be able to find a way to get out of farming. My brothers offered advice on selling and using the funds to invest in the stock markets. They said we could live well from those investments. We had done a great deal at Burdenshott and I wanted to try and keep the place.

There had been quite a bit of talk amongst local farmers about land being sold. I decided to quiz Jack Smythe, who was a neighbouring farmer. He had mentioned something about an American consortium of investors who were buying his place, along with several others in the area. I gave him a call and we decided to meet up in the Fox and Hounds, our local pub.

I was there first and whilst I was ordering a pint he came in through the heavy black doorway. Easily recognisable, he was a tall man in his fifties with pure white hair. He had to duck a little as he came through the doorway into the low-ceilinged pub. The dark brown exposed timbers, heavily stained with cigarette smoke, reached from the front to the back of the building.

'Hi, Jack,' I said. 'What can I get you, old fella?'

'Hello, Harry. I'll have a pint of my usual, thanks. Gloria knows what I drink. How are you?'

'I'm fine, thanks. How is the lovely Mrs Smythe?'

'She's fine, thanks. She is looking forward to us having time for ourselves when this deal goes through. Neither of us are as young as we used to be, so it is a bit of a godsend to tell you the truth.'

'I am intrigued, I must say,' I replied. 'I have been looking forward to finding out more.'

Pints were delivered and cash passed over the bar. We made our way over to a table in the corner. Although not a big secret, this was a rather delicate matter and we did not want to sit in the open for all to hear.

'So, how did it all come to light?' I asked.

'The deal is quite a way down the track now, but in brief we were approached by our solicitor. He gave me a call and explained that there was this consortium of investors who had set up a farming union here in the UK with a view to mass production of market garden produce. I'm not sure why they didn't get on to you. Everyone knows what you do at Burdenshott, Harry.'

'Perhaps because I am part of a bigger farming business with our interests in southwest London. Who knows, but I am looking at getting out, even if I just lease the land,' I said.

'Why don't you have a chat with our solicitor? He is handling our contractual side. They may still be interested in your farm. After all, your land sits right between mine and Alan's. They may well be interested.'

'I'll give old Phil a call tomorrow. If there is a deal to be done he will know about it. He's been the only solicitor around here dealing with farmland conveyancing since time began.'

We moved on to more general conversation and after a couple of pints we headed off home. The next day I called Phil Macintrye. He had been involved with my purchase of Burdenshott in so far as the vendor was keen to implement a restrictive covenant to prevent the land being built on. I managed to prevent the covenant being written into the title deeds and Phil Macintyre was the man who had dealt with it.

'Hello, Phil. Harry Barker,' I said.

'Ah, hello, Harry. Long time no hear, my dear chap. How are you?' he asked.

'I'm fine, Phil. How is the legal profession these days?' I asked.

'Busy, busy as usual, Harry. What can I do for you?'

'I was chatting with Jack Smythe yesterday about this American consortium buying up farmland round here. He told me you have the inside track on this. I may be interested in being involved.'

'Ah, that is most interesting,' he replied. 'Funnily enough, I had them on the phone just a few days ago asking about your place, but, to be honest, well, I told them you are highly unlikely to be interested, with your London association and all. It was left at that.'

'That's fair enough,' I said. 'But something has come up and I am now in the market to look at leasing out or selling Burdenshott. Do you think they may still be interested?'

'I am sure they will. I'll get on to them straight away. It may take a day or so to get hold of them, but I will put it at the top of my list. I am sure they'll be interested. I'll get back to you. Are you still on the same number?'

'Yes I am, Phil. That is good news. I'll look forward to hearing from you.'

Two days later, Phil called me back.

'In simple terms, Harry,' he said, 'they are interested in leasing. They don't want to buy right now, but would offer a deal including five years' rent up front and some shares, with an option to buy after five years. It is a bit unusual, but a good deal, Harry! Have a think and let me know. We need to move fast, though!'

I talked long and hard with Alexander and Abbi. It was the right thing for us to do. The offer was to be part of a multinational company with the parent company operating out of the United States, investing in a European vegetable farming syndicate. They were willing to front-up five years' rent with an option to extend the lease or buy after that. We would receive four percent of the shares of the company and be entitled to dividends after two years. In addition, we would continue to own Burdenshott Farm, but they would lease the land. After five years they would have an option to buy at the value of farming land per acre at the time, or to extend the lease for a further five years, or I could have the land back but relinquish my shares at zero value. It was a play-off against the value of the shares and the value of arable farming land at the time. The overall project was a four million dollar investment in farming in England. It seemed that good fortune had handed us a way out. Five years' rent up-front invested wisely would be plenty enough for us to live on for several years. Abbi and I could move to Brussels and look for a quieter life. Our first child was due in December and we could begin family life and see where it would lead.

Two weeks later I was sitting in Phil Macintyre's office signing an exchange contract to lease Burdenshott Farm. In late October the deal was completed and we began to prepare for a move to Belgium. Five years' rent totalling £12,000 arrived in my bank account on 29th October as cleared funds. My brother John set about preparing an investment programme with a view to obtaining a regular income for us to live on. By late November we had found a flat to rent in the suburbs of southern Brussels, near Abbi's parents, and arranged for some of our belongings to be shipped out. There was little work available for me in Brussels and with my language limitations I needed the money to provide us with a good income over the longer term. I was not getting any younger. With Abbi very pregnant, we left for Belgium three days into December 1928.

CHAPTER THREE

Between Christmas and the New Year of 1929 at the Red Cross Hospital in Brussels, our first child was born. A bouncing baby boy with a full crop of dark hair and big brown eyes. Our son was duly christened Paul Derrick Barker. Abbi had struggled with her health during the pregnancy and, following his birth, the doctors diagnosed symptoms of tuberculosis. With this news we redirected our focus for a home in the countryside with plenty of fresh, clean air.

After much searching we found a lovely villa in the small town of Spa in southeast Belgium. The town was surrounded by the beautiful, lush forests of the Belgian Ardennes, sometimes referred to as the Pearl of the Ardennes. The undulating hills and countless rivers and springs made this the perfect spot for Abbi to have the best chance of recovery. Plenty of fresh air and, most important, quiet and rest. Spa was not far from Abbi's family in St Gilles and it was in the ideal place for all three of us to settle while we addressed the symptoms of tuberculosis.

The house, called Villa des Nids, was situated on Rener Boulevard on the outskirts of the town. It was a beautiful, timber-framed building with a few steps leading up to the covered wooden porch. Four thick posts held up the roof of the porch, which housed the front door. It was a large house over three floors and a basement. The ground floor had huge windows in each room with a wooden arch featured on the frame. The first floor and gable ends of the roof had a timber-frame structure in typical Tyrolean style. It was a magnificent home with plenty of light pouring in from all directions and was surrounded by forest. Perfect.

A deal was struck to rent the house and Abbi, Paul and I moved in. It was a brave move, but I thought it was essential. Abbi was struggling to cope with Paul, increasingly finding herself tired and weak. What she needed most was rest and clean air. Brussels was busy and the atmosphere filled with industrial smoke. We needed to find an alternative and this was it.

A housekeeper in the form of Jeanne Briffaud was recruited to assist in the running of the house. Jeanne was in her mid-thirties and a spinster. She had dark brown eyes and a full head of black hair which she always kept tied up in a bun at the back of her head. A scarf would be tied over her head when she went outside. At about five foot four, she was a little on the short side, but her personality made up for any deficiency in height. She was quite loudly spoken with a clear diction. Every word was clearly spoken and pronounced. Some may have interpreted it as sounding a bit cocky, but I needed someone who was sure and confident. Most important, she had a good grasp of English. Her natural tongue was, of course, French, but even with her distinctive accent I could understand every word she spoke in English.

She was a Swiss girl from the French-speaking sector of Geneva and had been living in Spa for several years. She came with excellent references and had been a housekeeper for a wealthy family in the town. They had recently returned to Geneva but Jeanne wanted to stay. She had lost her father in the Great War and her mother had died shortly afterwards. She had a brother who had married a French girl and moved to Provence, but she had not heard from him for years. They had not been close and Jeanne had gone on to make a life of her own. She was engaged by a family with connections in Spa and came with them when they moved from Geneva. She had no reason to return to Geneva as there were no family connections any more. She lived alone in a rented flat in the centre of town. Her life was in Spa, but she would walk to Villa des Nids every day.

Spring and summer passed and the leaves on the trees which saturated our surroundings began to turn gold. Autumn sunshine brought a colour to the woodlands that is hard to describe. By late October the leaves were beginning to fall.

On Wednesday 30th October Jeanne had made her regular walk up to the villa from town, but on this occasion she came in bursting through the front door.

'Madame! Monsieur! There is important news!'

I was sitting in the lounge chatting with Abbi. Her calling out surprised us. It was not usual. I stood up to meet Jeanne in the hallway. She virtually pushed me into the lounge, falling over herself.

Gathering herself and standing in the middle of the lounge, she took a deep breath to recover from her running.

'Monsieur, there is bad news from America!' she gasped.

'What news?' I asked. 'Calm yourself, Jeanne. Just slow down. What is it?'

'Monsieur Harry,' she began again. 'The stock market in America has crashed. There is chaos in the streets of New York! The financial markets have collapsed! It is on the radio and in the paper.'

'Oh my God!' I exclaimed. 'My investments may be at risk. It is what we live on,' I said to Abbi. 'I need to get on the phone to John and find out what is happening. He prepared all my investments and should know what to do.'

Three days later I was on the train to Calais and then back at Tangier Lodge. By then the crash in the States had continued and the run on the banks had begun. There were reports that some people had thrown themselves out of windows, having lost everything. The story was all over the British press and it was just getting worse.

I met with John the day after I arrived and he went through my investment portfolio with me. Most of the money we had received from the American deal was still in the bank and we had not invested in American stocks. For now the money was safe, but the value of my shares in the consortium that leased Burdenshott Farm was on the slide. There was nothing I could do about that, other than sell, which would relinquish ownership of the farm. Perhaps something good was to come of this disaster for me as, after five years, I could reclaim Burdenshott in exchange for the shares. If the share value fell, the decision to hand back the shares at nil value would be simple. I was just lucky to already have the money in the bank. Steps could be taken to protect the funds. John was on the case. I returned to Spa to let Abbi know we were not going to be victims of the American stock market crash.

Christmas came and went and the effects of the crash were spreading around the world. People all over Europe were suffering from the collapse of banks and businesses. The depression was beginning to bite, although we had not really felt its impact here in Spa.

Suddenly, out of the blue came a telegram from Alexander that mother had been taken ill. Since the passing of father, her lifestyle had slowed considerably. Alexander and Bee had been responsible for her day-to-day care, but during the busy season had little time to attend to her. She spent much of her day in the sunroom reading, but the loss of her lifetime partner had hit her hard.

I left Abbi with Jeanne and travelled home to Tangier Lodge. Mum was looking very frail and had lost weight. She was drawn and grey and I felt that she had given up. All of her sons were busy with their businesses and her daughters were involved with their own interests. She had lost purpose.

Over the following few months she became increasingly poorly and made several trips to hospital. In early July 1930 she, too, passed away, in her bed at Tangier Lodge.

We travelled over for the funeral, which was a very solemn affair. Black suits and grey ties. People wandering about aimlessly. I hate funerals. No one seems to know what to do or say. Jeanne chasing two-year-old Paul around everywhere. Everyone so sorry. The day finally passed and we returned to Belgium to continue our life in Spa.

Over the next six months Abbi became more involved with Paul. She would read him stories and play in the lounge. A wonderful mother-and-son relationship developed. To my surprise, in September 1931 Abbi reported that she was pregnant again. In May 1932 our second son was born and christened Victor Stephen Barker. We were a close-knit unit and were happy in our home in Spa. It turned out that Jeanne had some difficulty pronouncing the name "Victor". It took on several different sounds, but none were close to the English version, so she decided he would be referred to as "Stephen". A much easier name to pronounce. From that moment on, Victor became known to all family and friends as "Stephen".

During the winter of 1933, Abbi's health took a turn for the worse. Her breathing became increasingly laboured and I had to find a way to come to terms with the inevitable outcome of the disease. By the following summer, Abbi had weakened to such an extent that most of her day was spent in the high-backed chair in the lounge. She tired easily and the walks in the forest had been reduced to a short stroll around the garden. The boys were oblivious to the events unfolding around them. Jeanne was unbelievable and took complete control of their day-to-day lives. She was almost a full-time resident at the villa, but was insistent that she retain her independence in her flat in town. She walked back and forth every day, regardless of time and weather. She was as committed to the boys as if she had been their mother.

In October I had to make a trip back to Tangier Lodge and met up with John to sort out Burdenshott Farm. The five years were up and after the crash in 1929, the shares I had were worth nothing. The decision to keep the farm was a no-brainer, so that is what I did. I took back the farm, relinquished my shares and leased the land to another nearby farmer. I placed the house in the hands of a local estate agent to rent it out. The income would be more than enough to take care of financial matters for me in Belgium. A deal was done and I was able to return to Spa and take care of Abbi and the boys.

The atmosphere in the house became increasingly gloomy as Abbi's health deteriorated. Our weekend trips to St Gilles to see her parents had changed to alternate weekend visits by Leon and Stephanie. I decided that we needed some cheer in the house and one Saturday on a trip to town an unexpected opportunity arose. We passed a pet market that was being held in the town centre. A pen with five little Lurcher puppies was spotted by Paul.

'Please, Dad. Please can we have a puppy?' he pleaded. 'We could give it to Mum as a birthday present.'

I decided to have a closer look and found it difficult to resist the cries of Paul. They were undoubtedly adorable little creatures. The five little puppies sat with faces turned upward, as if asking to be rescued. They were so cute and irresistible. Perhaps a little distraction would bring some cheer to Abbi. For sure, Paul thought it was a great idea, but he gave little thought to the consequences of taking one of these little puppies home. Jeanne looked at me with a slightly bewildered expression on her face.

'Why not, Monsieur?' she said.

That was it. Decision made. To hell with the consequences. Within a few minutes a choice had been made and a box containing our new family member was passed to me.

The fifteen-minute walk back home saw Paul dancing along the pavement. Stephen was simply confused by the behaviour but fascinated by the little creature in the box. Paul was so excited that both Jeanne and I had difficulty containing his exuberance. He carried the box up to the front door and burst into the entrance lobby calling out, 'Mama! Mama! Where are you, Mama?' She was not sitting in the chair where she spent most of her day. I made my way upstairs to our bedroom and found her lying in bed.

'How are you, my sweetheart?' I asked.

'Not so good, Harry. I felt a little tired so I decided to take a nap. I'm sure I will be feeling better soon.'

'As it's your birthday tomorrow, Paul has found a special something for you. Do you mind if he comes up with our surprise?'

'No, of course not. Tell him to come up. What is it, Harry?'

'I can't tell you, darling. I'll call them both up.'

I moved to the door and called down the stairs:

'Paul! Stephen! Come on up and bring Mum her surprise birthday present.'

Paul bounded up the stairs, carrying the small brown box. Jeanne followed with Stephen. Paul stumbled, almost falling over in his excitement as he entered the bedroom and ran up to the bedside, where Abbi was now sitting upright.

'Mama, Mama. Here it is. Your birthday present. Open it, Mama. Quickly!'

He placed the box on the bed as Jeanne and Stephen entered the room. I stood at the end of the bed, watching the show.

A broad smile came across her tired face. She had not done much smiling in recent months and it was uplifting to see her lighten up like this. She looked up at me and then leaned over towards Paul and Stephen, who now stood beside the bed, jiggling with excitement.

She slowly opened the box and looked in to see the small puppy looking out at her.

'Goodness me!' she exclaimed as she dipped into the box, lifted the little creature out and held it up at arms' length. She then drew it towards her face and kissed it right on the nose.

'Oh, boys. He is just gorgeous,' she said, lowering him into her lap. 'What shall we call him?'

'Titou,' Paul cried out. 'Let's call him Titou.'

'Titou it is then. Welcome to our family, Titou,' she said.

It was a wonderful moment.

The summer of 1934 passed quickly. Abbi became increasingly short of breath, with endless coughing, and her energy levels were falling by the day. Doctors visited and prescribed various potions and lotions in an effort to rekindle her spirits, but to no avail. By September, as her symptoms developed, there was little doubt about what we were dealing with. Her coughing was accompanied by blood now, and increasing phlegm. The fight against tuberculosis became a pattern of diagnosis and prognosis. I knew it was only a matter of time, but I was not going to let the horror of losing the love of my life turn our happy home into a place of morbid depression.

Jeanne took hold of the situation, ensuring that life continued as normally as possible. Abbi attended dinner less frequently, but we continued with tradition at mealtimes as best we could. The boys seemed to accept that Mum was not well and adjusted their lives accordingly. It became increasingly normal for her to remain in bed, and both Paul and Stephen simply included our bedroom as one of the regularly visited and played-in rooms of the house.

As Christmas approached, we decorated the house and adorned the lounge with a fine tree covered in tinsel and baubles. It was the best tree yet and we all had fun dressing it, as Abbi looked on from her chair, wearing that gorgeous smile. It took me right back to the moment I had first seen her in the medical tent in France, sixteen years earlier. Much had happened during those years, every one of them as precious as the last. We had courted, married and lived on the farm. Then we had moved to Brussels and brought up our two boys. These years in Spa had been some of the most wonderful. Time to walk in the forests, hand in hand. To talk and share family time with Leon and Stephanie. Time to be together with our children, away from the daily pressures of running a busy business.

Christmas came and went. The boys were increasingly left to Jeanne to look after as I sat beside Abbi's bed and took on the responsibility of daily nursing care. Abbi grew weaker but rarely showed any signs of pain. She had lost weight and hardly had the strength to sit up in bed. Daylight hours began to merge with the night as she drifted in and out of sleep. I had adopted the high-backed chair that she used in the lounge and placed it in the corner of the bedroom. From here I read to her and spoke softly, recalling the times we had enjoyed together. How we had laughed while celebrating the end of the war. How she was terrified when introducing me to her parents. How she had smiled when I told my family we were to be married. The sparkle in her eye, when she had told me she was pregnant with Paul. The expression of happiness as we watched the boys open their Christmas presents, and how she held up Titou at arm's length and kissed him on his wet nose. There were so many special moments. She smiled as I whispered.

At 4 p.m. on the afternoon of 13th January 1935, the love of my life took a deep breath, made a long sigh and then lay still. Her eyes were already closed and a calm, comfortable expression covered her soft white face like a contented smile. She had slipped quietly away. A tear trickled down my cheek. I raised my hand and stroked her soft hair, moving down over her cheek and on to her shoulder. This was the end. I felt the pain stab into my heart. She was gone. I thought I had been prepared for this, but I was not.

CHAPTER FOUR

Staying in Spa was not an option. Too many memories. Too many thoughts. It was time to move away and begin again. I couldn't face the prospect of returning to England. I was not ready. I needed time to reflect, to consider and assess. The boys spoke almost no English and knew nothing of England.

My links with home had also weakened and my relationship with Beatrice was very prickly. The falling-out over the bloody Wimbledon finals just would not go away. To be honest, I was a bit of a sulker and I had never managed to get past the row between Beatrice and Abbi. It was always there in the background and as Mother and Father had passed away and Bee had taken up the senior role at Tangier Lodge, the thought of going back there was not really an option. I needed to take some time, so I decided that we would all, including the dog, move back to the St Gilles area, where I was quite familiar with the locality and knew my way around.

I found and rented a villa called Clos Normand in Avenue de la Sapinière in St Gilles. The area was typical Brussels suburbia consisting of avenues of houses, all with large gardens. Paul and Stephen were enrolled at the nearby Ecole Decroly Primary School. I employed a young local girl by the name of Yvonne de Vries. She was just seventeen years old and was engaged as the housemaid to assist Jeanne. She did, however, spend a considerable amount of time looking after the boys and joined in many of their games inside and outside the house.

I have always been somewhat of a disciplinarian. My father had always been strict and traditional and I had inherited these characteristics. The children were to be bathed and bedded by 6 p.m., summer and winter alike, including school holidays. They should always wash their hands before meals and sit properly at table. Permission to leave the table was granted only when everything that had been presented had been eaten. If they did not finish their food, they would have it re-presented at the next meal. Any nonsense resulted in the offending child being sent to his room. When tears abated, a sermon was delivered and the child was left to reflect for a further half an hour. Sundays, as in the true tradition set in my father's home, included lunch with the grandparents, followed by a walk in the nearby Forest of Soigne. These were my rules.

The neighbourhood was ideal, with many children resident in the houses in our adjoining roads. When playing outside, the boys were always accompanied by Yvonne. On the pavement they had obstacle courses through which to race their scooters and bicycles. Just down the road lived the Brichant family who had a tennis court. Jacques, the younger of the two sons, honed his tennis skills here and was later to represent Belgium and participate at Wimbledon. The boys used the court for roller-skating and frequently played hockey there, using my walking sticks. It was not long before I invested in hockey sticks for them as my walking sticks took quite a battering. There were enough children in the immediate neighbourhood that soon two teams were fielded and matches were organised.

Through the summer of 1935 we settled in and began to enjoy a family lifestyle, despite the political rumblings in Germany. Hitler had openly started rearmament and in both his speeches and *Mein Kampf* made it clear that he intended to break the terms of the Treaty of Versailles and reunite all

Germans into one nation. It was worrying, but it seemed a long way away from us.

A terrible tragedy hit Belgium in late August when Queen Astrid was killed in a car accident whilst on holiday in Switzerland with the young King Leopold. I decided to take the boys, along with Yvonne, to the funeral. It was a damp day with drizzling rain. The horse-drawn carriage carried the coffin shrouded in a black canopy. King Leopold walked behind, from the Palace to the Church of Notre Dame at Laeken, with his arm in a sling and a white surgical dressing on his chin, which covered a wound sustained in the accident. The streets were filled with mourners in black. Military uniforms lined the streets as the cortege of royalty followed the procession. The boys and Yvonne stood silently watching as the kings, queens and other royals of Europe passed by. This was the first time I had been reminded of the sorrow of death since losing Abbi. Seeing King Leopold following the coffin of his lost love brought back memories for me. It was an emotional moment.

During the following two years the boys became very good friends with our near neighbours, the Dejong family. Albert Dejong ran his own plumbing business, with many of his sign-written vans cruising the streets of St Gilles, installing central heating and servicing the needs of both industry and the general public.

Paulette Dejong looked after their daughter Monique. The relationship with the Dejongs grew quickly as a direct result of the almost permanent presence at our house of Monique. Monique, about the same age as Paul, was like a sister to the boys. Attending the same school, she shared their toys and was present at almost every party, game and family gathering. My association was limited as my French was totally inadequate and their English was nonexistent. We smiled and nodded at one another and the children just got on with it. Yvonne and Jeanne did all the communicating.

The relationship with Abbi's folks was difficult to sustain. My French was limited to say the least and their English – well, there was none. When we met up it was a real struggle. Jeanne, once again, had to do all the translating. The boys were the only reason why we met up at all. It was not really until we had moved back to St Gilles, after Abbi had passed away, that I noticed how little I actually spoke to them and them to me. With Abbi there it seemed we all got on just fine and had lots to say, but when she was not there, it was very apparent that there was a serious communication problem. We simply grinned at one another between sentences. It became very awkward. We kept in regular contact but fortnightly Sunday lunch ceased after just a couple of months and our meetings were reduced to occasional brief visits by them to see the boys. The relationship with the boys' grandparents dwindled – and all because I did not have the gumption to learn French. A pretty poor show really. I was losing my way.

During these first few years after Abbi passed away I became somewhat of a recluse. I hid away in the house and simply could not find a way to get over her. I could cope in a superficial way and on the surface I appeared fairly content, but within I was unsettled and lonely. The children did offer some respite, but language was a constant problem. Paul was beginning to pick up some English, but his native tongue was undoubtedly French, with a little Flemish thrown in. It just made it even more confusing for me.

Time flew by, even though I had done little but read and potter about. Two years passed. I was taking the boys for one of our regular walks in the Forest of Soigne when I heard the familiar sound of the English language being spoken by some people walking behind. I turned to look, but the group of three just behind us were now chatting in French. I could have sworn I heard English being spoken. They were an elderly couple, well into their sixties I thought, accompanied by a lady who, I guessed, was in her mid-thirties. She looked familiar. I had seen her before but could not place her. We walked on a little and then again I heard English being spoken. This time clearer and it was from the younger woman. I slowed to let them pass. The boys were playing amongst the trees, chasing one another. Now that Stephen was a little older, Paul spent quite a bit of time playing with him. I had seen her before, that's for sure. She was an attractive woman. About five foot eight in height with red hair tied in a ponytail and wearing round-rimmed spectacles. She wore a plain dress to just below her knees, black shoes with a sturdy heel and a tartan beret. Not exactly the height of fashion, but then they were just out for a walk on a Sunday. The tartan beret gave me some assurance that there might be a British connection. Why would someone in Belgium be wearing a tartan beret? I racked my mind to try and place her. Then I remembered. I had seen her sitting outside a café in town, alone. I had noticed her precisely because she sat alone and was wearing a tartan beret. One did not often see women sitting alone in a café, let alone with that beret. I remember thinking at the time that it was unusual. It was definitely her and she was definitely speaking English.

I was pretty desperate to have some level of adult communication in English. There were a few around town who spoke a little and I was able to speak to some people. The baker had married an Englishman, who had sadly been killed in the Great War, but she spoke pretty good English. A few words about bread and cakes were all we had managed to say between us. We joked each time I went into her shop. The mayor spoke good English, but I had no need to spend time with him. A little pidgin English with some locals, but that was about it. Sometimes I wondered why I was here, but soon remembered that it was about the boys and not just me.

I decided I was going to take the bull by the horns and just walk over to the three and introduce myself. It was not like me at all, but times were tough and I really needed to find someone to talk to. Perhaps I would finally find some friends and become normal again. Struggling with French was tiresome and extremely frustrating. As soon as I managed to get a few words out, I got lost in the response. If I dared to say, 'Bonjour, comment allez-vous?' I received a barrage of French and had absolutely no idea what had been said. It was awkward and embarrassing. It was a great deal easier not to say anything or to try in English. At least I had a chance to respond then. Someone to talk to in my mother tongue would be hugely satisfying.

I sped up a little to catch up with them and as I passed I turned to glance at the three, who were walking with their arms interlocked. The woman with the beret looked across at me and smiled. It reminded me of the smile offered by Abbi. This was my chance. I smiled back and enquired in a questioning but friendly tone:

'Do you speak English by any chance? I thought I heard...'

I was interrupted with:

'Oh yes. Are you English?' from the younger member of the trio.

The ice had been broken.

'Yes I am,' I responded. 'I live here with my two boys. How about you? I thought I saw you in town the other day?'

'Oh yes. I live here with my parents,' she said.

'Please forgive me,' I said. 'May I introduce myself. I am Harry Barker and those two running about over there are my sons. The older is Paul and his little brother is Stephen. We live nearby in Avenue de la Sapinière and are just out for a walk. To let them burn off a little energy, you know.'

'How nice,' came the polite reply. 'We live just down the road from you. I am Antoinette, but my friends call me Toni, and these are my parents, Maria and Henri Pergator.'

It was the beginning of a special relationship. I had finally found new friends in the Pergators. Because they had a good grasp of English, I began to spend more and more time with them, and with Toni, who had never married and had remained close to her parents.

Over the next few months Toni became an increasingly frequent visitor to the house, particularly whilst the children were at school. We would sit and discuss the rumblings of Hitler and the books we had read and talk quite a bit about her sister, who had married a Welshman and moved to Aberystwyth on the west coast of Wales. We had a great deal in common and I looked forward to her visits.

It was after an evening out, whilst I was walking her home, the flicker of moonlight playing on her soft white cheeks, that my emotions changed from platonic to sexual. I had not really encountered such emotion since Abbi passed away, probably because I had not had much contact with the opposite sex.

After a warm kiss on the doorstep of her parents' house that evening, my sexual emotions were aroused and whenever I saw her over the following weeks I noticed her soft breasts moving gently under her blouse. Her legs took on a new look and watching her natural swagger sent a shiver through my body. I couldn't wait to discover what lay beneath her clothing. The thought of lying beside her naked body, my hands caressing her soft skin, filled me with excitement. Feeling the warmth of her body against mine would be a dream come true. I simply had to have her. My fantasy became reality two weeks later and we became passionate lovers, taking every opportunity to tear each other's clothes off and indulge in lustful and passionate sex. My libido had gone into overdrive, perhaps making up for lost time, and Toni was game for it all.

The Pergators were quite a wealthy family, but all I knew of their background was that there was some connection with Luxembourg. They had a holiday house in Mimizan, a small town popular with holidaymakers on the southwest coast of France, about halfway between Bordeaux and Bayonne. Over the following years we would spend a few weeks there during the summer. We would drive down together and enjoy sunny days on the beaches with the boys, as well as excursions to nearby resorts and sights. We would sit on the terrace and talk for hours, a particular shared interest being the history of the area.

On 30th September 1938, at Heston Aerodrome, the British Prime Minister, Neville Chamberlain, returning from a summit with Hitler, declared that the Munich agreement meant "peace for our time". Few believed him.

For me, my evenings were generally spent listening carefully to the BBC international broadcasts and looking forward to Toni's next visit. As winter set in again, our day-to-day lives continued to pass by normally. Spring came and went. German troops moved into Czechoslovakia in March 1939 and in the summer the boys, Toni and I went off to Mimizan once again. It was on this holiday that Toni told me that her family had decided they would be leaving Belgium. There were rumours that Hitler was planning to attack Poland and it was considered by many that the agreement between Hitler and Chamberlain was not worth the paper it was written on. There was war in the air. Naturally I was very disappointed to learn of her departure. I tried to persuade her to stay, but she insisted that she had no choice. Her family in Luxembourg felt under threat as German troop movements on their borders increased. Maria and Henri had decided to leave and head to England. They had already made arrangements for them all to travel together. She was leaving five days after we returned from holiday.

It was something I also needed to give careful consideration to. Should we also leave now? The boys were happily enrolled at school and their lives were here in Belgium. Belgium was, after all, neutral. Hitler would not invade Belgium, I thought. I decided I would wait and see how things developed, but keep the idea on the back burner.

When we got back from ten days in Mimizan the boys returned to school and I had a farewell dinner with Toni at our favourite restaurant in St Gilles. We made love several times that night. I was going to miss her, but my priorities lay with Paul and Stephen.

CHAPTER FIVE

On 1st September 1939, Germany invaded Poland and Britain presented her with an ultimatum to withdraw. Hitler ignored the threat. At 11 a.m. on 3rd September 1939, with no response to the ultimatum, Britain declared herself at war with Germany. Within six weeks, Poland had been crushed and the country divided up between Germany and the Soviet Union. This battle was over, but the war was soon to begin. Concerns grew amongst other European countries. Where would Hitler turn next? Belgium, Holland and Luxembourg declared themselves neutral, but there were few among us who truly believed that we would not be caught up in the fighting.

During the following weeks, Hitler secretly called together his generals and explained that his intention was to invade France. This decision was not welcomed by the generals. Britain and France had much bigger armies, with more tanks, ships and aircraft. The German military might was outnumbered in both strength and technology. To invade France would be a dangerous move. Hitler, though, was known for his determination and enthusiasm for the unexpected. And his belief was absolute. His commanders came up with a plan to execute a successful attack on France and Britain. The idea was risky, but he was convinced that it would work.

They would attack on three fronts: from the northeast through Holland, from the south through Luxembourg and the southeast by the Albert Canal. A huge tank assault from the south would advance through neutral Luxembourg, bypassing the Allied and French defences along the Maginot Line. The tanks would sweep up through the forest of the Ardennes in southern Belgium and into France, heading north behind the Allied lines and entrapping their forces. From the southeast, the single major obstacle was the River Meuse. The best point to cross was at the Albert Canal. There was no significant defence here and, once over the river, there were no geographical obstacles until the shores of the English Channel. The attack and capture of crossings at the Albert Canal would be followed by a 1,200-strong Panzer division, led by the then little-known General Erwin Rommel.

For the first few months there was little fighting, but both sides began gathering defensive forces.

On 10th May 1940 Hitler launched his Western Offensive with the radio code word "Danzig", sending his forces into Holland and Belgium. Two thousand five hundred German aircraft set off and bombed airfields in Belgium, Holland, France, and Luxembourg, and 16,000 German airborne troops parachuted into Rotterdam, Leiden and The Hague. A hundred more German troops, employing air gliders, landed and seized the Belgian bridges across the Albert Canal. The Dutch army was defeated in five days. The Belgian campaign, code named "Blitzkreig", saw the Germans invade Luxembourg and move on into the forests of the Ardennes in southern Belgium. Allied forces poured into Belgium to confront the advancing enemy.

Within days there were soldiers and mounted horses everywhere. The local football club had become a centre for the army and the pitch was full of horses. British troops were arriving in Brussels in their thousands. I took the boys to see them marching on their way to the front. The locals were very amused at the sight of British officers marching ahead of their men with walking sticks swinging in time with their step. English gentlemen to the last.

Instead of advancing up towards Brussels, the German tanks turned left into France, breaking through the now lightly defended front line. The Allies had fallen into Hitler's trap. The Panzers headed northwards, behind the defending forces, entrapping tens of thousands of Allied troops in Belgium.

Three days after the launch of the Western Offensive and now in control of the bridges on the Albert Canal, General Rommel and his Panzer division began racing, virtually unchallenged, towards Brussels. The German pincer movement would ultimately push the defending forces up into the top corner of Belgium, trapping them on the beaches of Dunkirk.

On the news of the collapse of the defences in the south and seeing the chaos developing amongst soldiers and citizens in Brussels, I decided that there was no time to lose. My constant indecision had landed us right in the middle of a bloody war zone. Time had run out and we had to pack up and get out quickly. God help us if we got caught up in this fight. I was a Brit after all. Why in God's name had I not left months earlier? How could I have been so naive? Everyone had been talking about it. Toni had left. What had I been thinking? Too late now. We had to move, and fast.

'Jeanne!' I called out. 'Where are you, Jeanne!' I shouted louder and with some desperation in my voice.

'Oui, Monsieur Harry,' came her reply as she appeared through the doorway into the lounge. 'What is it?'

'For goodness sake, Jeanne. Please stop calling me Monsieur Harry! I am Harry. Just Harry. OK?' I pleaded.

'Oui, OK, Monsieur Harry – excusez-moi, 'Arry,' she replied. 'What is it, 'Arry?'

'You have heard the news?' I enquired. 'That the Germans have moved into Luxembourg and all hell is breaking loose?'

'Oui 'Arry.'

'Well, I have got to get the hell out and quick!' She sensed the desperation in my voice. 'Go round to Monsieur Dejong and ask them to come round this evening. I must make arrangements with them about the house and things. Please go now. Right away!'

'OK,' she said, 'I go right now,' and she disappeared out the way she had come in.

Ten minutes later she returned, saying that they would be here at nine o'clock.

I could hear the sound of gunfire and tank shells exploding in the distance as night began to fall. The boys were upstairs, having been put to bed by Jeanne.

It was dark outside when the doorbell rang. I moved from the lounge where I had been sorting through the paperwork that would be needed on our journey: passports, birth certificates, resident permits, identity cards, etcetera. Money also would be needed – as much as I could gather together. I entered the hall and opened the door to Albert and Paulette. Albert was wearing the usual dark-coloured jacket that seemed to accompany him everywhere. White shirt, collar and tie, plus his shiny black shoes. Under his arm was a folder. Paulette was shrouded in a long charcoal coat which hung all the way down to her ankles. She had a scarf around her neck and a black handbag over her shoulder.

'Come in,' I said, bowing my head slightly and gesturing to my side. 'Jeanne has prepared some tea in the dining room. Please go on through. You know the way.'

'Thank you,' said Albert, as he moved aside to let Paulette enter ahead of him. 'This is such a dreadful affair,' he continued. 'God only knows what will happen next. Paulette and I are terrified. We're not sure what to do.'

They made their way through the hallway into the lounge and then through the double doors into the dining room.

Jeanne entered the room from the kitchen, together with Yvonne.

'Good evening, Madame and Monsieur Dejong. Welcome. How are you?' said Jeanne.

'Very well, thank you,' they replied in unison.

'Please sit,' said Jeanne. 'Yvonne will bring some tea.'

Yvonne disappeared back into the kitchen.

We drew back the dining chairs and sat ourselves around the table. I had some papers already there and Albert placed his folder in front of him as he sat.

'This is very kind, Harry,' said Paulette.

'No, it is nothing,' I said, as I pulled in my chair.

Yvonne had reappeared balancing a tray containing a large china teapot, a small pot of milk, a bowl of sugar lumps and a plate with a few biscuits.

We all sat round the table looking at one another in a brief moment of silence. I interrupted the moment.

'Well, I think the time has come for us to leave Brussels. This impending war seems to be right on our doorstep now and I, as a British subject, simply cannot stay. I don't have much time, but I wanted to talk to you all about what we are to do. You all realise that, if I was to stay, I would be taken prisoner, and I fear for the future of the boys. I don't see that I have any choice but to make my way back to England.'

'I understand completely, Harry,' said Albert. 'You have no choice. Paulette and I have been giving the matter some thought. You must leave urgently. Tonight would not be too soon. What we can assure you is that we will take care of things here and look after Titou. You need not concern yourself with the house or anything here. We will take care of things, but you must leave as soon as you can.'

'That's very kind of you, Albert. I know you will do whatever you can, but you must not, under any circumstances, put yourself or any of your family at risk on my account. This is not your responsibility – but I appreciate your kindness.'

'So what have you decided, Harry?' asked Albert.

'I think it is best that we leave tomorrow before dawn. We will have a bit of a head start and may be able to get out of Brussels before the rush. I will take the boys and make for the coast. We should be able to get passage across the Channel and back to London. One of my brothers will meet us and we can take it from there.'

'But Monsieur,' piped up Jeanne, 'you will not be able to manage the boys alone. What if you cannot get to the coast, or are caught up somewhere along the route? I will come with you.'

'No, Jeanne. You have done enough. You must try to find your way back to your family. I could not possibly expect you to run the risk of travelling with us.'

'I have given this much thought,' said Jeanne. 'My brother is my only family. I don't really know where he is now and I have not had any contact with him for several years. The last I knew, he was in the south of France and I do not wish to go there. My life is with those boys and I simply could not live with myself if I did not know that you had all escaped safely. I will not discuss this further. My mind is set.'

'Please, Jeanne...' I pleaded.

'No. My decision is made. I will travel with you until I know the boys are safe. I do not wish to go to England, so once I know you are away I will make my way back to Brussels. Albert and Paulette have said I can stay with them, but I shall return here and see how things develop. I am Swiss, so have nothing to fear from the Germans.'

'All right. I understand and will be pleased for your support. Yvonne, what about you? Have you considered what you will do?' I asked.

'For now I shall stay here,' she replied. 'The house will need to be maintained. I shall make enquiries with my family in the south, but shall stay here for now. Monsieur and Madame Dejong are nearby and they have offered to let me stay with them if needed.'

'Are you sure?' I asked.

'Sure. This war will be over in a few months. I can wait.'

'Harry,' enquired Albert, 'I have a very big favour to ask.'

'Fire away,' I replied.

'First, I must explain,' he said. 'When the Great War broke out in 1914, the Germans came to Brussels. The Belgian people responded as best they could. Civilians fought from their homes, in the streets and from the rooftops. I was there, fighting for my country. The Germans were vicious. I remember vividly the day that they rounded up six hundred civilians and paraded them in the town square. As a reprisal for the loss of a few soldiers, they murdered all six hundred. This was a lesson for the Belgian people not to resist. Who knows what may happen this time? I fear for Monique. She is like a sister to your boys and we feel that she would be safe in England. Would you take her with you?'

'Good heavens, Albert,' I exclaimed. 'Are you sure?'

'Yes, we are sure,' Paulette replied. 'Please, Harry. Take her to England where she will be safe. Please!'

'Well... Jeanne, what do you think?'

'It would be fine by me,' said Jeanne. 'I will take care of her like my own. If there are any complications en route, I will bring her back safe.'

'Albert, I am honoured that you ask and have trust in me. I am surely shaken, but of course I will.'

'That is settled then,' said Albert. 'I have brought all the documentation you will need for her to travel with you, plus some money.'

He opened his folder and began to draw out the various papers and a wad of money bound together with string.

We sat together late into the evening, talking and planning our journey, which would begin early the next morning. Albert and Paulette left about midnight to pack up a few things for Monique. We would meet again at 3.30 a.m.

Daylight was beginning to break at four in the morning. The Studebaker had been loaded with a few bags and a number of baskets containing food and refreshments for the journey. The boys and Monique were running between the house and the car, very excited about our impending journey. They seemed to be completely unaware of the reasons for our hasty departure, but enthusiastically joshed with one another about who was to sit where in the car. As far as Monique was concerned, she was going on holiday.

Albert, Yvonne and Paulette stood alongside one another, trying desperately not to give away their emotional turmoil. I could sense their pain and fear. Was this going to be the last time they saw their daughter? It was the right thing to do, but it undoubtedly hurt deeply. I could feel their anxiety.

The three children piled into the back of the Studebaker, wriggling and chatting excitedly. After I had shaken the hand of Albert and gently kissed Yvonne on the cheek, I moved towards the car. Three kisses was the norm, but my English ways made me embarrassed, so a single kiss was all I could manage. Jeanne was hugging Paulette. I turned the ignition and the engine burst into life. This prompted Jeanne to complete her farewells and she jogged round to the passenger side and pulled the door closed. I reversed out of the drive, glancing back to the front of the house where the three stood in a row looking grey and glum, but with raised, waving hands.

Over the next eighteen days, the retreating Belgian forces fought bravely all through the country, from the Albert Canal near the German border to the North Sea. The Belgians both suffered and inflicted heavy losses, but after their capitulation on 27th May 1940, they were forced to surrender. The Belgian King, Leopold III, in his capacity as Head of State and Commander-in-Chief of the Belgian Army, had asked the Germans for a suspension of arms as he wished to spare his people further bloodshed. The King was made a prisoner of war and the Belgian cabinet (which had dissociated itself from his actions) set up a government-in-exile in London and announced its resolve to continue the war at the side of the Allies.

CHAPTER SIX

We set off around the outskirts of Brussels, with our planned route taking us up to Ghent, and then on to Ostende. As we made our way out of St Gilles, despite the early hour, the roads became increasingly congested. Brussels was in panic, with more and more people gathering together their possessions and making an escape northwards. Word was out that the defending Allied troops had flooded into Belgium, with the intention of halting the German advance. The evidence was clear from the number of soldiers, military vehicles, tanks and horses filling the roads – all heading south. We negotiated our way onto the main road for Ghent, where our pace slowed. A line of traffic stretched out ahead as far as we could see. The southbound road was packed solid with military vehicles of all shapes and sizes. Progress for us had slowed to walking pace. There was no sense of panic, just a calm resignation from drivers and passengers alike. It took several hours to travel just a few miles to where the main arterial road out of Brussels reduced to a single lane.

As we approached Aalst, a sizeable town about thirty kilometres north, the real picture began to unravel. Heading south were soldiers on foot and horseback. Trucks filled to the brim with men in a variety of uniforms and helmets. As many French as English, some Poles and the easily identifiable Scots with their kilts and fabric tartan hats.

More and more civilians made up the numbers travelling in our direction. The civilian population had obviously had a head start as, the further north we travelled, the greater the numbers there were fleeing. The scenes became increasingly desperate as more and more people joined the slowly moving queues along the roadside. Horse-drawn carts with tethered cows behind, bicycles, tractors and prams began to appear. Elderly women alongside children pulling trolleys piled high with blankets and clothes were accompanied by dogs, pigs and donkeys. People had taken everything they could carry, plus whatever might be valuable as food or shelter. Despite there being many cars and trucks, the route had become crammed with people walking beside the road. People of all ages, from babies being carried and in prams to elderly folk being helped or even pushed along in wheelchairs and carts. It was a sight I had not seen since the end of the first Great War as thousands of displaced people appeared from nowhere, jamming up the broken roads as they began to make their way home.

I felt somewhat uncomfortable in the now not-so-shiny Studebaker. The children spent most of our several hours on the road with their faces pinned to the windows, watching the incredible sights we slowly passed by. By nightfall we had not yet reached Ghent. Normally, this journey would take no more than a couple of hours. I decided to turn off the main road, which had slowed to a snail's pace, and seek a quiet spot in the countryside to park up for the night. The children could eat a few of the sandwiches we had brought with us and get some sleep. Our journey onwards was going to be long and arduous. Perhaps by the morning the roads might have eased and we would be able to make speedier progress.

A quiet spot beside an old wooden barn was found. I pulled up alongside and as I turned off the engine, silence filled the air. Jeanne unpacked the sandwiches, which were hastily devoured and washed down with milk. Within half an hour we had bedded the children down in the front and back seats of the car. Jeanne set herself down beside the Studebaker within easy reach and hearing of the children. I wandered into the barn. It was a hay barn, but with little in it, given the time of year. Harvest had not yet arrived and the stocks remaining from the previous year were low. I found some loose straw and kicked it together to create a covering on the dirt floor. A blanket and cushion was all I needed. I lay gazing into the dimness, wondering where tomorrow would take us. Sleep.

I was awoken by the rumbling of military vehicles on the road we had turned off the previous evening. I felt that we had travelled further into the countryside in our search for a resting place than we actually had. Deceptively, the road was only a short distance away. Jeanne already had the children up and was rearranging the bedding and seating in the Studebaker. I was grateful that she had let me sleep a little longer – I was going to need it. A glass of juice accompanied a dry croissant and then we were loaded up and on our way again. As we approached the main road, we could see that the situation had only worsened. There was no choice but to join the entourage heading north.

As it approached midday, the sun was directly above us. We had resigned ourselves to being stuck in the slow-moving traffic jam – there was nowhere else to go if we were to get to Ghent. All of a sudden, people began to run from the roadside into the farmland edging the road. Soldiers on vehicles travelling in the opposite direction jumped from their trucks beside us and disappeared into the long grass. I glanced into the rear-view mirror and saw people scattering in all directions as puffs of smoke appeared in the background from the vehicles behind us. For a few moments I heard nothing – and then the screaming of Stuka dive-bombers overhead. Within seconds they had passed as stones and grit flew up from beside the car. Rat-a-tat, rat-a-tat as bullets hit the ground along the roadside. There was no time to jump out of the car.

'Duck down!' I screamed. 'Everybody get down!'

No one seemed to understand why I was shouting, but the children covered their heads with their hands and Jeanne bent forward with her head in the foot-well. Stephen began to cry with terror and Monique peered at me, her face filled with fear and confusion. I peered back at them through the gap between the front seats. The roar was deafening and the gunshots ear-piercing as the two Stukas, one ahead of the other, disappeared down the road, wildly shooting at the stranded vehicles. Cars swerved off the highway and others splintered into bits as the bullets ripped at the metal chassis. Refugees dragged their animals into the adjoining fields and others abandoned their carts and horses to take cover. Within seconds they were gone. The children were crying and Jeanne got out from the front and opened the rear door, leaned in, and comforted the three little children who were crouching, terrified, in the back seat. Some vehicles had exploded and were burning fiercely. Slowly people began to reappear and, as if nothing had happened, gathered together their few possessions, which had been discarded as the planes approached, and re-formed their lines to continue the walk north.

It seemed that no one had been hurt in our vicinity. The traffic began to move again. I was numb. Confused and thanking God that we had not been hit. A close-run thing, but would they return to strafe the refugee lines and military queues again? Everyone was heading for Ostende. Would we be able to get aboard a ship there? If the whole of Belgium ended up in Ostende, what chance would we have of finding one? The place would be heaving and my children could not even speak English. After consideration, I concluded that they would not take us. Our chances were slim to none. We had transport and our chances would be improved if we could avoid the obvious point of crossing. Most people had no choice. I decided to turn off the road and head for Lille and up to Calais. As we reached the outskirts of Ghent, I turned left to Kortrijk.

By comparison with the road to Ostende, this was clear in the direction we were travelling. It was still busy with many vehicles and pedestrians, but not forming a solid traffic jam. We made good progress and reached Kortrijk by nightfall.

I had no intention of stopping after our experience earlier in the day. This time I was going to drive through the night. Luckily we found a refuelling station in Lille and filled up the car. Instead of heading up to Dunkirk, I cut across country to Bethune.

It was still dark as we approached Calais. I skirted the town and made for the port. I had been here several times before, when Abbi and I visited my family in England during the days of our courtship and marriage, so I knew my way around. Things seemed eerily quiet as we approached the harbour. My passengers began to stir as the street lights disturbed their sleep. There were a couple of fishing vessels, but no ferries or ships in port. I drove to the passenger terminal, from which a few lights sparkled. It was quiet, with only a few people about. The sky had begun to brighten as the sun rose. I parked alongside the terminal in an empty car park. Jeanne and I climbed out of the car and made our way into the terminal. A man in uniform approached us as we entered the building.

'Bonjour,' he said. 'Can I help you?'

'I hope so,' I said. 'We have travelled up from Brussels and hope to get a ferry to England.'

'Have you not heard, Monsieur?' he interjected. 'The Germans have broken through the Maginot Line into France and are heading up here. Everyone is leaving and all ships and boats have already left the port. There is chaos in Ostende and Dunkirk. You must leave immediately and go west. There is no chance of escape from Calais, Monsieur.'

'Are you sure?' I asked. 'When did this happen?'

'Just yesterday. Everyone is leaving, except for those who don't have the choice or are determined to stay. You must go west, Monsieur!'

It seemed we had little choice. Jeanne and I walked back to the car, where the children had their faces pressed up against the windows.

'Let's get out of here,' I said to Jeanne. 'We don't have much time. We'll take the coast road and make for Dieppe. We'll try again there.'

The sun was up and the sky was once more a clear blue. We drove out of the port and into the centre of Calais. The main crossroads displayed the signs. Dunkirk left. Bethune straight on. Abbeville right. At that moment, it came back to me. The time I had spent hiding in a cold, wet hole at the end of the Great War, looking at that dagger protruding from the muddy wasteland ahead of me. "Abbeville 72kms". Not again, I thought. Not all over again.

I turned right and put my foot down.

By noon we had reached Abbeville and turned off towards Dieppe and Rouen.

Dieppe was a main port almost as large as Calais. The main difference was that Dieppe was used primarily for commercial shipping and had no cross-channel passenger facilities. That we might not be able to take the car, board a train or find a comfortable seat was of no concern to me. Just to get out of France was the first priority. I did not wish to even think about the consequences of being taken by the Germans. Who knew how this war would pan out. Just get the hell out.

It was mid-afternoon as we approached the town, with the sun casting parallel shadows from the trees lining the road. It was probably best, I thought, to head for the centre-ville and ask. That was the plan. Jeanne was wide awake and the children were restless in the back. A walk around the town centre would do us good, anyway. It would be a chance to refuel and gather some food stocks. Perhaps we could get a meal.

Following signs to the centre-ville brought us to the Church of St. Jacques, a 600-year-old building and a superb example of gothic architecture, featuring huge, flying buttresses complete with scowling gargoyles and intricate stained-glass windows. I parked alongside, near a row of shops. We dragged ourselves from the car, stretching as we stood upright, and then made for a small café some twenty metres ahead of us. We passed a patisserie displaying a few chocolate figurines and then a toy shop with a wide selection of puppets that filled the window display. It reminded us of a performance of *Snow White* the children had performed a few years ago. They stopped, pointing their fingers at various characters hanging from strings and sitting hunched on pedestals. A large wooden puppet version of Pinocchio featured in the centre of the display. His wooden head tipped back and his loose arms hung from his side as he sat slumped on a three-legged stool. The character brought a smile to our faces and all three children looked and pointed as they recognised the bright-coloured character from the books we had at home.

The children did not want to leave, but were ushered away by Jeanne, their heads steered by her hands. We entered the café next door. Chairs screeching on the tiled floor, we filled the table nearest the window. We were soon tended to by a tubby Frenchman with a wispy moustache.

'Oui, Monsieur, Dame?' he quizzed.

The café was dimly lit, with the only light coming from the window fronting the street. A layer of smoke could clearly be seen hovering at head height across the room. The strong aroma of Gauloises cigarettes and pipe tobacco drifted through the café.

The three men propping up the bar spoke loudly, arguing about the impending German occupation. News had obviously reached Dieppe that the Germans had broken through into France and were racing northwards. Nobody knew if the Allied forces would be able to stop them. If not, it was just a matter of time before they began their invasion of France. Fear was in the voices of the three – and a clear sense of anger. Between us and the bar was a table occupied by four Frenchmen, each wearing dark-coloured jackets and flat berets. Two were smoking cigarettes and the others had spindly pipes. The familiar small glasses of cloudy white pastis, accompanied by a jug of water, adorned the table. The men were deliberating the fact that all shipping vessels had left the port and had not offered to take anyone with them. We ordered coffee for Jeanne and I, orange juice for the children, plus a croque monsieur each.

As we waited for our refreshments, Jeanne translated the gist of the conversation and I concluded that there was no likelihood of a maritime escape. What had become more apparent was that I was in trouble. If I were not able to make an escape, I would be taken prisoner sooner or later. What might happen to the children then was not worth thinking about. Our capture was not an option. I had to find a way out.

As we sat in silence, thoughts ran through my mind. Go west. But that led to Brest, a huge naval base. The Germans would make directly for there that was for sure. Stay and wait? Not really an option. Go south into Brittany and see what happened over the coming days and weeks? Things might settle down. Oh, what to do!

A screech of tyres interrupted both my thoughts and the noisy debates in the bar. The back doors of a small Citroën van flew open and three men, scarves covering their faces, jumped out, brandishing bricks and sticks. There was a loud crash, followed by the sound of the glass of the main display window shattering. Then the glass door to the puppet shop was smashed by a flying brick and the three men rushed into the shop, shouting:

'German pig! Get out of here, you German pig!'

Jeanne grabbed hold of the children and crouched in the corner beside our table. I retreated, placing myself between them and the café window, shaking with fear. The remaining customers all made for the front door to see what was happening.

A few moments passed with loud banging, crashing, shouting and screaming coming from the shop next door. Within moments a tall man suddenly appeared in the street, stumbling over and falling to his knees. The three men followed, wielding their sticks and beating him about his body and head. A stricken woman followed, screaming at the men who were beating her husband. She was waving her arms about in a chaotic frenzy, trying to stop the attack upon the man who was now huddling on the cobbled street, attempting to protect his head from the blows.

'German pig! Go home, we don't want your kind here!' the three men yelled as they pounded the man about his body. He slumped to the ground while clutching his side, having received a kick in the kidneys, but this only left his head undefended from further blows from his attackers. Crouching over their victim, and seeing the man resigned to his fate, with a final flurry of verbal abuse the three masked men raced to the back of the van and jumped in. The woman scrabbled about on the pavement, picking up the bricks which had smashed the window and hurling them at the van as the back doors slammed and it sped off down the road.

The woman returned to her beaten husband, who was trying to get to his feet. Blood covered his face and seeped from his head as she wrapped her arms around his chest and helped him up. The men in the bar had gathered at the doorway, pushing and shoving as they tried to see over one another. We remained huddled in the corner, terrified at what we had just witnessed.

The woman helped her bleeding husband back into the shop as quiet settled in the street once more. The clientele of the café gathered together in a group at the bar, gesticulating as they re-enacted the event. No one went to the aid of the woman or her husband. I was paralysed with shock. I had not seen anything like this before. My experiences in the war had been awful, but I had never witnessed a cold-blooded attack on a single man by a pack of angry thugs. The children were crying once again and Jeanne was doing her best to comfort them, offering reassurance that it was all over and they were safe.

The experience had been very frightening and, with appetites lost, we made our excuses and ushered the children out of the café, with our shoes crunching on the broken glass littering the pavement. We hurriedly jumped into the car and made off out of town, leaving Dieppe behind us. The shock of what had happened had scared us all so deeply that no one seemed able to say anything. I drove on, deep in thought. The appalling events of the attack outside that bar and the terrifying thought of what might befall us if we were captured by the Germans filled my mind once more. I had to get out of France. But how?

It was not far to Le Havre from here. We would be there in no more than a couple of hours. Le Havre offered another opportunity to find a ferry or boat across the Channel to safety. It was a major industrial harbour situated on the mouth of the River Seine which ran all the way into Paris. It was one of the largest commercial ports on the northern coast of France, bringing in and taking out vast quantities of produce from all over the world. Surely there would be some form of shipping there which would take us out of France?

We soon reached the approaches to Le Havre. The port was situated on the northern side of the river, so if we were unable to secure a passage it was a long drive back inland to get across the Seine and further west. It was worth the risk. Every hour we remained in France made it more likely that we might end up being captured by the Nazis. The consequences of that were not worth thinking about. Somehow I had to find a way. Le Havre offered a possibility.

As we entered the town from the north we drove along the beach-front promenade. There were hundreds of small white wooden beach cabins filling the first thirty metres of sand. I had never seen so many little huts. It reminded me of Brighton beach when we went there for the day in the twenties. The main difference was that the beach was long, there were many more huts and they stood six or more deep. The beach, however, was almost deserted, with a few people walking along the sand, some with dogs. It was late in the day and my objective was not one of sightseeing but rather ship hunting. I continued on towards the port which lay ahead, clearly identified by many large cranes reaching up into the sky. As we drew nearer, the cranes multiplied in number and stood in rows along the quayside. There were a few people milling about. They looked like seamen of some kind. Not military, as none had any kind of uniform. They stood in small groups wearing caps and heavy jackets and smoking pipes. Several ships were moored alongside and that gave me hope. How to enquire about passage aboard one of these giant ships was another matter. I had no idea where to go or who to ask. With my very poor French it seemed the only option was to ask Jeanne to do the enquiring. That was not such a good thought. These men looked rough and tough. Weathered by the sea. Not likely to be responsive to a gentle woman or look sympathetically at the plight of wide-eyed children. I thought they looked more as if they might like to have the children served up as a hearty meal than offer them refuge and comfort. I was scared.

Regardless, I drove into the docks, through a heavy iron gate which had no security guards, although there was a hut and descending bar which stood erect to the side. I scanned the area and spotted a large building off to the left with people hanging around the entrance, either side of which there were parking spaces. I drove up slowly and pulled to a halt in one of the spaces. Jeanne and I both got out together and stood beside the car, looking around and then at one another.

'Let's go in there and ask,' I said.

'OK,' she replied. 'You stay here,' she said in French to the children, who were all sitting staring at us as we stood beside the car.

We walked over towards the main double-door entrance and entered into a lobby area. We were met by a uniformed man who stepped forward and asked in French:

'Yes, sir and madam. How can I help you?'

'This gentleman and his three children are refugees from Brussels trying to find a ship that might take them to England,' said Jeanne.

'Not possible, I am sorry to say,' replied the uniformed man. 'The last ship left yesterday, bound for America. Since midnight three British warships have arrived in the Channel and are patrolling the waters for German naval ships and U-boats. No ships are to leave port until they have been given clearance from the navy. I am sorry.'

'What? No ships at all. But these people are British. They must get out of France. Surely there will be some ships taking refugees?' Jeanne enquired.

'I am sorry. For now there are no ships leaving port here, or anywhere along this coastline as far as I am aware. The danger is too high. Until the events in Belgium become clear, no one is going anywhere. I am sorry. You can wait if you wish.'

'For how long?' enquired Jeanne.

'I don't know. Perhaps a few days, perhaps a few weeks. I don't know.'

We looked at one another. I got the gist of the conversation. It was not good news. We turned and walked towards the heavy wooden doors and out into the car park.

'What do we do now, 'Arry?' asked Jeanne.

'We go on. Perhaps we go south into Brittany. Maybe we will find something further south. Maybe things will settle down. Maybe refugee ships will be sent. Maybe not. Lots of maybes. We can't stay here, so we go on.'

We climbed back into the car and drove out through the heavy iron gate, the stop bar still pointing to the sky, and headed out of Le Havre. Following the banks of the Seine inland, we came to a bridge which allowed us to go further west, away from the fighting and into uncertainty.

It was soon sunset and dusk began to fall. It became increasingly difficult to follow the lanes through the Normandy countryside with the sun directly ahead of me. The search for departure ports along the northern coastline had proved fruitless and our day in Dieppe and Le Havre had been hugely stressful and disappointing. We had been travelling for three days now with no real rest or sleep.

The three children were soon asleep on the back seat of the car, with Monique slumped backwards, her head resting on the small, rear fixed window. Her mouth was slightly open and there was a shiny, silky moisture-glaze on her bottom lip.

I glanced to my side, where Jeanne sat upright, gazing directly ahead. She did not react in any way to the turning of my head or the humming of the engine. She gazed ahead into space and I realised her thoughts were elsewhere. Her complexion was pale, with a grey sheen that made her appear much older than her years. Her hair was swept back into a bun but looked a little bedraggled. It was unkempt and in need of a warm-water wash to bring back the sheen and natural bounce. I had not really looked at Jeanne in any other way than as a hired hand. To me she had never been a woman with the attractions and personality that would catch the attention of men. Glancing back into the rear-view mirror, to the three youngsters lined up on the back seat, suddenly made me think about how such a woman had given up so much for the care of someone else's children. She was undoubtedly perfectly able to have her own children and a family with a home and husband. Why had she decided to leave that aside and commit herself to caring for Paul and Stephen?

When she rested, there was a natural smile forever present on her face. Some people rest with a grimace or frown. Jeanne rested with a Mona Lisa smile. It was gentle and subtle, but unmistakably there. She seemed content, but she couldn't possibly be. We had hurried away, leaving behind all she knew in Brussels, and headed in the opposite direction to where she came from, to a place she knew nothing of, and with people she only knew through her association with me.

She was intelligent, and an attractive woman from head to toe. She seemed to have a natural affinity to engage the boys in her creativity and always delivered her instructions and requests in a tone that it was impossible not to obey. There was a relationship between the boys and Jeanne which seemed quite unique. They were perhaps even more attached than most mothers and children. At this time the relationship between mother and child was expected to be distant. Children were to be seen and not heard, which restricted the emotional attachment. Jeanne was feared but revered by the boys. During these past few days I had seen a side to Jeanne I had never seen before. I had never realised her love and devotion for my children. In a strange way this endeared me towards her. Was I beginning to see Jeanne in a different way?

I was alone in control of our destiny, with little real plan of what to do or where to go. I was terrified of what lay ahead, but could not let my fear show.

I checked the fuel gauge and noted that it was half-full. I thought it should be good for another two hundred kilometres. I was not too familiar with Normandy, but did know that there was not much here. There was some agriculture and a little sheep farming, with much of the landscape featuring apple orchards with small villages dotted between the hills. Houses of typical Normandy style, timber-framed with clay peg-tile roofs, or grey-stone with slate roofs and window shutters of all colours were scattered across the landscape.

The next main town was Caen and as we approached, I came across a main junction. My options were Bayeux and Cherbourg to the north, Paris to the south or St Malo and Rennes to the west. Heading up to Cherbourg seemed pointless. All our efforts to seek cross-channel shipping had failed, so a further excursion up to that port did not offer much hope. I decided to continue towards St Malo, where we should have been able to refuel at the very least. If we had no joy with cross-channel transport there, we would be able to get to the next main town without the worry of running out of fuel. My next priority was to find some sort of overnight accommodation. We had not enjoyed the luxury of sleeping in a proper bed for several days. It was time to give my weary passengers some proper rest and a decent meal. We had been living on bread and fruit. I, too, was tired. The war was behind us for now. We had not heard the sound of gunfire or artillery shelling for three days. All the fighting was in Belgium and the northeastern corner of France. There were no signs of refugees here: the roads were empty and life appeared normal. The next small hotel or house showing accommodation was my objective. And the sooner the better.

As I drove through the Normandy countryside, all four of my passengers remained still. Weariness had overcome them. Paul and Stephen, with their eyes firmly shut and heads bowed, slept quietly.

After another two hours of driving, my passengers began to stir. It seemed that our best chance of finding accommodation would be the coastal town of Avranches. We should reach there before it became dark and would all welcome the shelter and comfort.

By eight in the evening, the sun, which had shone into my eyes for two hours as it descended to the west, began to break the horizon. A bright streak of scarlet spread across the darkening sky as we approached the outskirts of Avranches. Within minutes there was a sign saying "Chambres d'Hôtes" and I turned left onto a small gravel lane leading up to a large square house.

The façade had a grey, rendered finish with pale grey frames around the windows. The building stood three-storeys tall with four sets of windows on each side of the main centrepiece of the building – a large wooden door with an arched top and a heavy, black, circular knob in the centre. There were two stone steps leading up to the door, which was shrouded by a wrought-iron arch covered in twisted wisteria in full blossom. The gravel road opened up into a small, open, car-park area, flanked by grey rocks. Alongside the grand house stood a barn with an old cart standing in front of the large wooden doors. It was hard to tell if it was part of a display or whether this was a working cart that had been left outside.

We pulled up in the far corner of the parking area and Jeanne got out and made her way up to the great wooden entrance. For the first time I noticed the sway of her hips. Beside the door, there was a chain, hanging from an oval bell. She pulled it and a chiming sound rang out. She turned and glanced back at me. A soft smile.

The door opened and before her stood a short, slightly stooped elderly lady. She wore a pale blue pinny and brown slippers. A conversation took place and after a short while Jeanne turned towards us – we had our faces pinned up against the car windows – and signalled with her hands, beckoning us to come. I knew then that we had found a resting place.

The sun shone through tall windows into the dining room, where we were gathered round a large cloth-covered dining table. It was eight forty-five on a crisp sunny morning. We had all slept soundly, grateful for the softness of a comfortable bed. Breakfast was croissants and small baguettes with apple jam and black coffee. The children washed down their warm bread rolls with fresh jus de pomme, their smiling, spotless faces and busy hands a sight to behold.

Soon we were all back in the Studebaker, clean and refreshed and ready for the next leg of our journey into the unknown. I had decided that we would make a quick stop in St Malo on the off chance that there might be a ship to England. In fact, our visit to the town was also made compulsory by the need for fuel. With a quiet but powerful engine, the Studebaker was a thirsty beast. It had the capacity to hold twenty gallons of fuel but that would only carry us three hundred kilometres. On the narrow, twisty lanes of Normandy, that distance would be even less. And fuel was both difficult to find and expensive. St Malo offered us the security of a certain fuel supply and an outside chance of an escape back to England.

The streets in the town were busy with vehicles and carts laden with a variety of produce, mainly agricultural. I followed the signs to centre-ville, hoping to come across a petrol station or shop where we could replenish our food stocks. St Malo was a sizeable town and there was little evidence of the war present on the streets. People seemed to be going about their business in a normal, everyday way. I soon found a petrol station which had plenty of fuel, with no signs of panic. It was right at the entrance to the harbour and probably the best located to fuel the many small fishing boats littering the waterfront. While I filled the tank to the brim, Jeanne enquired whether there were any ships that were due in or which had recently left the harbour carrying refugees or soldiers. The answer was that no ships had been in the harbour for several days and most fishing boats had ceased to fish. News of the events in the north had filtered through and the fishermen had decided to stay in port until things settled down. British warships in the Channel had also been reported in St Malo. No one was setting out to sea for the foreseeable future. An escape from St Malo seemed unlikely, so I made my way into the centre of town, seeking shops. I drove into the main square and parked. Shops lined the sides, with tarpaulin-covered carts, filled with fresh farm produce, bordering the pavement. I handed Jeanne some money and asked her to buy everything she thought we would need for the next three days: fruit, bread, cold meats, salad, milk and water. I also asked her to get some sweets for the kids. She disappeared into the crowds while I sat in the car with the children.

Fifteen minutes later she returned, her arms filled with paper bags brimming with fruit and bread. Unloading her bounty into the boot of the car, she headed off again into the crowded market place.

After a few more trips she had bought all we needed and, giving me a thumbs-up, made her way to the passenger door and jumped in. We knew we would be fine for several days and could continue our journey south. I fired up the Studebaker and slowly headed out of town, looking for signs to Rennes.

As we travelled south towards Rennes, the Brittany countryside was very reminiscent of England. The roads were straight and narrow, and often either protected by hedgerows or left open, with trees spaced equally on both sides, creating a kind of corridor. These kinds of roads were only seen between larger towns and where the landscape was flat. They had been built by the Romans, with their uncanny knack for building in straight lines, and they generally planted trees on either side, marking the route. Many years before, when I was a child, my father occasionally took us to the beaches of Cornwall on brief summer breaks. The journey was long and I don't recall much of it, but the beaches were sandy and the sea icy cold. The countryside of Brittany seemed similar to that of Devon and Cornwall. A hilly landscape with miles of green fields, stone hedgerows and large trees. The main difference was that the villages in Brittany were clusters of rendered symmetrical buildings surrounded by rickety, huge timber-framed barns flanking simple, thatched farm cottages on the outskirts. As I drove on through the countryside, it seemed strangely familiar, which made me feel a little more comfortable when considering the reality of our situation. Perhaps the familiarity of the environment had tricked my mind, offering me a false sense of security. It made me feel reassured, but I did not really know why.

As we arrived on the outskirts of the larger town of Rennes, the familiar signs of clusters of houses began to become apparent. Rennes was located more or less in the centre of this northwest corner of France. The main ports of Brest in the far west, St Nazaire in the south and St Malo in the north gave Rennes the ideal geographical location for all-round distribution of the region's goods.

I stopped on the roadside to have a look at the map. Where to from here? My idea was to find a quiet corner somewhere on the south Brittany coastline. This was as far as we could go from the fighting and well away from major towns. If the Germans were to invade, it would take some time for them to get to a small village in southern Brittany. There would be bigger fish for them to fry first. Vannes seemed a good place to head for. It was relatively small and out of the way. Situated on the Gulf of Morbihan, we could find a secluded spot, sit tight and wait to see what develops. I selected first gear and edged my way back on to the road. I skirted Rennes and followed directions to Vannes, about 130 kilometres south. We would reach Vannes well before nightfall.

The children were hungry and weary by the time we reached the outskirts of the town. I decided we would try once more to find a place to stop and get a hot meal. The memories of Dieppe had faded and I sensed a feeling of safety once again. We stopped at a roadside routier restaurant. The food was simple but excellent. We feasted on hot meat and potato stew and I treated Jeanne and myself to a carafe of local red wine. By the time we had filled our bellies, the experience of Dieppe seemed almost forgotten. I placed the map on the table as the children devoured île flottante, their favourite French dessert.

The most secluded spot we could find that was within a day's reach was the small fishing village of Port Navalo, just beyond Arzon on the furthest point of the Gulf of Morbihan. If the Germans were to eventually reach this side of France, they would have to go some to find us in this remote fishing village. The location also gave us the option of going south if necessary, plus the possibility of rescue by sea. The northern side of the gulf would see us cornered, but the southern side gave us an escape route, if needed. That is where we would go.

It was dark as we entered Arzon and drove through the centre-ville out towards the tiny fishing village of Port Navalo, only a kilometre or so beyond Arzon. There was hardly a soul to be seen. A couple of hundred metres on from what looked like Port Navalo village square we reached the small fishing harbour. We could go no further.

With few signs of life in Port Navalo itself, we returned to Arzon and found a small chambre d'hôte, which would become our base for the next few days while we sought more permanent accommodation. On the advice of the owner, we made the short walk into the town centre and into the one and only shop, which doubled up as a letting agency for a few summer holiday cottages rented out in the locality. Our luck was in and two properties were available. The first was a two-bedroom flat on the northern side of Arzon and the second a three-bedroom holiday cottage situated on the Chemin de Petit Mousse next to the beach and close to Port Navalo harbour. Arrangements were made to view the two properties later in the day. We were keen to see if either would give us shelter and somewhere to stay.

The cottage was ideal. It overlooked the beach and had a wonderful sea view. We could see Quiberon, situated on the end of the peninsula jutting out from the mainland on the western side of the Quiberon Bay. Only about fifteen kilometres across the bay, as the crow flies. It was about a kilometre to Arzon town centre and its shops and only a short walk to Port Navalo Harbour. The cottage was typically French, with shuttered windows and tiled floors throughout. It was fully furnished with a double bed in one room and two singles in the others. I could have my own bedroom, Jeanne and Monique would share, as would the boys. The kitchen was fully fitted-out with pots, pans and plates and the main lounge area housed three single, comfy chairs surrounding a dark, well-worn rug. It was as if the house was waiting for us to turn up. Perfect! We struck a deal.

Within a few days we were settled in and stocked up with food. I sent a telegram to Albert, telling him that we were safe and where we were. I could but hope it would reach him in Brussels. We would sit it out here for the time being and see how things developed. I could also find out more on options of escape and whether or not refugee ships were planned.

CHAPTER SEVEN

The people of Arzon were welcoming and warm. Cut off from most of the goings-on in France, they lived an independent lifestyle and everyone knew everyone. Our arrival did not go unnoticed and we soon became well-known in the community, as we became the subject of great debate. The few shops in the town consisted of a café, grocery store, patisserie, boulangerie and a repair garage which doubled up as a maison de la presse, selling cigarettes and beach accessories that catered for holidaymakers.

The town was run by two families. The local shop was the life of Monsieur Leclerc and he had some influence over several of the retail shops in the square. He was a short, stocky man with a pencil moustache and a very welcoming face. He and his wife had run the village shop since his parents had passed it on about fifteen years ago. 'Once a shopkeeper, always a shopkeeper,' he used to say. His family had lived in the village for generations and he was known by everyone and knew everyone. His brother was the mayor and had married a girl from Saint Nazaire, a coastal town about an hour further south. They had a beautiful teenage daughter and, as well as being the official representative of the commune, Monsieur Leclerc was also the local builder. If any development were to take place in Arzon, or Port Navalo for that matter, it would need to be approved and built by the mayor, as would any extensions or refurbishment.

As the main shopkeeper in the village, Monsieur Leclerc was also the only retailer who sold locally caught fish. His relationship with the few fishermen was absolutely solid. He and his brother ensured that the locals would always be the first to receive fresh fish from any catch before the bulk of it went to market. It was one of the priorities that Monsieur Leclerc insisted upon. In this way, he would ensure that his business was always profitable.

The fishing fraternity was under the management of Jean-Paul Lafayette. He skippered one of three fishing boats operating out of Port Navalo. Monsieur Lafayette had lost his wife four years earlier, and was the father of three children, all girls, who were now in their late twenties. All had married and moved south with their husbands, close to Bordeaux, and it had occurred to him to take himself south if the war came to Port Navalo. The younger two girls had married brothers from a well-to-do winery in the Medoc. The eldest had adopted a life of self-sufficiency in the pine forests of the Landes, where she lived on a smallholding with her artist husband, a few chickens, a dozen ducks, some pigs and a horse.

Jean-Paul was a burly figure, his face showing the scars of many years facing the harsh winds and weather of the Bay of Biscay on his small fishing boat. His clothing rarely changed. He wore an old, thick-knitted wool jersey, sleeves pulled up to the elbow, and a heavy leather belt holding up dark baggy trousers that were tucked into a pair of well-worn leather boots. A flat cap listing to starboard sat on his head and he always had a Gauloises cigarette hanging from his mouth, sometimes lit and sometimes not.

We settled in, and the pressures of running from the threat of the Germans diminished. We had no way of knowing what was happening outside of the small town and fishing port. The locals seemed not to care or be interested. Whatever was going on was all too far from here. I, though, needed to know, so I enquired at the shop for a radio. It would be a few days, I was told.

It was a warm summer's evening and we had all enjoyed a meal on the terrace overlooking the beach. There remained just a bottle of wine and two glasses on the table plus a pack of cigarettes and an ashtray. I lit another cigarette and topped up the two glasses. The sun had set and the sea was lit by a bright moon, sending a streak of light over the water and lighting the white foam of the small breaking waves as they gently washed up on the sandy beach. The children had settled in bed after a busy day playing in the garden and building sandcastles on the beach. Jeanne and I sat looking out across the water.

'It has been a difficult time this past two weeks,' I said.

'It has, 'Arry. The children have been very good, really. What they have been through! And still, we do not really know what will happen next,' said Jeanne.

'It is very difficult to know what to do. When I get that radio I have ordered it will give us a clearer picture about what is going on. Hopefully we will have a better idea of what to do.'

'That's true. I really hope things have calmed down a bit, but I am not optimistic. I just hope to God that we can find a way out of this mess.'

'What are you going to do if I do manage to find a way to escape with the children, Jeanne?'

'Oh, I don't know. I know I will miss you and the children. I don't like to think about it really.'

She leaned over to reach for her glass of wine. The moonlight fell upon her face. She was quite beautiful, I thought. My eyes moved down her neck towards her breasts, moulded by the tightness of her blouse. She looked up and caught me staring. She smiled. I looked away, embarrassed.

'Do you miss Toni?' she asked, continuing to smile.

I was taken aback by the question. She had never asked anything so personal. I didn't know quite how to respond. Of course I did and I missed our closeness and the passion.

'A little,' I replied. 'Haven't you had anyone in your life, Jeanne?' I asked. 'You are a beautiful woman, but you have never said anything about your personal life.'

'You have never asked, 'Arry. I have had a few lovers but it has never worked out,' she said, looking down towards her knees with a frown. I have found what I wanted here with you and the boys. It is special and enough for me.'

She looked out across the sea and took another sip from the glass.

'We all need people in different ways,' she said. 'I have been able to get what I need from you.'

'How do you mean?' I asked.

'I have never mentioned this before, but I am not able to have children. When I was a teenager I became ill and the result of that illness meant I would not be able to have children. As I said, I have had a few lovers, but it always ended because I could not get pregnant.'

She sipped at her wine.

'I wanted to have a family of my own, but it was not meant to be. I discovered that I could find that inner contentment by doing what I do. It has worked for me so far.'

'I am so sorry, Jeanne. I had no idea.'

'It is not your fault, 'Arry. It is as it is. You don't realise what you have given me. Do not feel sorry, please. I don't want you to feel sorry for me.'

'You have always been special to me and I have always wanted to be sure you would remain with us. I don't know how I could cope without you,' I said.

'There's no need to say that 'Arry. We all need people, perhaps in different ways, but we all need people. That is what I think anyway.'

We talked on late into the evening. The bottle was empty. I had smoked about ten cigarettes and consumed a glass of brandy when Jeanne declared she was off to bed.

'Goodnight and thank you,' I said, as she stood up to leave the terrace.

'Thank you, too,' she replied. 'It was good to talk.'

And with that she disappeared through the doorway into the darkness of the lounge.

I finished my cigarette, collected up the two glasses and empty bottle of wine and stumbled slightly unsteadily through the lounge into the kitchen. Having placed the items in the sink, I made my way into the bathroom, brushed my teeth, which was a ritual I had practised since being at school, and crept into my bedroom. The room was lit by the brightness of the moon shining in through the open window. I discarded my clothes on the chair beside the bed, pulled back the bedding and slipped in between the sheets. Pulling the blanket up to my chest, I laid on my back with both hands behind my head, thinking about the evening I had just had with Jeanne.

A squeak of the bedroom door handle turning and the door opening interrupted my thoughts. I looked straight down the bed towards the door as it opened. In the doorway appeared the image of a woman lit by the light from the moon. I sat up, gazing across the room at her. She moved into the room and closed the door behind her. She turned and looked at me. I whispered, 'Jeanne?'

She moved towards me and raised her hand up towards her face. With her index finger close to her lips she gently whispered, 'Shhhh.'

She glided over the floor towards me. I stared in amazement, my heart pounding. She climbed on to the bed and straddled me, only her nightdress and the bedclothes between us. She leaned forward and our lips touched. Her soft lips against mine. A gentle kiss. With her face just an inch or so from mine, she stared into my eyes, her hair falling down over her shoulders, and spoke quietly:

'It's you, 'Arry. It has always been you, and tonight you are mine.'

She sat back upright, squatting upon me, wrapped her arms around herself and slowly lifted her nightdress up and over her head, revealing her naked body lit by the moonlight from the window.

I was awoken by the bright sunlight streaming in through the window and lighting the room. I turned over to wrap my arm around her, but there was no one there. She had gone and I was alone in the bed.

Several days passed before the small radio I had ordered from the shop in town turned up. News of the debacle in Dunkirk filled the airwaves. Bulletins on how thousands of soldiers had been trapped on the beaches and how hundreds of small boats had crossed from England to rescue the stricken men. The story was a tragedy. Thousands lost and thousands taken prisoner. We had only just managed to escape in time. Belgium had fallen, as had Holland and Luxembourg. The allies had suffered a massive defeat. The huge German fighting machine was moving towards Brest in the west and south to Paris. There were no armies to stand in their way and there were no signs that Hitler was going to stop the pace of invasion and occupation. We would soon need to move, but to where?

Two weeks after our arrival in Port Navalo, the children were playing in the front room when their game was interrupted by a loud knocking at the front door. Jeanne, who had been preparing food in the kitchen, made her way towards the door, wiping her hands dry on her pinny as she walked, closely followed by Monique. I stood looking down the corridor, wondering who was calling on us. As Jeanne opened the door, my view was obscured and I couldn't quite make out who was there, other than that it was a man wearing brown trousers and a dark grey coat. I recognised the figure and stature, but he stood with his back to me, so I couldn't quite identify this tall, dark-haired man.

As Jeanne opened the door, the figure turned towards her. She raised her hands to her face, cupping her cheeks, as her eyes widened. A gentle cry of 'Mon dieu' came from her lips. Monique peered round Jeanne's hip to see who was there and then jumped forwards, holding up her arms. The three disappeared from my view behind the slowly closing door as they fell outside into the arms of the surprise visitor. As I moved towards the entrance, Jeanne called out, ''Arry! Come quickly!'

Paul skidded on the wooden floor in his socks, turning the corner and bumping into me. Then I saw him. Albert Dejong. Paul couldn't believe his eyes.

'Monsieur Dejong!' he cried out and ran into his arms as Albert bent down to catch him in his embrace. Behind us stood the solitary figure of Stephen, with his toy still clutched in his hand. Albert broke our embrace and moved towards the confused-looking Stephen, with arms outstretched. 'Mon petit garçon!' he said, as he swept him up off the floor and held him up to the ceiling, looking into his bewildered eyes. A smile swept across his face as he recognised the warm, familiar face of Albert.

'How did you know where we were?' asked Jeanne.

'Harry sent me a message telling me you were here in Port Navalo,' he replied.

'But how did you get here?' enquired Jeanne.

'On my bicycle,' said Albert, turning away and pointing to a bicycle resting up against the garden fence.

'On your bicycle! But it is hundreds of kilometres from Brussels. How did you make such a journey?'

'I knew you were here in Port Navalo and I also knew that the Germans had invaded France and were moving across towards Brittany. I also heard that there were no ships leaving from the French north or west coast and I was very worried that you would not be able to get away. So I decided to come and find you. I managed to get on the train for some of the journey, so it has only taken five days to get here. I could not leave my daughter alone in France – not to mention you, Jeanne. It was my duty to come and get you or at the very least know that you had managed to get to England safely.'

'Come in, come in,' I said. 'I will explain, Albert. Come and sit in the lounge and Jeanne will get something to eat. You must be exhausted and starving.'

We all made our way into the lounge and stood for a few moments, gazing at the man who had travelled for five days by train and bicycle to find us.

That evening after supper the children were put to bed and we three sat at the table. The next three hours were spent telling Albert the story of our attempts to cross the Channel, and then listening to him recount the journey which had brought him to Port Navalo.

CHAPTER EIGHT

I had been listening every day for news reports on the evacuation of troops and civilians from the west coast of France. There was little to go on, but I knew the Germans were moving west quickly. An obvious exit port was Brest, but, with all the naval activities surrounding this major port, I was not confident about heading into what either already was, or was soon likely to become, a war zone.

News had come through that a couple of troop carriers were on their way to assist with the evacuation of stray soldiers and civilians on the west coast of France, but I did not know of their intended calling ports. We had to sit tight and wait. Gossip was rife that the Germans had now reached Brest and begun filtering down towards the southern part of Brittany. I had become increasingly concerned for our safety. There were few options available. Heading south was probably the only realistic choice, but I had very little money and fuel enough for only about one hundred kilometres.

With the arrival of Albert, the situation had become even more complicated. We were now six, but Albert was not of the view that he would accompany us in an escape to Britain – and my staying was not an option. The approaching threat in the form of grey uniforms would undoubtedly result in me being taken away as a prisoner, with inevitable long-term incarceration. Perhaps even the children would be taken into care of some sort, and the idea of this was deeply troubling. We had to find a way of escaping the threat. The news of refugee ships en route had brought some hope. This seemed our only option. Let's wait a day or so, I thought, before we make any other decision.

The morning of Sunday 16th June was clear and sunny. We kept vigil out to sea as the sun rose and then, as the afternoon wore on, began its descent towards the horizon. Tension was building. How long would it be before the invaders arrived in this small fishing village? The Germans knew that there were many soldiers and refugees scattered across western France. It was a clear-up operation and we were quickly being caught in the net. We had little else to do but sit tight and hope a rescue ship would offer us a last-minute escape.

At about 4 p.m., we saw the smoking funnels of two ships appear on the horizon across the bay west of Quiberon. Quiberon was at the tip of the peninsula which stretched out from the mainland like a long curved finger. Gradually, the silhouettes became clearer and we were able to distinguish the shape and size of the two troop carriers. The appearance of the two ships across the bay brought a surge of excitement and a flood of adrenaline into our bodies. We all turned to look at each other with disbelief on our faces. We were neither smiling nor crying – unable to know whether or not to believe our eyes. Stephen and Paul stood beside me with expressions of confusion. The two ships turned the corner and began their careful approach into Quiberon harbour.

Although I could clearly see the ships across the bay, only about fifteen kilometres away, the route by road was more than eighty kilometres around the Gulf of Morbihan. A journey by car, from Port Navalo to Quiberon, would be long and through dangerous territory. Reports had confirmed that Vannes was already occupied by the Germans and we would need to skirt around the town. I looked at the people surrounding me.

Jeanne, with her Mona Lisa smile, and the weather-beaten face of Albert, who had travelled many miles by train and bicycle to find and secure the safety of his daughter. My two sons and Monique, innocent and in danger. I had to get us to the rescue ships. To do whatever was necessary.

The choice was simple. Gather together a few basic things and head for Quiberon. There should be just enough fuel in the Studebaker to get there. It was probably our last hope.

'Albert – we are going to Quiberon to get on one of those ships. We need to go into the house and get the boys' things together quick. Pack up their small suitcases. Nothing more.'

We all rushed back into the house.

The small brown suitcases which had carried the few toys and clothes were quickly filled – no folding or discussions. Clothes were pulled from drawers and thrown into the suitcases. We had to move fast. Within minutes, we were running from the house across the small garden towards the open doors of the car. It seemed frantic, almost a panic. The boys were confused, but excited by all the rushing about. With suitcases thrown into the Studebaker again, we looked across the bay to see our escape-route ships. 'Let's go! Let's go! Hurry! Hurry!'

My shouting was suddenly interrupted by the scream of an aircraft engine overhead. Flying low, a Stuka dive-bomber tore overhead in the cloudless blue sky, heading directly across the bay towards Quiberon.

The first of the two ships had already turned the corner, skirting the small harbour. The second stood still in the water just offshore. The Stuka skimmed across the glistening water of the bay directly in line with the first of the two ships. I tried to picture the scene on the *Franconia*. There would be panic:

'Take cover! Incoming bomber to starboard approaching! Take cover!' bellowing out of the internal speaker system. Crew members rushing from all directions, disappearing into doorways.

They had no defence from any attack, let alone from the air. How could the bomber miss? They were stationary in the water – a sitting duck. The plane had appeared from nowhere. The Stuka grew smaller as it few away from us and towards the ships at high-speed fifty metres above the ocean. As it approached the ship, two bombs appeared from its undercarriage. They were clearly visible as they fell directly towards the aft of the ship. We watched as the Stuka roared over the ship, climbing steeply skywards. Then a massive shower of water rose from the sea as two bombs detonated simultaneously. The rear of the ship lurched upwards out of the sea.

The Stuka rose into the sky and disappeared northward, away from Quiberon harbour and us. We knew that the attack had been a success as smoke began to rise from the stern of the ship.

The injured vessel had not sustained a direct hit. The bombs had fallen slightly short and detonated beneath the ship on the shallow sea bed. The blast had lifted her upwards out of the water and caused damage to her underside. She was undoubtedly taking in water through the buckled steel plates of the hull. She was still afloat, though, and able to move – albeit slowly. She turned slowly towards the open sea and limped away.

We all stood agasp, watching the aerial attack on our only hope of escape. Now we continued to stand in silence, waiting for another Stuka to tear across overhead. But there was nothing. It was quiet.

The second ship turned away from Quiberon and made its way across the bay, heading in our direction, southwards, billowing black smoke into the cloudless sky. She was heading directly for Port Navalo at full steam. Was she going to stop outside our small port?

She passed us by only a few hundred metres off the beach. We could see the crew on the deck, but she was not going to stop at Port Navalo. We all waved from our position on the beach, trying to attract attention. She steamed past us with all funnels blowing, leaving a trail of dark smoke in her wake.

The option of a treacherous drive to Quiberon had been shelved. Our only chance now was to find some way of following the evacuee ship as she made her way to another port on the Brittany coast to pick up lost and weary soldiers and refugees. I ruled out the idea of trying to follow her by car. La Rochelle seemed the likely destination and we did not have enough fuel to make it that far. Following by sea was the only option.

We were not the only people to witness the appearance of the two ships, nor the attack which had put paid to our hope of escape. I needed to head into town to find a fishing boat that might take us south in pursuit.

Paul, Stephen and Monique were taken into the house by Jeanne. She was to unload the Studebaker and prepare a meal while Albert and I went into town in search of a fisherman. My spoken French was not good, so the support of Albert was essential. We had become friends with many of the locals during our stay these past few weeks. They had seen us in the village buying food and playing with the children on the beach.

Monsieur Leclerc, the local shopkeeper, had taken to us and he seemed the obvious first place to go.

Albert and I walked down the cobbled road with great gusto and into the small town square which housed the few shops and café. It was about 6 p.m. and the village was well populated by locals all discussing the incident that had happened just a couple of hours ago. Several stood outside the entrance to the small village shop and quite a crowd had gathered in the terraced area of the café. We made directly for the shop and Monsieur Leclerc.

I was not to be disappointed. Our arrival in the shop had not been unexpected. Monsieur Leclerc was well aware that I was English and that Paul and Stephen were my sons. He was almost expecting us. Albert took the lead and broke into an explanation in French with a great deal of head nodding and intaking of breath.

After a brief debate, the nodding of heads was interrupted by a vigorous shaking of hands. I understood the gist of most French conversations, but I had never been able to express my own words fluently. I had always struggled with the tenses and silent letters. In my efforts to learn this language, it regularly seemed to me that what was written was not said. This continued to baffle me and perhaps was why I had never really managed to master French. Albert explained that it had been arranged for us to meet Monsieur Lafayette, the fisherman, at 9 p.m. in the café across the square. Albert and I made our way back along the cobbled road to the cottage for food and an anxious wait until our rendezvous.

The children had been fed and were being read a story by Jeanne when we quietly left the cottage and made our way down the darkened lane back into town. It was a good walk.

There were no street lights, so only the glow of the moon showed us the way. It was a warm midsummer evening without a cloud in the sky. The stars were bright and, looking up, the universe looked impossibly vast. Such beauty above and such ugliness below. I was scared and tense. I knew that this walk into town was leading me into the unknown – either escape to England or a terrible internment. What would become of my children if escape were not possible was a thought I did not wish to have. Fear ran through me like a river of blood. I had to secure a fishing-boat escape. What would it take to convince Monsieur Lafayette to take us away? We approached the dimly lit café.

As we opened the door and entered the bar, we saw a gathering of men, one in a grubby Polish military uniform, in the far corner. Sitting behind a round table with a small, glass tumbler glowing with white pastis, was the large figure of Monsieur Lafayette, cigarette protruding from his bearded face. Beside him sat Monsieur Leclerc. Deliberations appeared to have begun and we made our way across the linoleum flooring. Monsieur Leclerc stood up as soon as he saw us, a broad smile on his face, and beckoned across the table with his hand outstretched, welcoming us to the gathering.

Our only chance now was to get aboard a fishing boat and track the route of the southbound ship in the hope that we could get aboard. Travelling by car was no longer an option as we would not know where to go and would have no idea of the destination of the ship. What we did know was that the Germans were near and our options were limited. Travelling by road would be too risky. Jean-Paul Lafayette was our last hope.

Albert did all the talking, translating as he went. It was well understood by Jean-Paul that the Germans were closing in. To continue to fish seemed folly as the chances of them permitting things to carry on as normal were considered highly remote. He had therefore decided to head south to his daughters in the Medoc and take it from there. He had agreed to take the sole Polish soldier, who stood leaning against the wall just behind him.

The conversation centred on the importance of us following the ship by sea, and the best time to leave. After just ten minutes, Jean-Paul agreed that he would take the boys and me but could not take Monique. Albert accepted his decision. We would leave at 4 a.m. the next morning. It was a small boat, but he said we should all get aboard. Albert would make his way back to Brussels with Jeanne. There was to be a financial settlement of 500 francs, payable in cash before we boarded. It was most of what I had left, but this was a life-or-death decision, so I had no problem with it. I would have given him the shirt off my back if he had asked. He would take us down the coast until we could transfer to the refugee ship and then he would continue to Bordeaux. It was agreed that we would meet at the end of the pier at the harbour. Smiling faces and handshakes all round. Thank God! At last, we had finally secured an escape!

CHAPTER NINE

Albert and I made our way back up the darkened lane towards our holiday cottage. The light from the front room lit the window through the thin, cheap yellow curtains. We did not talk. I was bursting with enthusiasm to tell Jeanne and the children, but I knew Albert would tell her and I could not tell the boys until we woke them in the early hours of the next morning. Together we walked through the small wooden gate bordering the front gravelled garden and opened the front door. Jeanne was standing alone in the hallway, her face distorted with anticipation. What had been decided? Would Harry and the boys escape or were they to be interned? Fear was written across her face.

As soon as Albert walked through the door, though, the smile on his face gave away the fact that an agreement had been reached. I, too, wore a huge smile, but one of relief rather than excitement. This part of the job was done, but not the whole job. Tomorrow had yet to come and we were yet to get aboard the ship. So many obstacles remained to be overcome before we would be out of danger. At least we had managed to get to this stage. Another hurdle had been jumped, but we were still a long way from the finishing post.

An hour later, I retired to bed. I would need the sleep. There was a long journey ahead and it would be just the boys and me. A family again, together, on our way home. Back to England, where I should have gone years before – when I lost my Abbi. That had been the moment. I had let it pass and now I was going to pay heavily unless we could get on that ship. I now had no money, no fuel and no other options. I was cornered like a helpless fox hiding in a hedgerow with the fearsome pack of hounds drawing ever nearer. Was my fate sealed and possibly that of my boys, too? Was God going to let us survive? Would that last-chance, outstretched hand be grasped? Would we make it? The suitcases were packed, the remaining money and our papers were in my coat pocket. Nothing else was needed. It was just me, what I stood up in and my two boys. We were ready to go, and tomorrow we would leave.

At three in the morning Jeanne woke the boys. 'Get yourselves dressed up warm,' she said. 'You are going on a boat. How exciting for you.'

I had decided that we should all go in the Studebaker to the harbour. A final journey in the car that had brought us this far. At 4 a.m. we rolled quietly into the harbour and drew up alongside a pile of old fishing nets. At the furthest tip of the pier, a hundred or so yards away, I could see a lone fishing boat and a small gathering of people on the quayside. A set of steps led down to the boat on the inner sidewall of the harbour. We climbed out of the car and took the boys' small suitcases from the boot. I led the way, with Paul on my left and Stephen on my right, holding their small hands firmly in mine. In their free hands they carried their suitcases. We began our walk along the narrow pier towards the gathering, with Albert, Jeanne and Monique following closely behind. The cobbled quayside was lit by the bright moonlight. As we approached the group, I could make out some Polish soldiers in worn and tattered uniforms, a few locals and the burly figure of our captain, Jean-Pierre Lafayette. A heated debate appeared to be in full flow. I could not hear the argument, but I knew that was what it was from the gesticulating and pacing going on. There was some head nodding and then an aerial wave of the hands and a stepping back.

As we drew closer, Jean-Paul suddenly noticed us and, drawing both hands up to chest height, he silenced the arguers. 'Attendez. Attendez-vous!' he said, and broke away, heading towards us. All the heads of the group turned towards us and then away again.

'Bonjour, Monsieur Barker,' he called out as he approached us.

'Bonjour,' I replied.

'We have a problem, Monsieur,' he said. 'This morning two more Polish soldiers arrived here and I have little choice but to take them with me. If they are caught, they will be taken as prisoners. I cannot refuse!'

'That's fine with me,' I said.

'No, you don't understand,' he said. 'I can only take four people as my boat is small and fully loaded. There is only space for four. I am very sorry, but because your children are Belgian and they will not come to any harm from the Germans, I cannot take them.'

'But we agreed last night, Monsieur Lafayette,' I pleaded.

'I know,' he replied. 'But last night there was only one soldier. Today there are three. I am very sorry. I can take you, but I cannot take the children. If it makes you feel better, I will not ask for 500 francs, Monsieur Barker.'

'Oh my God,' I muttered under my breath. 'Oh my God.'

What could I do? This had been our only hope of escape, but now it had been dashed.

'The soldiers have said that the Germans are already in Vannes,' said Jean-Paul, 'and they are due here today. There is no escape for the Poles. None! I must take them, Monsieur Barker. I have no choice. You must understand.'

I looked down at my two boys, and then behind at Albert and Jeanne.

'What should I do?' I asked Albert.

He had always been a fast thinker and quick to assess a situation. He had been through this when he decided that I should take Monique. I looked into his eyes for some guidance. For a solution. Albert looked down, as if trying to avoid my glazing eyes. Then he looked up again and said:

'Harry, you must go. Jeanne and I will look after the boys.'

'No,' I said. 'I can't put that on you. They're my responsibility. They're my children. I can't just leave them here. It's not an option.'

''Arry,' said Jeanne, her eyes filled with tears. 'You have no choice. If you stay, you will all go to an internment camp. If you go, at least the children will be safe. We can take care of them until things become clearer.'

'Oui,' said Albert. 'You must go and we will take care of the children. I can return the favour and repay you for what you did for me. When we asked you to take Monique, we had no choice, but now it is you who has no choice. Please, Harry. You must see that this is the only option. Go!'

I looked down at my two sons, who were gazing up at me, bewildered and confused. Stephen was puzzled. Paul, on the other hand, understood well. He knew I was going to leave them here on the quayside. The reason why would not be so clear. Why we were even here was not so clear to him. And nor was why we were scared of the Germans. What was obvious, though, was that he was to be left here with his brother, Jeanne, Albert and Monique. And his father was leaving him. His eyes filled with tears. It was the first time I had really witnessed pure emotion from Paul. And, as I saw his eyes moistening, I felt, for the first time, too, that we really understood each other. He had grown up and I had not even noticed. The time was now. I knew it, and so did Paul. We were father and son at last – but not for long.

I knew now that it was me alone, or none of us. I had to make the most difficult decision of my life. But, as Albert had said, I really had no choice. Standing on the quayside, a mist engulfed my mind. I reached into my coat pocket and pulled out my black leather wallet. I drew out the 500 francs and a bundle of papers. I handed them all to Albert and said:

'A vous, Albert, je laisse Paul et à vous, Jeanne, je laisse Stephen.' (To you, Albert, I leave Paul and to you Jeanne, I leave Stephen.) 'Here is almost all the money I have left, with the birth certificates of the boys and their mother's paperwork. It should keep them safe. Make your way back to Brussels and I will be in touch as soon as I get back to England. Take good care.'

I looked across at Jeanne. Tears rolled down her cheeks. There was something special between us now. We had just become lovers and I was leaving her behind. I might never see her again. I was leaving them all behind. My children and my lover. Everything that was important to me. Those I loved most. My reasons for being. My heart ached. I turned and walked towards the fishing boat, my breath short, choking on emotion. I dared not look back.

CHAPTER TEN
PAUL

The small fishing boat and father's dark figure gradually disappeared into the distance as we stood at the end of the pier. Stephen and I were side by side, with Albert, Monique and Jeanne behind us, their hands on our shoulders. The tears which had trickled down our faces dried, leaving crystallised lines down our cheeks. Our watery eyes gazed out to the ocean. We turned and fell into the warmth of our carers' embrace. Although alone and confused, we were reassured by the familiarity of Albert and Jeanne, who had cared for us since our mother had passed away.

We turned and, with our heads bowed, walked slowly back towards the car. It seemed a long walk in the dawn breeze. The grand Studebaker stood proudly on the grey, cobbled surface of the quayside.

'We must get rid of the car,' said Albert. 'The registration is in the name of Harry, so we must destroy it.'

'Push it into the harbour,' said Jeanne. 'That's it. Push it into the sea. They will never find it there.'

We knew that the Germans were close and, as the sun rose, we could hear the occasional sounds of small-weapon gunfire in the distance. We did not want them to have the car.

Albert climbed into the driver's seat and disengaged the handbrake. Together we gathered at the back and pushed with all our might, but the heavy vehicle did not budge.

And then, from a small cobbled lane which led to the harbour, two men dressed in dark coats appeared, heading towards us. As they approached, one called out, 'Qu'est-ce qui se passe?' (What's going on?) We turned and looked at them. We could tell from their accents that they were locals. Our greatest fear was that they would be Germans and that we would have to offer some explanation as to why we were there and whose car this was. As the two young men approached, Albert stepped forward to engage them.

'What's going on here?' they asked. 'Who are you?'

Albert explained that we were refugees from Brussels and had been staying in a cottage by the beach. The father of the two boys had left from the harbour an hour ago and we were alone here now. The car was the boys' father's, but we needed to get rid of it. We had hoped to push it into the harbour, but it was too heavy for us and we did not know what to do.

The two men looked at one another and a short discussion took place between them. Turning to Albert, who had remained steadfast between them and us, the taller of the two said:

'We agree that it would not be right for the Germans to take the car, but it would be a shame to push such a magnificent vehicle into the harbour. I have a farm not far from here with a large hay barn. We could drive the car out to my farm and hide it in the barn. You may not be able to keep it, but at least the Germans won't get it.'

Albert had little choice. Despite the fact that we did not know these two Frenchmen, we preferred that the car did not fall into the hands of the approaching German soldiers. It was agreed that they could take it and hide it in their hay barn.

The two men climbed into the grand car and fired up the engine. It growled into life and then settled into a gentle purr.

'Can we take you anywhere?' they asked.

'Please. Back to the cottage,' said Albert. We all squeezed in and off we went.

At about three o'clock the very same day, we heard the rumblings of heavy trucks making their way along the uneven road that led into the town centre. Together with Jeanne and Monique, I went into town to witness the arrival of the German troop trucks. The soldiers sat in rows of six or seven on each side of the open-topped vehicles, with their grey uniforms and a machine gun resting on the lap of each one. The entourage of three troop carriers was led by an open-topped saloon car, with a smartly dressed driver at the wheel and a helmet-clad soldier beside him. In the back sat an important-looking officer with round-rimmed, gold-framed glasses and a flat-topped hat that proudly displayed a gleaming silver eagle above the visor.

From our position we had a clear view of the village square where the entourage had come to a halt directly in front of the typically French-styled Mairie which stood in a prominent position in the centre-ville. Outside the wooden double doors of the Mairie stood the mayor of the village, dressed in a dark suit. He was flanked by an elderly looking woman on his left and a young girl, about sixteen years of age, in a blue-coloured frock, on his right. His wife and daughter.

The helmet-clad soldier quickly exited the saloon car and moved round to open the rear passenger door where the officer sat, upright and stern-looking. The officer stood up in the car with his hands behind his back, before looking around ominously and then stepping out on to the gravel square in the direction of the waiting mayor.

The troop-carrying trucks filled the small square and the soldiers began climbing hurriedly from the rear of each vehicle, forming a circle around the perimeter of the square.

They were officious and aggressive, and acted as if this intimidating procedure had been done many times before.

Villagers began to appear from their houses as curiosity got the better of them. They filtered into the shadows of the outer edges of the square, looking at the circle of soldiers, who stood with legs apart, their machine guns at the ready and directed outwards at the assembling villagers.

Soon the mayor, his family, the important-looking officer and two soldiers disappeared into the shadows of the great wooden doors.

CHAPTER ELEVEN
HARRY

I stood on the stern of the fishing boat as we chugged away from the harbour, watching as the silhouettes of my two sons grew smaller and smaller, until I could only just make them out as they turned and walked away beside Albert, Monique and Jeanne. I stood there for what seemed like an eternity as my mind raced and rocked. Was I doing the right thing? Should I have stayed and tried to head south in the car? Would they be safe in the hands of their carers? What would the Germans do to them when they found them? How could I get them back to England?

I had connections with Brussels, but nothing with Port Navalo. When I got back to England I could make enquiries as to their whereabouts. I hoped that the communication channels would still be open. Somehow I would find a way – I had to believe that.

My choices had diminished drastically now from those available to me when we had arrived in Port Navalo. We had all thought and hoped that the war would end quickly. That we could return to Brussels and continue where we had left off. The rapid German advance and invasion of France had been so fast. Through the radio I knew that Dunkirk had been a catastrophe for the British forces trying to hold back the German advance. After Dunkirk the German progress through France was rapid as they moved south towards Paris and west towards the naval base in Brest.

What was I to do? If I had been captured, I would have been interned as an enemy of the Reich and at the very least separated from the boys. Then who knew how the Germans might have categorised the boys? Were they British or Belgian? God only knew. The only option was to do everything possible to escape from France and then reassess on my arrival in England. It was a rapidly changing situation, but at least I now had a chance to get home and review it.

Our small fishing boat remained within eyesight of the French coast as we headed south, our main objective being to catch up with the refugee ship. The weather was clear and sunny with a calm sea. Our vessel chugged on relentlessly, carving a channel through the blue waters of the Bay of Biscay. The Polish soldiers were laid out on the deck, flanked by their green rucksacks and basking in the warm sunshine. The morning had passed quickly as the sun had risen high into the sky. By midday the events of the last twenty-four hours kept my mind buzzing. But I was just beginning to feel weary. I looked round for a clear space to rest a little. Between the mooring ropes and a collection of crabbing baskets I found a clear space. Using my coat as a pillow, I lay on the deck, looking up at the cloudless sky. Within a few moments I was asleep.

I was abruptly awoken by a shout from the captain, booming out across the wooden decking:

'Alors! Voir là-bas, mes amis!' (Hey! Look ahead, my friends) his throaty voice growled out, coloured by countless cigarettes and his outdoor life. We all stood looking forward as the horizon began to reveal the outline of a large ship. We had not expected to catch up with it until the next day, but as we drew nearer it became obvious that she had dropped anchor outside St Nazaire. The funnels were clearly visible, but there was no smoke coming from them. She was stationary. We all looked at one another and began to smile. Within a few moments, the soldiers were performing some kind of dance, with their arms round each other's shoulders, forming a circle and kicking their legs into its centre whilst they sang. The little boat rocked from side to side. I stood where I had been sleeping trying to keep my balance, captivated by their enthusiasm and smiling, perhaps in embarrassment. This was not a British way to behave. I was a little uncomfortable and unsure quite what to do. I switched my gaze between their joyful show and the outline on the horizon.

It was mid-afternoon and the sun was hot on my shoulders. We were now within a few miles of our escape-vessel and the fishing-boat continued its persistent chugging. We began to make out the flotilla of small boats of all sizes, bobbing in the gentle swell as they sailed to and from the ship, transporting soldiers and civilians from the quayside at St Nazaire. The ship itself was crawling with tiny figures hanging off its rails as more boats pulled up alongside and people scrambled up the stairs beside the steel hull. Would we be able to get aboard? She seemed full to the brim already. Somehow we had to. I unravelled my coat and folded it over my arm. The Polish soldiers were still dancing and singing as we drew nearer. Only another couple of hours and the first leg of my journey would be over.

It was four o'clock in the afternoon, clear blue sky and calm sea. The perfection of the day was suddenly disrupted by the piercing shriek of German dive-bombers as they flew over St Nazaire, diving towards the ship. The two Stukas had appeared from nowhere, but were already as clearly visible as the passengers aboard the ship. Moments later, the Stukas were within metres of the stationary vessel. Before those aboard had a chance to move, two large explosions blasted the timber forward decking, shooting fragments into the sky. Panic and chaos flooded over the passengers. People began running in all directions. Some jumped off the side into the water below. Black smoke filled the air and flames quickly appeared among the billowing fumes. I could hardly believe my eyes. I stood there, staring in shock. This large ship, with its calm security, the ship that was to be my escape, had become a burning inferno. It was packed with passengers. Soldiers in a variety of uniforms and civilian men, women and children filled the ship. There was little time to lower the lifeboats and she began to list to port, spilling people into the sea.

A few moments later, there was another shriek from the sky as a third Stuka appeared from the mainland. Its bomb landed square at the base of the forward funnel, sending shards of red-hot metal fragments across the deck. The top half of the funnel fell sideways into the sea, sending a shudder though the whole ship. Some areas were now ablaze and an oil slick surrounded her. Lifeboats with frantic rowers were trying to escape the inferno. Through the roar of the blaze we could hear singing as the ship slowly slipped over, exposing her red hull. The words of "Roll Out the Barrel" and "There Will Always Be an England" could be heard between the explosions and the suction sounds of invading water as she began to sink. Within twenty minutes, she had gone. There was a strange calm as the ship disappeared below the surface and into the blue waters. We all stood on the forward deck of our fishing boat, watching in sheer amazement and disbelief. We were frozen by the shock of what we had just witnessed. Our thoughts of imminent escape had turned in an instant to horror and terror at the events unravelling before our eyes. We were only a mile or so away but, although we immediately headed towards the scene, we would not be in time to be able to help.

The waters around the oil slick left by the sunken vessel were soon filled with small boats of all sizes, pulling people from the water.

By the time we approached, all we found were bodies floating facedown, most covered in black oil. A few boats still zigzagged over the area looking for survivors. But there were no signs of life, just those bodies, and flotsam from the sunken ship, drifting on the surface. A discarded white lifebelt bearing the ship's name floated by: RMS *Lancastria*.

There was no point in us disembarking at St Nazaire. We could see that the town was in chaos. Our arrival there would help no one. Captain Lafayette made the decision to sail on to La Rochelle. There might be a chance there of another ship or, at worst, we could make our way south to Bordeaux by train.

As evening approached, there was the most spectacular sunset. A calm sea reflecting a bright orange sky and cirrus clouds splitting the colours from bright yellow to deep crimson red. It felt as if all was calm in the world. But my life – like so many others – was in complete turmoil. Night came and I was unable to sleep. Mind racing, I was constantly tossing and turning. We were expected to reach La Rochelle by morning. Several hours yet in which to endure the mind games.

It was 4.30 a.m. and still dark. I stared into the distance, looking for signs of glimmering lights on the shore, an indication that we were nearing La Rochelle, but there was nothing. I looked back to the dimly lit bridge window, where I could see the silhouette of the bulky man manning the wheel.

A glow from the tip of his cigarette briefly illuminated his face as he inhaled deeply. He did not see me looking at him and continued to gaze fixedly ahead.

There was a slight brightening of the sky from the east, as sunrise approached. All eyes focused fore and towards the coastline on our left. And then, finally, we glimpsed a glint and glimmer at about ten o'clock ahead. The first signs of La Rochelle.

The sky brightened, but only slowly, as the morning brought a thick cloud-covering from the south. The lights of La Rochelle were shining brightly now. The diesel engine gently chugged on and the waves splashed against the hull as the bow cut through the sea.

We slipped into a small nearby marina. Following our Polish guests, I threw my coat on to the wooden jetty and climbed ashore. Lafayette leaned out of the side door of the bridge and called out, 'Bon chance, Monsieur Barker!' followed by a wave of his left hand. He did not dock, but instead there was a grinding of gears as he selected reverse and slid away again from the wooden jetty. My new Polish friends and I made our way into the town centre in search of food and drink.

We found a quiet café where we could breakfast and consider what to do next. The Poles' uniforms reminded me of those I had seen during the time when I served in the Great War. They spoke a little English and told me how they had marched all the way from Poland to fight Hitler. When the Germans had broken through into the forest of the Ardennes, the Poles had headed west, and were now seeking an escape route back home.

The rapid departure from Port Navalo had left me with little money. Furthermore, I had not anticipated an extended journey. Joining up with the soldiers, whose French was good, would give me a better chance of escape, particularly as my own command of the language was limited. And at least I would not be alone. In some ways it was a blessing that the boys were not with me. It was risky to travel in France, even now in these early stages of occupation. You never knew when you might run into a German checkpoint or come across enemy soldiers moving around the country.

In La Rochelle we heard that there were ships leaving from Bordeaux, carrying refugees and displaced soldiers. We decided that was where we would head. Time was of the essence – the quicker we could get to Bordeaux, the better chance we had of getting aboard one of the last ships. The Germans were now spreading across France quickly and, once they got to Bordeaux, there would be no more refugee rescues. Rail seemed the fastest way and it was still possible to travel by train without too much worry of German intervention. The main German advance had been in the north and northwest, and they had a huge military presence in Paris. There was a window of opportunity now, before they flooded down into the southwest.

My newfound friends and I made our way to the station to get on the next available train.

We arrived at La Rochelle Station and made enquiries as to the next train. We discovered that we would have a two-hour wait before it departed. The bad news was, that after paying the fare, I was down to my last few francs. If I did not get aboard a ship, I would soon run out of cash.

The train's first stop was the famous town of Rochefort and from there we travelled on through the beautiful Charente Maritime. As we moved south, the vineyards of Cognac filled the rolling countryside on both sides. There were rows and rows of crooked brown stems shrouded in bright young green leaves, and tiny bunches of grapes hanging in the shadows. The sun was bright, feeding the valleys, which were awash with tiny lime-green grapes that would later be harvested to become the finest brandy in the world. Would the coming German occupation allow the harvest to be brought in? What fate awaited these fields of fruit?

On we went, into the Gironde and the vineyards of Bordeaux, arriving in the town in the early evening. We stepped on to the platform of the mainline station, somewhat anxious that there might be a German checkpoint at the station. Glances towards the exit, though, revealed a clear route. There were no enemy soldiers, simply a cascade of people with all types of bags and suitcases. Everyone seemed to be carrying all they could. They used sheets and blankets, too, filled with their personal possessions and hanging over their shoulders. It became obvious that the sea of people filling the station and platforms was almost exclusively made up of refugees. We stumbled along towards the exit, passing through the main hall. The front of the station was in chaos, people everywhere, some sitting in small groups, others rushing to and fro. The Germans were on their way and these desperate people needed to get away before the men with guns arrived. I could smell the fear and see the terror in their eyes. What to do?

Rumours had filtered out that rescue ships were available in Bordeaux, and many people had left their homes to seek passage to the safety of Spain or further afield – with some, like me, hoping to get to England.

A discussion with a station guard soon revealed that my hopes were to be dashed – the last refugee ship to England had left two days ago. The Port of Brest, in northwest Brittany, had been occupied by the Germans and it had become too risky to sail around Finisterre, the northeastern point of France, back to England. There was only one small ship in port and it was bound for southern Spain. It was due to depart at dusk, sailing under cover of darkness, hoping to escape the U-boat predators. Spanish citizens were prioritised, so there was little or no chance of getting aboard.

We decided that we had to make for Bayonne and try to get to Spain. The question was how?

CHAPTER TWELVE
PAUL

Over the next few days, things changed in Port Navalo as the new arrivals began to enforce their rules and presence. A curfew was applied that prevented anyone from being on the street after nightfall and before dawn. Those found breaking the rules would be arrested and possibly shot. The locals found it difficult to continue to go about their daily business and it was impossible to ignore the intimidating presence of the German soldiers on the streets. We did not venture from the house during these first few days and were very wary of the soldiers, who made no effort to befriend anyone. They looked at us with distaste and a threatening intimidation. Few spoke any French and thus the segregation between the soldiers and the locals was obvious and apparent. Clearly the mayor had been evicted from his post. By the entrance of the Mairie two uniformed soldiers now stood, night and day. The commanding officer had taken up residence and we would watch his comings and goings from the upstairs bedroom window of a friend who lived on the square. There was no sign whatsoever of the mayor or his family.

Four days after the arrival of the German military, we were awoken at seven in the morning by a loud knocking at the front door. Albert and Jeanne were already up, preparing breakfast. Albert opened the door and was confronted by two German officers, who clicked their heels and stood to attention with right arms pointed up and outwards.

'Heil Hitler!' they shouted.

Albert was unsure quite what to do, so repeated back to them: 'Heil Hitler.'

They both removed their hats and tucked them under their arms.

'We have some questions,' one of them said in French.

Albert was surprised to find that they spoke quite good French and showed them into the front room. Stephen and I crept down the stairs and, remaining out of sight, listened in on the conversation.

'We understand that you are not local to Port Navalo and that you have two young boys and a young girl here with you. Is that correct?' the officer asked.

'Yes, that is true,' Albert replied. 'We are Belgian and have three children here with us, who are refugees from Brussels.'

'We are here to establish the origination of those resident in the town. We are aware that many people fled the combat zone in the north and refugees are now scattered across western France. As you may know, Germany has now occupied France and it is our duty to notify all refugees that they must return to their homes. There is no danger to you or the children. Are you and the children Belgian?' asked the officer.

'Yes, apart from Jeanne, who is Swiss. We were all born in Brussels,' Albert replied. 'We fled when the fighting began. Paul is ten years old, Stephen is nine and Monique, my daughter, is eight. The mother of the boys died some years ago and we do not know where their father is, as he fled, too, when the fighting began. We came here with the children for safety and have been here for just a few weeks.'

'Do you have papers?' asked the other officer.

'Yes, I will get them for you,' said Albert, and disappeared out into the bedroom in which Dad had slept and which was now occupied by Albert. Returning with a bundle of papers, he rifled through them, sorting out the relevant documents, and handed them to the two uniformed men.

'Thank you for this information. That is all we need to know for now,' said the officer as he stuffed the papers into his briefcase. 'We will notify you within the next few days as to the transit arrangements for your return to Brussels. That will be all for now.'

They moved towards the door and, on the doorstep, replaced their caps upon their heads, turned to face Albert and once again shouted 'Heil Hitler!' with hands raised.

Stephen and I had scuttled back upstairs to our bedroom as Albert showed the two soldiers to the door. We peered out from our bedroom window to see the German officers march down the short path to the roadside and then, to our amazement, climb into Dad's Studebaker car!

The next day, at noon, there was another knock at the door. There stood the same two officers who had visited the day before. Behind them, the Studebaker was parked at the gate. Albert answered the door and was greeted by the usual 'Heil Hitler!' and salute.

'We have checked your papers, Monsieur,' the first officer said. 'There is some discrepancy about the father of the two boys. His name is not Belgian, Monsieur. We believe he is British. Where is the father, Monsieur?'

'As I said yesterday, sir,' Albert replied, 'he fled when the fighting began. We do not know where he is. We think he went back to England... but the boys are Belgian. They were born in

Belgium to a Belgian mother. I have her birth certificate and death certificate here. They have lived in Belgium all their lives, sir.'

'Why are they here in Port Navalo?'

'As I said yesterday, sir, we all fled from the fighting. The children are young and scared.'

'Give me the papers about their mother!' the second officer shouted.

'I have them here,' said Albert, having selected them from the remaining papers on the table.

'Merci,' the German replied. There was a brief silence as he scanned the documents.

'All right, Monsieur Dejong. We will take these papers and have them verified. Please prepare for your return to Brussels. A train will be departing from Vannes tomorrow, taking refugees to Paris, where you will transfer to another train for Brussels. You may only take what you can carry and a truck will collect you from the village centre in Arzon at 2 p.m. to take you all to Vannes. You must all come to the Mairie tomorrow at noon, where you will be issued your travel documentation.'

At that, they turned and headed back towards the Studebaker. Albert, noticing the car, said nothing and closed the door behind them.

CHAPTER THIRTEEN
HARRY

It was soon dark, so we decided to find a place to sit out the night. We would move on at dawn. Together with hundreds of others, we sat beside our few belongings against a wall inside the main station, watching the mass of refugees milling back and forth. As the hours passed, more and more of them formed groups and sat on the floor with their bags and boxes beside them. Children with their heads on the laps of their mothers slept quietly. The hall was a sea of people laid out across the floor. I wondered where they would all go. Where they had come from. I drifted in and out of a light sleep as I sat on the tiled floor. It felt like a long time before dawn broke and light began to fill the hall. My three friends lay beside me, still asleep. Another hour and they began to stir. The hall was full of weary people. It was time to make a move. We stood up and gathered our bags.

Together, we left the main building of Bordeaux station, pushing our way through the crowds and out into the open concourse. This, too, was filled with people, mostly standing beside their bags and belongings. A family of four caught my eye as they stood huddled together. Two adults dressed in tired and tattered clothing, accompanied by two young boys. The boys sat on their small suitcases and my mind returned to the scene on the quayside at Port Navalo. I wondered where my boys might be now.

We moved on over the tram tracks that were sunk into the dull grey cobbled roadway, across the road filled with cars, trucks and carts and into more crowds of refugees clogging the pavement. The street was lined with cafés, bars and small shops. With little money, we looked enviously at those sitting at the tables with their coffee and pastis, watching the crowds drift by. We stopped on the next corner, facing each other, as the three Polish soldiers lit up cigarettes. Where to now?

We glanced left and right, wondering which way to go. The three Poles chatted between themselves, still looking back and forth as they spoke. I had no idea what was being said and stood quietly, waiting for a lead. Finally, one of them tapped me on the forearm. He said to me in broken English:

'Mister, we go alone now. Germans coming. We go east. You go south.'

I looked inquisitively into his eyes as he drew on his cigarette and blew smoke out of the side of his mouth.

'I go alone now?' I asked, to confirm I understood correctly.

'Tak, (Yes),' he said. 'Alone now. You go south. Hiszpania (Spain). OK.'

'Yes. I understand,' I said.

And with that my three new friends turned and walked away. I stood alone, my coat hanging over my arm. That coat and the clothes I was wearing were all I had. My pockets were empty, bar a few coins, a few cigarettes and a box of matches. Although I was surrounded by thousands of people, I don't think I had ever felt so alone. I was cast away in the middle of a foreign country with little idea of where to go. Pull yourself together, I thought. This is no time for self-pity. I had a responsibility to find a way back to England. A responsibility to my children. And to those who were taking care of them. Think straight! I told myself.

I had one thing in my favour. I was, after all, familiar with this part of France, having spent summer holidays here with my lover Toni and the boys.

Just south of Bordeaux the region had been sparsely inhabited and consisted mostly of swampland, where the few residents walked on stilts to stay clear of the water. In the mid-nineteenth century, wide-scale reforestation had taken place in order to rehabilitate the landscape and provide for regional economic development. It was now the largest maritime pine forest in Europe, stretching from the outskirts of Bordeaux right down to the foothills of the Pyrenees. There were few towns, tiny roads and thick forest. It was the perfect camouflage. I knew the main roads and the main towns. My chances of navigating my way down through to the Spanish border without a map were good. I needed to get to Bayonne. Which way was south?

I began my walk down Rue Amédée Saint-Germain, which ran parallel with the railway track. This led me to the junction of Cours de la Somme. Some irony in that, I thought. It seemed a lifetime since I had fought in the trenches of the Somme, which had led to my meeting Abbi and having my two sons. It was a very strange coincidence. I turned left and walked on to the next junction, which led me to Route de Toulouse. I knew I was heading in the right direction. Just follow this road, I thought, and I will eventually be presented with the option to head towards Arcachon, through the forest of Landes, and towards the Pyrenees Mountains.

My walk along this empty road was suddenly interrupted by the increasing rumble of fast-moving heavy vehicles appearing from behind me. I turned to look and, for the first time, saw the dull grey colour of German trucks, preceded by a jeep speeding towards me. I ducked into a recess between the buildings and dipped my head, hoping not to be noticed. The convoy approached quickly and the ground shook as they passed me by. About fifteen in all. They were travelling too fast for me to count. The first ten or so loaded with soldiers and those which followed carrying boxes and crates. Once they passed, I moved back out on to the street and continued my journey. Just a few minutes later there was another roar as more vehicles and motorbikes passed me. I hid in the shadow of a porch. I knew that the Germans had now reached Bordeaux and were heading south – in my direction. I needed to be much more careful from now on. I couldn't afford to be stopped and checked. My first priority was to get off this main road and find a quieter route.

By the time I reached the outskirts of Bordeaux it was late afternoon. I was hungry and tired. I had not had a meal of any substance for several days, having survived on a little bread and fruit. Food had not seemed a priority over the past few days, but now my stomach was telling me I needed it.

The road was quiet and the crowds that had filled the station concourse and streets of Bordeaux seemed long-gone. My priority was to try and find something to eat and a place to sleep. It was fortunate that this journey was taking place in the middle of the summer – there would be fruit or vegetables around. Meat did not seem to be an option. The idea of trying to slay a chicken or some other living animal filled me with horror. As I ventured further out of the suburbs of Bordeaux, countryside replaced the houses and the chance of finding something to eat became greater. Making my way towards the small village of Leognan, I began peering over garden walls, looking for a vegetable allotment or fruit trees. My progress was slow now and I was tired, but good fortune was on my side. A vegetable garden beside a plain single-storey house on the edge of town boasted a selection of vegetables bursting from rows of neatly turned soil. Tall stick-tripods supported a plethora of long, ripe runner beans, hanging from the green foliage. Alongside the row of beans grew red, ripe tomatoes. I couldn't believe my luck. It was dusk and the dim lights from the windows of the little house were beginning to glow. I stepped over the fence and, crouching as I went, tiptoed into the vegetable garden. And there I sat, amongst the plants and leaves, picking green beans and soft juicy tomatoes, enjoying a meal never to be forgotten.

Before leaving, I gathered together a few more tomatoes to take with me on my journey. I did not know when or where my next meal might be.

I stepped back over the fence on to the road and headed further out into the countryside. A barn or even a bale of hay would suffice as a bed for the night.

It was not long before I found a barn. There was no hay, unfortunately, but at least it had a roof. I was reminded of our overnight stay the day we were attacked from the skies on our journey northward from Brussels. This, though, would not be quite as comfortable. Sleep.

I was woken by a beam of sunlight piercing the weathered wood-cladding of the barn and warming my face. I sat up, blinking and shaking my head. For a moment I was completely confused by my surroundings. None of it was familiar. I was in an empty old barn with an ancient wooden cart alongside me. I rubbed my eyes and slowly recalled how I had ended up here. Things fell into place as I looked around, remembering the previous day's events.

I stood up, glancing around the barn, trying to remember how I had entered and looking for the way out of this tall, wooden structure. Streaks of sunlight burst through gaps in the cladding, lighting the cavernous structure. There was not much around me. A few bales of hay discarded in the far corner. The wooden cart parked almost in the centre. The dirt floor strewn with leftover hay, a few empty sacks, an old pram, and a bicycle propped up beside the door.

It was another sunny day, warm and bright. I stepped through the small gap between the heavy wooden doors and looked out across a dirt track that led from the road to the barn. I did not remember walking along this path the previous evening, but I knew I must have. As I made my way along the track to meet the road from Leognan, it suddenly struck me. 'The bicycle!' I said out loud. I ran back to the barn, through the gap between the doors, stopped and gazed at the old bicycle. It might have been old but, on closer inspection, it had solid-enough rubber tyres – very worn, and cracking around the rim, but good enough for me. The chrome on the handlebars was flaking off from rust and the saddle was worn, too, with rusty brown springs breaking through the leather seat. I pushed it around the barn to see whether the wheels turned, if there were any brakes, and whether the pedals were intact. It all seemed to work. The brakes were pretty dodgy, but it was rideable. Someone is looking after me, I thought. I pushed the bicycle out through the gap between the doors and scanned the vicinity to see if anyone was about. I felt like a guilty young boy, hoping not to get caught. I decided not to attempt to mount the bike until I reached the road.

When I got there, I turned away from the village and continued my journey on my new form of transport. The fresh morning air rushed across my face and through my unwashed hair as I pedalled fast to get clear of the village.

I needed to cut across country, towards Arcachon, and intercept the main route south. I recalled again the visits we used to make to Mimizan. It had crossed my mind to head for there, but I knew that Toni had already left Europe. The likelihood of finding refuge in that quarter was slim. The journey to Spain would be a long one and a diversion to Mimizan was not an option. Finding food and shelter was going to be difficult enough. If the weather turned, it would become even more difficult. With my new form of transport, though, my chances of making it to the border had improved significantly.

It did not take long to arrive in the next village and, choosing to avoid the main road in case I came across any more German military, I turned south. The landscape began to change from small, nondescript farms, surrounded by what seemed to be dilapidated outbuildings, to a more forested area.

Arriving in the next small commune, I decided to use a few of my remaining francs to buy some basic provisions. I knew that the next stage of my journey was going to be a long one, through the kind of territory that would provide little opportunity to stock up. I wanted to stay away from the few main towns in the area.

Having strapped a small bag holding my supplies to the rack behind the saddle, I left the commune on a single-track road flanked by forest on both sides. The road stretched straight ahead for what looked like miles, before turning away, dead straight again, and fading into the distance.

There was no sign of life anywhere. The air smelled of pine and damp. The sun flickered between the trees as I pedalled on. Beneath the trees little grew, apart from a few small sprouting ferns in a sub-terrain that was mostly covered in brown pine needles. There was a feeling of freedom out here, but contained somewhat by the walls of tall pine-tree trunks on either side, with not a clearing to be seen. Tonight would be cold and damp, and all I could hope was that it would stay dry as I made my way through the forest. My mind filled with thoughts of my two boys. I cycled on, filled with optimism. I could do this!

As the sun set and dusk threw its shroud over the forest, it quickly became dark. It was not long before I could see little before me. Clouds had hidden the moon and the forest had almost become black. I had to stop and find some sort of shelter for the night. With few options, I just pulled off the track and walked a few paces into the forest. Parking the bicycle up against one tree, I sat leaning against another. I took out a few tomatoes left from my garden incursion and some of the bread I had bought. Tomato sandwich! It was sweet and tasty. The darkness fell deeper. I wrapped my coat around myself tightly, pulled up my knees close to my chest and hoped I would drift off. It was quiet. Nothing but the gentle rustle of pine needles high above.

It was a restless night. I lay on my side in an effort to get some sleep, but the ground was damp and cold. Worst of all, a light spray of rain began to fall between the pine trees. There was no real shelter and no way of moving on because it was so dark. I sat in silence, thinking again about where my boys might be. My thoughts drifted towards the summer holidays we had taken in Mimizan with Toni. Of them running in and out of the surf, calling out to one another. They had been so filled with enjoyment and so reliant upon one another to make the day fun. I remembered chatting with Toni on the terrace, drinking gin and tonic as we watched the sun turn the sky bright orange, before falling into the sea. When the boys were asleep we would make love. How different it was now. It seemed such a long time ago.

By four thirty the forest began to brighten. The dark shroud had lifted and the surrounding trees became visible. There was no time to waste and I got to my feet. I felt the stiffness in my body as I stretched to release the tension in my muscles. I picked up the bicycle and took it back over to the road. Pushing with my right foot while my left rested on the pedal, I gathered enough momentum to keep upright. I swung my right leg over the back of the bike and lowered myself on to the saddle. The air blew into my face once more as I pedalled on into the forest.

It was an overcast day with low, dark cloud. The forest was damp and the road glistened from the light rain that had fallen during the night. After about a mile the road turned to the left. I hoped that I would soon arrive at some sort of junction with signposts. I was a little anxious to check that I was still travelling in the right direction. I pedalled round the bend, but all I could see before me was a continuous track, disappearing into the distance. No junction. Just more road. I leaned forward on my bike, head down into the wind and cycled on.

By the end of the day I had arrived at the edge of the small town of Labouheyre. It was here that, when we visited Toni's holiday home, we would turn right off the main road towards Mimizan. I had approached the town from the east on a rural road, having previously passed through Pissos. I needed to get to the coastal side of the main road from Bordeaux to Bayonne. If the Germans were using any roads in this region, it would be this one. Labouheyre was a relatively large village on the

147

route south. I was concerned about being spotted, so I decided to wait until nightfall before entering. I pushed the bicycle into the woods and found a quiet spot to sit back and wait.

During the day I had not seen a single soul. Not even a car or tractor. I had been the only visitor on the narrow road that cut a path through the forest. I was hungry again, so I took the opportunity to eat and drink from the few supplies I had left. Finding more food would soon become a priority, I thought, as I consumed my last tomato.

Once darkness had fallen, I began the short ride into town. My approach would bring me in on the north side, where the small road slowly swept round from left to right, running parallel with the main route for about three hundred metres. All seemed quiet as I cycled slowly towards the village lights, past the junction leading from the main road. In the distance I saw the flickering of headlights on the main road, approaching quickly. I jumped off and ran into the undergrowth, crouching down beside my bicycle. The approaching diesel engines and the rumbling grew louder. I couldn't make out how many vehicles there were, but I could see from the headlights that there were several. They slowed as they approached the junction of the main road about thirty metres from where I hid.

As the trucks turned from the main road on to the road into the village, their headlights swung from right to left. There was the sound of slowing engines, grinding gears, and then revving as they changed up gears, one after the other. Within a few moments the vehicles were upon me. The first was a car, followed by trucks covered in tarpaulins. As they passed, I could see soldiers lined up inside, lit by the lights from the following vehicle. I counted four as they passed me by. Germans. A cold shiver ran through my body as I peered through the weeds and bramble surrounding me. The trucks rumbled on down the road towards the village. I remained still for a few minutes, not sure what to do next. Then I stood up, looking left and right. Heading on into the village was no longer an option. Perhaps, if I went back along the route that the trucks had arrived from, it would lead me away from the danger and over the main road. That made sense. I quietly made my way out of the undergrowth on to the roadside and walked back up towards the main road. All was quiet.

As I approached the junction of the main road, I saw more lights coming, from the south this time. I darted off the road into a ditch. The car passed by. Once it had disappeared into the distance, I climbed back out on to the roadside. At the junction there was a road opposite me, leading into the darkness. A sign showed that Escource and Mimizan were straight over, Bordeaux to the right and Bayonne to the left. Looking left and right, I ran across the main road pushing the bicycle beside me. As I ran into the narrow road opposite, with my momentum I mounted the bicycle and immediately pedalled as hard as I could into the darkness. I was across the main route and back in the forest.

I cycled hard. My heartbeat was racing and I quickly began breathing heavily. I was not a fit man – I had little interest in sport and activity. I had led a lazy existence for several years and was beginning to regret it now. It was not long before I was almost out of breath. Visibility was very poor in the darkness, but I had pedalled as hard as I could, not looking any further than a few metres ahead.

Suddenly I felt the front wheel dip sharply and I was thrown headfirst off the bicycle, landing on my right shoulder and coming to rest in a heap beside the trunk of a pine tree. My face had grazed the pine floor and I felt its dampness on my cheeks. There were pine needles in my hair and a sharp stabbing in my right knee, from where I had connected with the handlebars as I flew over the front of the bicycle. I sat up and looked around, running my fingers through my hair. Then I pressed on my knee to see if there was any real damage. Nothing serious. I bent my leg back and forth and everything seemed to be in working order. The bicycle lay on its side just a few feet from the road. I had been travelling at full pace and had neglected to take account of the fact that the road had a sharp bend to the left. My momentum had carried me straight off the road, where the front wheel had dropped into a small gully and stopped the bicycle dead. I had continued over the handlebars, into the forest. I gathered myself together and brushed myself down. I was shaking and needed a smoke to calm me. I rummaged through my pockets to find my cigarettes and matches. Cupping my hands around the lit match, the cigarette glowed. I took a long drag and inhaled deep into my lungs. The nicotine rushed into my blood. Calm.

I picked up the bicycle and made my way back to the road. Looking in the direction I had come from, I could see nothing but darkness. Looking to the right, in the direction that the road had turned, I saw the same blackness. I stood beside the bicycle for a few moments, catching my breath. My heartbeat had slowed and my breathing was now more regular. I recalled the sign on the crossroads. I knew now that I was still travelling in the right direction. Remounting the bicycle, I pushed off into the darkness, accompanied by a small squeak from the front fork on each rotation of the wheel.

CHAPTER FOURTEEN
PAUL

It was mid-June, warm and bright with a few puffy clouds
scattered across the blue sky. The five of us – Albert, Jeanne,
Monique, Stephen and I – had packed up our few belongings
and were on our way from the holiday house, which had been
our home for the past weeks, along the short road into the town
square. Stephen and I had our small suitcases, which we had
packed for what was due to be a sea journey a few days ago
but was now to be a train journey. Below our coats were knee-
length socks and tired-looking leather shoes. Monique wore
ankle boots with laces running up the centre, while Albert had
his heavy coat and a rucksack over his shoulder. Jeanne wore
a long dress and black shoes that became visible beneath her
as she walked, and she carried her brown suitcase which she
had packed with food for our journey.

As we approached the square, we could see two large trucks
with the familiar tarpaulins covering their rears. German
soldiers stood at the side of the square with guns poised, as if
ready for battle. Their heavy, grey helmets and leather chin-
strappings gave them an intimidating and threatening
appearance. As if we could be a threat in any way! Two other
German soldiers with guns in holsters were striding between
the Mairie and the trucks, carrying papers. One beckoned over
to us, waving officiously.

'Hurry,' he shouted. 'Hurry. We have little time. You go to
that truck,' he continued, pointing to the one furthest from us.
'Round the back and get in! Your papers!' he said, thrusting a
bundle of documents into Albert's' hand. 'Go! Quick!'

We shuffled towards our waiting transportation, the armed guards gesturing with their guns in the direction we were supposed to move, stern expressions on their faces. They all looked angry and avoided any eye contact. In most of the doorways facing the square, locals stood, with their arms folded across their chests, watching as we were ushered around to the back of our truck. A German soldier dropped the tailgate of the truck and there was a loud bang as it bounced off the metal framework. The rear tarpaulin was rolled up and a row of wooden benches could be seen lining the sides of the empty space. Albert was pushed towards the truck and threw in his rucksack before stepping back to help Jeanne. The soldier moved forward to block his path and pushed him back towards the truck, poking him with his gun. He climbed in, looking back as if scared that the rest of us might be diverted to the other truck. Jeanne was helped in, followed by us three youngsters, who were lifted under the arms by the guard. Our suitcases followed. We moved into the darkened space and found a place on the wooden benches, Albert on the right, with Monique beside him. Stephen and I sat on either side of Jeanne, who wrapped her arms around us, pulling us close. I looked out into the square as soldiers moved around hurriedly. One guard climbed in with us and sat down at the back. The tailgate was slammed shut and we waited. A few more commands were shouted out by the two officers carrying paperwork, after which the remaining soldiers clambered into the second truck. Engines burst into life with loud roars. Doors slammed and we moved forwards.

As we drove out of the square, I saw the curious and glum faces of the locals as they stepped out of their doorways and turned their heads to get a clearer view of the departing trucks.

We passed Dad's Studebaker, parked in front of the Mairie. I grimaced as my thoughts turned to him. I wondered where he might be now. The vehicles bumped and bounced along the uneven road as we left Port Navalo behind us.

The grinding of gear changes and roar of the diesel engine made it impossible to talk. We sat in silence, looking across at one another and glancing out of the rear of the truck as dust obscured the road and thick, dark smoke poured from the exhausts. Once we were on the main road the dust and smoke cleared and we could make out the countryside. We sped along the road towards Vannes, tall reed banks bordering the inland seawater lagoons that flanked both sides of the road. This scenery continued for several miles as we made our way towards the mainland.

Our first stop was the small village of Sarzeau, about half an hour from Port Navalo. The trucks rumbled into the town square and stopped in a line outside the Mairie. Three plain-clothed men in their sixties stood on the pavement with suitcases beside them. The shouting began again. 'Papiers!' bellowed one of the soldiers. Our guard pushed open the tailgate, which fell with another loud bang. He jumped out on to the road and stood to attention. After a few more orders, he rushed off towards the three men. Prodding with his gun, he ushered the three towards our truck and shouted for them to get in.

We shuffled along, deeper into the truck, to make a little space as more suitcases were thrown in, landing just in front of us. The three men were soon sitting beside us, two alongside Albert and Monique and one beside me. The tailgate slammed shut once more, the guard moved back into position, and the engines roared back into life. Onwards we went, gears crunching and grinding again as we lurched forward. No words were spoken.

An hour or so later, we entered the outskirts of Vannes. The road was smooth here and we had acclimatised to the noise of our transportation, which nevertheless still prevented us from communicating with one another. We remained silent, therefore, looking across at one another, occasionally glancing over at our unfriendly guard or out of the back of the truck. I looked at the guard a little more closely now as he stared directly ahead. He had blue eyes with dark eyebrows and what seemed to be a permanent frown. He also seemed more uncomfortable since the three men had joined us, apprehensive and a little tense. Before they had arrived he had been happy to look around outside, but now he just gazed ahead. Perhaps he felt a little insecure now there were three more grown men in with us. He had a big nose, was clean-shaven and was probably in his early twenties. He was quite a good-looking man and physically in good condition. There were strong veins down his neckline and he had a tanned colour, probably from standing around outside during these past sunny weeks. When his head moved with the motion of the truck, his tightly fitting helmet followed. His uniform was sharp-edged, immaculately clean and close fitting, almost as if it had been tailor-made. His boots were shiny clean and his machine gun glimmered in the light. He was clearly a fastidious man, proud of his appearance and of being a German soldier, but very unfriendly.

We bumped across a railway track and through a deserted factory zone. And then suddenly we were in the midst of a mass of German vehicles of all shapes and sizes – trucks, jeeps and motorbikes. There were soldiers packed inside lorries and marching along the roadside. We turned into a concourse filled with trucks similar to ours. Around us stood hundreds of people in groups with bags and suitcases of all sizes, mostly elderly or very young. There were very few adult men. We had arrived at Vannes railway station. It seemed there had been plenty of others trying to escape the advancing German army as well as us. Hundreds had been rounded up and brought here.

Our truck came to an abrupt halt. Once more the tailgate was unlatched and fell open with a loud bang. The guard jumped out on to the cobbled concourse. Turning towards us as we sat bewildered and confused at what was to happen next, he shouted while waving his machine gun. 'Aussteigen! Schnell!' he bellowed. We looked at him uncomprehendingly. 'Sortez! Vite!' he tried again. We understood that, so we got to our feet and gathered our bags. The three men climbed out first, followed by Albert. They all turned to help Jeanne. Once she was clear of the truck, the men held out their arms to help Monique, Stephen and me out.

Before we knew it, we were all standing together in a group at the rear of the truck. Our guard stood proudly beside us, as if we were his very own possessions. Moments later, an official-looking German officer appeared dressed like those who had first come to our holiday cottage door. Carrying a wooden board with a large black bulldog clip at the top, and a few pages of papers which looked as though they contained a list of names, he strutted over to us, stopped beside the guard and shouted, 'Papiere!' Albert reached into his inner coat pocket and pulled out the bundle of papers that he had been given by the German official in Port Navalo. Unsure whether he wanted some specific paper or all of them, he just handed over the whole lot.

The three men dipped into their pockets and handed over their own papers. The officer looked through them, sifting and reshuffling. He appeared to be looking for something in particular.

'Gut,' he mumbled, finally. Turning to us he said, 'Vous êtes Belges?'

'Oui,' replied Albert.

The officer folded up our papers and added a sheet headed with an eagle logo, below which was some bold, black text and then a list of all our names.

'Là-bas, à la zone verte,' (Over there, to the green zone), he said, pointing towards a large group of people gathered at the entrance to the station. 'Vite!' he yelled.

We picked up our bags and scurried off towards the indicated gathering, with Albert clutching the new sheet of paper, our three fellow travellers and guard left behind.

As we approached the station, another uniformed soldier approached us and demanded 'Papiere!' once again. This time Albert handed him the sheet given to us earlier. The soldier snatched it from his outstretched hand. 'Danke,' he mumbled. A quick, expressionless inspection of the papers was followed by a finger pointing towards a queue as he handed back the eagle-headed sheet. 'Transport neuf,' (Transport nine), he said loudly. We moved on towards a large metalwork gate that was flanked on each side by soldiers, brandishing their machine guns.

We were soon absorbed into a mass of people squeezing through the gateway leading onto the station platform. The platform was filled with people struggling with their various forms of baggage while trying to clamber on to the waiting train. Once we were on the platform, we could see that the carriages had been numbered with large, handwritten, chalk digits on the dark blue background. We made our way towards the carriage marked "9". It was almost the last carriage and was made up of several separate compartments. As we approached the doorway, our guard for the journey stood at the foot of the step. 'Papiers!' he ordered. With a quick glance at our documents, he ushered us in. Albert led the way as we moved along the corridor, looking into each compartment, our bags bumping along the sides as we went.

About halfway along the carriage, Albert led us into an empty compartment. Having hoisted his rucksack onto the overhead baggage rack, he turned to take our suitcases, which followed his bag onto the rack above. We sat together, Monique beside the window, with Albert alongside, and Jeanne, Stephen and I sitting opposite. We three children made ourselves comfortable, our legs only just able to reach the floor, wondering what was to happen next.

We were all looking out of the large window on to the platform, watching the anxious faces of the bewildered families making their way towards their numbered carriages, when we were interrupted by a uniformed soldier leaning into our compartment and shouting in German. After a few moments of gesturing and pointing, it became clear that we were all to move on to one side of the compartment. Albert and Monique squeezed into the remaining space on our side, nearest to the sliding door. Once they were *in situ*, the soldier beckoned to a family of four gathered in the corridor to enter the compartment. A man, a woman and two children – a girl and boy a little older than us – came in with a few bags which they kept on their laps rather than lifting them on to the baggage racks above. A small smile came across the boy's face as he looked at me sitting directly opposite. I smiled back. And then we sat in silence once again.

Half an hour or so passed and the platform gradually thinned of refugees, leaving just the German soldiers dispersed along the length of the platform. A whistle blew, our guard climbed in, and the main doors of the carriage were slammed shut, followed shortly by a jolt as the train shunted forward. We were on our way.

It was early evening as the train left Vannes and headed out into the Brittany countryside.

As the skies darkened the train slowed and we crawled through Redon station. We could see signs of a German military presence on the platform, but we did not stop, and picked up speed again as we left the small collection of houses behind. The clickety-clack as we crossed the track joints became a rhythm and our eyelids became heavy and began to close.

It was dark outside now. The light in the centre of our compartment was on and cast a dim glow around us. Heads had fallen forward and swayed from side to side. Our guard maintained his watch, his heavy boots passing by every half hour or so. We could occasionally hear him talking to another soldier as they met between patrols at the end of the carriage, where two wooden chairs blocked the way between the coaches.

I was awoken by bright platform lights coming in through the windows, followed by the screeching of steel on steel as we drew into Nantes station. A sudden jolt sent a domino effect the length of the train, the carriages pushing against each other as the train came to a standstill. Soldiers, spaced about twenty metres apart, lined the platform facing the train. They stood, legs slightly apart, glancing left and right, with their heads tilted forward so that we could not see the eyes beneath their steel helmets. Everyone in the compartment was awake now and we sat quietly looking out of the window and then back at one another, wondering what was to happen next.

It seemed an age that we were there, sitting and wondering, but finally we could hear shouting and boots running further back along the platform. Suddenly the train jolted forward, accompanied by a loud crunch. I looked out of the window. We had been coupled to a further ten carriages for our onward journey to Paris and then home.

The station guards had not moved, but suddenly there was another shunt, and the train began to move forward. Slowly we moved along the platform, its lights shining brightly from left to right across our window. A large sign reading "Nantes" passed us by, then another and then darkness as we left the station.

There was steel on steel again, and then a lurch to the right and a multiple cracking from the wheels as we negotiated a junction. We passed through a level crossing with its barriers down, red lights reflecting off the windscreen of a car waiting for us to pass. There was another tug as the powerhouse engine ramped up the steam to pull us away again. Slowly we drifted past industrial units and factories with their many windows lit, and then dark blocks of housing as we headed through the suburbs of Nantes.

Soon everything was dark once more and we settled back into our seats, huddled up close to one another.

CHAPTER FIFTEEN
HARRY

It was dark and I was cold. The adrenaline had subsided and I began to feel the effects of my crash – a stiffness in my shoulder and an ache in my knee. My hands had chilled in the breeze as I cycled through the damp forest and now my whole body was starting to feel cold. I needed a place to stop for the night.

I recalled the sign on the main crossroads at Labouheyre: Escource eight kilometres. I must have covered about three by now. There would be somewhere there to find shelter. Get to Escource, I kept repeating to myself, over and over, as if there was nothing else to think about. I was in a kind of semi-trance and my mind continued to repeat the mantra, almost in a singing rhythm. I could only see about thirty metres ahead now. The road was still shiny, but dark. Dead straight, but disappearing into increasing blackness. I knew I need not worry about sharp turns, as I was not cycling at full speed now. Continuous rotation of the pedals. Knees pumping up and down. Repeated squeaks of rubber on the front forks.

As I approached the small village that was made up of a few wooden farmhouses between clearings in the forest, I scanned ahead, trying to search out a barn or other suitable building in the darkness. A light shining from a window in one farmhouse shed illumination on to an adjacent wooden structure. That's the place to seek shelter, I thought. I was too tired to look for alternatives – and there seemed to be little choice, anyway. I dismounted my rickety bike and walked towards the dimly lit structure, squinting to see if I could make out the entrance to the building. As I drew nearer, I could see the outline of a door with a heavy bolt. The door, though, stood slightly ajar. I walked as quietly as I could round to the side of the building and leaned the bike against the wood-slatted frame. Then I crept back round to the entrance and gently pulled the door towards me, creating enough of a gap to squeeze inside.

I peered into the darkened shed, glimpsing various tools and farming equipment distributed around the edges. To my right was a pile of chopped timber, neatly stacked about a metre high. Beyond, just within sight in the darkness, a couple of discarded wooden chairs. I moved deeper into the darkness. As my eyes became increasingly accustomed to it, more items and some machinery became visible. At the far end were a few old sacks behind a tractor. Well, it's dry and a place to lie down, I thought. I brushed the dirt floor with my hand, clearing a small space, and lay down with my hands tucked into my coat. Sleep came quickly.

'Qui êtes vous?' (Who are you?) a loud voice shouted. 'Qui êtes vous?' the deep-throated rasp repeated, even louder.

I sat up sharply, not quite aware of where I was. Looking up through sleepy eyes, I tried to gather my thoughts and make sense of what was happening. Before me I saw a pair of heavy, well-worn black boots. I lifted my eyes to see a stocky man, dressed in a grey shirt with sleeves rolled up to the elbows and dark oversized dungarees that were held up by braces. He had a thick, dark-brown leather belt around his waist and a cloth cap on his head. In front of him, only a metre or so from my face were the twin barrels of a shotgun. I pushed myself up on to one arm and gazed up at the figure before me.

'Monsieur,' I said in my best French, 'Monsieur, s'il vous plait, excusez-moi.' (Sir, please, excuse me.)

He looked down at me, his gun getting closer to my face.

'Parlez-vous anglais?' I asked.

'Anglais!' he bellowed back at me.

'Oui,' I said quietly. 'Oui. Anglais.'

He lowered his gun and moved forward towards me. Bending down, he placed his arm under my armpit and pulled, helping me to my feet. He lifted me as if I was a feather – I could feel the strength in his forearm as it pressed firmly into my side. I stood before him, my hands beside me, completely helpless and vulnerable. He brushed the side of my coat and the dirt from the floor formed a cloud beside me.

'Venez,' (Come), he said, turning towards the door through which I had entered. He held the gun in his right hand as he beckoned me to follow with his left.

'Venez!' he said louder and I did what he said.

We came into a small courtyard. Dawn had just broken, but it was still quite dark. He led me through a heavy wooden door into a kitchen. A large wooden table occupied the centre space, with an open fire on one side, burning brightly, and an oval steel tub, filled with various cooking dishes and tin enamel plates, beneath a single tap attached to the stone wall. There were three wooden chairs, like those I had seen discarded in the shed, around the table, one on each side. On the table were a wooden chopping board with a half-consumed loaf of bread and a vicious-looking knife, a couple of used tumbler-like glasses and a dark-green wine bottle. All were dimly lit by a single paraffin lantern hanging above the table. The stocky Frenchman placed the gun beside the door, moved across to the table and pulled out a chair, which grated on the stone floor.

'Asseyez-vous,' (Sit down), he said in his deep, grouchy voice.

I understood enough French to be able to cope with a few regular words and phrases and sat down. He walked round to the other side of the table and took his place opposite me. He stared at me for a few moments and then said:

'Anglais, eh?'

'Oui, Anglais,' I replied again.

We looked at one another for a few more moments. I did not know what to say. I knew little French and he seemed to have no English. But then he looked up and said:

'You English.'

My eyes widened in surprise.

'Why you here?' he asked.

'I am from Belgique,' I said. 'I am going to Spain to escape the war. La guerre. Escape. Espagne.'

'Ah, oui. You go Espagne?' he repeated to me.

'Oui,' I said.

With my pidgin French and his pidgin English, this conversation was going to be difficult.

'Comment?' (How?) he asked.

'On my vélo,' (On my bicycle), I said.

'Vélo?' (Bicycle?) he questioned, looking slightly puzzled.

'Oui. Vélo,' (Yes, bicycle), I repeated.

'Quel vélo?' (Which bicycle?) he asked.

'I have vélo by shed,' I said, 'I'll show you,' and got to my feet.

'Non! Non!' he said as I stood. 'Asseyez-vous.'

I sat back down, not willing to unsettle him. He sat and stared for a few more moments.

'Mangez. Eat,' he said. 'You eat.'

Then he stood and made his way across the room towards some shelving near the open fire. He reached up and grabbed a packet from the shelf, unwrapping it as he returned to the table. It contained a lump of pale-red coloured meat. He leaned over, picked up the knife and cut a thick slice of bread from the loaf on the centre of the table. Then he placed the bread before me and set about cutting some slices of the meat. He leaned towards the bottle, reached over for his used glass and filled it to the rim with a deep yellow substance.

'Eat,' he said. 'Drink.'

Somewhat cautiously, I did what he said. The glass contained a sweet fruit juice, although it was difficult to tell exactly what sort of fruit. The bread was dry and I guessed that the meat might have been wild boar. It tasted good and I welcomed the nourishment. Fear had distracted me from my hunger.

Things settled then and, although not much was said, I felt less threatened as the Frenchman walked around the room, sometimes talking to himself and readjusting his cloth cap every now and then. The room brightened as daylight came in through the only window above the sink. Over the next hour or so, communication continued through brief sentences made up of a mixture of French and English. I did my best to explain how I had tried to escape from Brussels with Jeanne, Paul, Stephen and Monique as the Germans advanced northwards. How we had driven along the northern coastline and eventually ended up in Port Navalo. He sat listening intensely, interrupting occasionally to clarify his understanding. Unlike many French people, he understood quite a bit of English, but found it difficult to string together a sentence.

By telling my story, I had opened my heart to this stranger and he showed me sympathy, shaking his head in disbelief as I talked through the disappointments. In this way, the morning passed quickly. He offered no story of his own, but just listened and interacted with mine. By noon it was complete. He stood up from the table and moved towards the door, beckoning to me to accompany him. We walked back across the small courtyard and round to the side of the shed. He stopped and pointed at my bicycle leaning up against the wall.

'No good to go to Espagne,' he said, pointing at it. 'I take you.' And he turned and pointed to an old Citroën C4 truck parked beside the farmhouse.

It was dark blue with a black grille surrounded by a chrome frame. Two headlights were mounted on a chrome bar that spanned the front wheel arches. The single cab had deep side-runner plates and a flat bed on the rear. It was a very functional agricultural vehicle, clearly well-used and without doubt in need of a clean.

'I take you dans mon camion,' he said. 'Pas possible sur un vélo. Trop dangereux. I take you to Bayonne and Saint Jean-de-Luz. I have soeur là. Sister. We go ce soir. We voyage on petits chemins. Small roads. Come, we prepare for departure ce soir.'

During the afternoon I took a shower. It was my first for several days – basic and cold but invigorating. My newfound friend brought me some replacement clothes, explaining that I needed to look more French and rural. He explained that I was to be a worker on his farm. It turned out that he farmed ducks as well as doing a little financially rewarding wild boar hunting. His farm was small and very isolated here in the Landes forest. His wife had passed away a couple of years ago and he had a son who had moved to Bordeaux to find work. He was alone here now. He had one sister, though, who lived in Saint Jean-de-Luz, which was just south of Bayonne and close to the Spanish border. Her husband supplied fresh fish to the Bayonne markets, and the hotels in the popular holiday resort of Biarritz. My friend had very limited knowledge of what was going on in the world, but regular visits to his sister gave him more information. He knew that war was coming and he had little regard for the Germans. His uncle had been killed in the Great War, after which his aunt had returned to San Sebastian in Spain, where her family lived. Thanks to my new friend, I now had a good chance of making it to the border and crossing into Spain.

By dusk I had been re-clothed with musty-smelling dark blue dungarees, a well-worn check shirt with sleeves rolled up to the elbow, topped off with a replacement cloth cap. Plus I had a black tubular sack containing a thick polo-neck jumper, replacement trousers and shirt and socks, bound up with a rope. I kept my own coat and shoes but that was about it.

As night fell, we climbed into the cab of his truck and moved slowly along the muddied track towards the road from which I had arrived. Turning left, we passed the remaining few dwellings, only just visible in the fading light, and headed south into the forest.

The weak headlights threw two faint beams of light on to the shiny surface before us as the stocky Frenchman leaned forward, focusing his eyes on the road ahead. As he ground through the gears, I bounced up and down in my seat, feeling every bump shuddering through the truck from the uneven surface.

From Escource we travelled south towards Lesperon. This road was as straight as the others I had cycled along since I had entered the Landes Forest. It was too noisy in the cab to talk, so we sat in silence as my companion stared out into the darkness.

As we continued south through several small remote villages the roads became narrower, with the tarmac edges breaking up. We had to stay right in the centre to avoid unexpected potholes. Fortunately, we did not encounter a single vehicle coming in the opposite direction.

An hour or so later we approached Léon, where the road improved. We continued on through the tiny village of Messanges, heading southwards along the coastal route, which became increasingly twisty as we passed by Hossegor and Capbreton. It was three in the morning as we approached the outskirts of Bayonne.

There were three bridges crossing the River Adour that split the town in two. It would be quiet at this time in the early hours of the morning, but as we would be one of very few vehicles on the roads, we might attract attention. From our position on the coastal side of the main road, we could enter the town from the northwest and travel through the residential areas, rather than taking the main road which ran through the eastern side of Bayonne. My driver knew this route well and found his way without needing to follow signs. Soon we were on the Pont Grenet, crossing the great river that disappeared among the old town buildings beyond. All was quiet on the streets and there was no sign of any German occupants. We had had a clear run and soon we were out into the countryside once more and heading towards Biarritz.

The terrain had changed now. There was no more forest and the landscape had become hilly and undulating. A sign told us that we were seven kilometres from Biarritz. We needed to be careful now. I had somehow managed to inform my new friend that I had witnessed German troops travelling south in great haste. He had reassured me that I need not worry. If we were stopped he would do the talking, which did not fill me with confidence. On the other hand, why would the Germans be interested in a somewhat agricultural Frenchman in a flatbed truck?

As we entered the town, dawn was beginning to break. It was necessary for us to drive right into the centre of town in order to get on to the coast road that headed south to Saint Jean-de-Luz, the last town in France on the edge of the Spanish border. We hoped that the Germans had not yet managed to get this far south. All the fighting had been in the north of France and the invading armies had concentrated their efforts on moving west to Brest and into Paris. This far south-eastern corner was some way from these cities. Although I had witnessed some military presence just south of Bordeaux, we hoped that the main occupying forces had not yet moved south in numbers. My chances of crossing into Spain were looking good.

We drove on into the centre of Biarritz when, just as we turned a corner, immediately ahead of us was a German checkpoint. A single-person wooden shelter box painted with zigzag stripes stood on the pavement. Beside that stood two German soldiers with rifles hanging from their shoulders. A wooden pole with white and red segments spanned our side of the road. Twenty yards further on, another shelter and pole blocked the road from the opposite direction. I glanced across at my driver. He looked straight ahead. Two cars were ahead of us, the first passing paperwork out of the window to a single German soldier. We slowed to a stop behind the second car. My Frenchman looked at me and said: 'Silence. C'est moi qui parle. I speak. OK?' I nodded.

We moved forward slowly as the barrier rose and let through the cars ahead of us. It was our turn next. We were right alongside the two Germans by the shelter. They looked me straight in the eye. I looked away nonchalantly, dipping my gaze beneath my cap and into the footwell.

'Papiers!' demanded the soldier now at the opposite window.

'J'ai pas de papiers. Nous sommes en route vers l'usine.' he replied. 'Pas de papiers. Désolé.' (I have no papers. We are on the way to the factory. No papers. Sorry.)

'Papiers!' the soldier repeated louder.

'Pas de papiers! Usine!' the Frenchman repeated louder.

'Wer ist er?' (Who is he?) the soldier said, pointing at me.

'Frère!' he replied. (Brother!)

'Bruder?' the soldier said.

'Frère!' he repeated.

'Papiers prochaine fois!' (Papers next time!) the soldier said. 'Ja?' he shouted, as he leaned in towards the window.

'Ja,' my driver replied, leaning back towards me in response to the shouting soldier.

'Allez!' he said, stepping back and gesturing to the soldiers at the box to raise the barrier.

It seemed that they had only just arrived and this particular German had little to no French. Only 'Papiers' and 'Papiers prochaine fois.' We had been lucky this time.

First gear was selected and the flatbed truck lurched forward past the barrier. We slowly gathered speed as we passed the checkpoint for oncoming cars and carried on into town. We headed towards the harbour and the hotels which overlooked the sandy beaches. We turned left into Rue Gambetta, past holiday houses on our left and beaches on our right. Our flatbed truck must have looked a little out of place among the shiny modern cars parked outside the holiday homes. The holidaymakers must have been caught unawares by the sudden arrival of the occupying forces.

Soon we were back in the countryside on our way to Saint Jean-de-Luz. My French friend, who had said nothing during the past hours, looked across at me and smiled. I was in the hands of a stranger, but he had become a saviour. During the night we had covered ground that would have taken me days on that trusty bicycle. God only knew how I would have made the journey. Someone was taking care of me.

By mid-morning we had arrived in Saint Jean-de-Luz. It was a small fishing town not hugely dissimilar to Port Navalo and was broken into two by the Nivelle river, which flowed down from the foothills of the Pyrenean mountains into the Bay of Biscay. On the edge of the town was a small bay with beaches and the harbour hosted a strong fishing fleet of small independent fishermen. We drove through the centre-ville on to the south side of the River Nivelle.

Turning, soon afterwards, up a short, tree-lined driveway, we approached a large villa with terracotta roof tiles, deep-purple climbing bougainvillea and white arched terraces, on each side of a stairway that led up to the main entrance. The noise of the truck engine suddenly stopped and the silence was deafening. My ears were numb – I had become too accustomed to that roaring and its sudden end was a shock.

I opened the truck door and stepped out on to the runner plates and then the gravel driveway. I felt a little unsteady on my feet and had to delay releasing my grasp on the door. I stretched upwards and, placing my hands on my hips, bent over backwards a little to get the muscles in my back operating again. I stood for a few moments looking at the villa, and then over to the stocky man as he walked towards the stairway leading to the main door, the gravel crunching beneath his heavy black boots. Despite all my failed efforts to escape with my children from France, this man had brought me to safety. Although, of course, I did not yet know how I was to make it across the border into Spain, which was now only fifteen kilometres away. The journey here had been long, but England felt so much further away.

My friend tugged on the handle of a wall-hung bell, resulting in a high chiming deep inside the house. After a few moments, the main door opened, revealing a tall, elegant lady in a colourful dress that stopped just below the knee. She had a deep golden complexion and pitch-black hair that was pulled back behind her head, where a plaited ponytail with a red ribbon fell forward on to her chest. Strong red lipstick framed a warm smile that revealed a perfect set of pearl-coloured teeth. She was a spectacular specimen of Mediterranean beauty – a mixture of French elegance and Spanish style.

Despite her brother's grubby clothes and less-than-fragrant smell, she threw out her arms to greet him.

'Pascal!' she cried out.

This was the first time that I had heard my saviour's name. For one reason or another, we had never actually referred to one another by anything other than "Monsieur". It came as a bit of a shock. The English are generally quite formal and I had always been so. The French join them in this, with strict rules within the language to indicate respect for elders, family, friends and acquaintances. How we did not get round to asking the most obvious question of all, though, was most peculiar. It was perhaps because of our limited communication abilities, or maybe the unusual circumstances. Whatever the reason, I now knew his name. After a few words from Pascal, his sister stepped aside and called out to me, 'Monsieur. Come quickly!' There was a tone of anxiety in her voice. She looked around the driveway inquisitively, as if checking to see if there was anyone there who shouldn't be.

I hurried over to the lady, who opened her arms and kissed me on both cheeks. It was such a common French gesture, but it made me feel embarrassed and awkward. This was a natural English reaction – I had felt these things all my life. Although I had lived in Belgium for almost ten years, I had never quite overcome the discomfort when strangers greeted me with kisses.

She turned, tucking her arm under mine, and pulled me into her home, with Pascal following behind. Then she turned to me and, in almost perfect English, said:

'I am Collette. You must have had the most terrible time.' She turned and took one more look out into the garden, before closing the door. 'What is your name?'

'Harry Barker,' I replied. 'You speak good English.'

'Thank you, Harry,' she said. 'Come into the kitchen. I was in England for four years when I was a teenager, working in a hotel in London. It was a memorable time for me and I made many good friends. It was during the roaring twenties and we had a lot of fun.'

'Whereabouts in London?' I asked.

'I was in Kensington,' she said.

'Goodness me,' I said. 'I am from Barnes, a little further outside London. I know Kensington quite well.'

'That's amazing,' she said. 'I have heard of Barnes, but I did not go there. I spent all my time in central London working in the hotel. They were good times.'

We sat at the kitchen table and talked a little more about my hometown and how I left England for Belgium with Abbi. How we had raised two boys and how I ended up here. It was good to talk to someone who spoke English well. I had forgotten how much I missed it. She was warm and open. She spoke little about herself, but kept asking about my life. I think she enjoyed talking about her time in London. It was some time ago and a long way from Saint Jean-de-Luz.

After an hour or so, I was led down into the cellar. In the corner behind a double wardrobe lay an old mattress and blanket.

'You must try to get some sleep, Harry. There is much to do and we have little time. I will call on you in a couple of hours.' With that, she climbed the wooden steps, which led out of the cellar, and the door closed quietly behind her.

This was unbelievable. From sleeping under a tree, wrapped in my coat, cold, wet and hungry in the middle of the Landes Forest, to a mattress with blanket and pillow in a warm cellar. Things were improving, I thought.

I was woken some time later. I had no idea of the time or how long I had slept. I must have needed the rest. We sat at the kitchen table for dinner and were joined by Claude,

Collette's husband. The four of us sat and talked late into the night, Collette translating as we chatted.

The subject soon turned to the matter of crossing the border into Spain and where to go from there.

Claude explained that there had been many refugees arriving in and passing through Saint Jean-de-Luz in the past few weeks. Thousands had been evacuated from Bayonne, but more refugees turned up every day as the news of what was happening in the north spread south. German soldiers were due to arrive in numbers any day. There was considerable debate spreading through the town about occupation, and there was talk that some of the police were beginning to show signs of siding with the Germans, and of forming a local militia. The Germans had already taken control of the main border crossing and there had been reports of some locals being questioned as to whether they were Jews, and being detained. Crossing at the frontier would be difficult.

Claude had built a successful business trading fresh fish and had many friends and contacts in the fishing fleet of Saint Jean-de-Luz, as well as knowing Spanish fishermen from San Sebastian. He was acquainted with several who had been taking refugees across to Spain by boat. It was only a short journey and heavily populated by a variety of fishing boats regularly trading between the ports. This seemed like the best option, but we would need to be careful and move quickly. Arrangements would need to be made.

Late into the evening, I returned to the cellar. My mid-afternoon nap had quelled my need for sleep and my mind was wide-awake, speculating about the next phase of my journey. The last time I had tried to escape by sea, things had gone very wrong. The Germans were due to arrive here any day, so here

I was again in the same position. Would I get away in time? Thoughts of how I had left those closest to me on the quayside in Port Navalo filled my mind. Paul and Stephen standing beside their small leather suitcases, tears running down their cheeks. The image was crystal clear in my mind's eye. Where were they now? Were they safe? The uncertainty was unbearable. I sat upright, staring into the darkness. 'Please, God, keep them safe,' I said quietly.

I lay back, resting my head on the soft, warm pillow. There was nothing I could do now. My first priority was to get back to England. Once I was there, I could look into finding out where they were. In the meantime, I was once more in the hands of others. Finally, I drifted off to sleep.

I was woken by the sound of running water as it fell down the length of the drainpipes from the roof gutters. Dim light came from a small window at the back of the cellar. I crept over to look out. A thick film of dust coated the window. I couldn't see anything. With my hand I rubbed at the glass to clear away the dirt. I peered out. Due to the slope of the land, I could see out across the back garden as it fell away into a valley, revealing a wonderful view. A dull, grey sky stretched out over the terracotta-tiled roofs of far-away houses. A misty rain obscured the view, shimmering in waves as it was blown about by the breeze. I had been lucky with the weather so far, but this wetness looked like it was here to stay.

There was a knock on the cellar door, the handle turned and then the face of Collette appeared in the doorway.

'Harry!' she called out. 'Are you there?'

'Yes, I am here,' I replied.

'Good. You need to get up. We have made some arrangements. Claude made contact with a friend and we need to meet him in town as soon as possible. Bring all your things. We must go immediately.'

'Ah. OK. I will be up in a tick,' I said.

I gathered up my coat and cap, put on my shoes, grabbed the black sack supplied by Pascal in one hand, and then walked up the few steps into the kitchen. Collette met me at the doorway.

'Here,' she said. 'Take this,' and held out a cloth sack. 'You will need it.'

The sack was unexpectedly heavy. I could see the shape of a bottle within and assumed this was food and drink. She took me by the arm and guided me swiftly towards the front door. For a minute I wondered whether this was all a ruse to get rid of me.

'You must hurry,' Collette said. 'Claude is in the car, waiting. There is no time to lose. Go now. Good luck!'

'But what about Pascal?' I called out, as I walked down the steps to the waiting car.

'Pascal has gone,' she said.

Before I knew it, I was sitting next to Claude in his Citroën, on the way into town.

Five minutes passed as we sped along the main road into town. Yesterday we had come up this road on the way to his house. Just before reaching the main roundabout to town, he suddenly turned right along a tree-lined road which led away from town into the forest. A kilometre or so further on, we turned left on to a dirt track which led to a small farmhouse nestling between the trees. An old grey van was parked in the driveway. The back doors were open.

We came to an abrupt stop. 'OK, Harry. Jean-Pierre will take you to a safe house in the mountains for a few days until we can arrange a route for you. Don't worry. It will be OK. Go on. Out. Quick!' he said, pushing my shoulder.

'But...' I began to speak, but was quickly cut short.

'No time, Harry. You must go now. Get into the back of that van. Please. Go now!'

I climbed out of Claude's car and walked across towards the van. A large man in grubby clothes, with a cap on his head, a pipe in his mouth and a shotgun slung over his shoulder, followed by a large black dog, came out from the farmhouse, walking quickly towards the van. 'Entrez!' he called out. 'Vite!'

I wasn't going to argue and climbed into the small space. It was a little cramped, but I managed to get in and sat on the corrugated steel floor. The back door slammed shut, after which the dog jumped into the front passenger seat and the van tipped to one side as the heavy man got in, and then his door slammed closed. The engine sparked into life and with a bump we moved off. I bounced around inside the van as we moved along the potholed track. I had no idea where we were going. I had to trust these people. What other choice did I have?

Fifteen minutes or so later, after a bumpy ride, we came to a stop. The large Frenchman climbed out, came round the back and opened the door. Light flooded in. I had to squint and hold my hand over my eyes to get used to the brightness. We were now deep in the forest. A wooden shed stood before us, hidden amongst the trees and covered in bramble. You would not see this hut unless you knew it was there, I thought.

'You stay here,' the Frenchman said with a broad accent. 'I come tomorrow.'

'OK,' I agreed. Where would I go from here? I thought. I have no idea where I am or how long I might be here for. Within moments the man, his dog and the van disappeared between the trees and out of sight. I was alone in this forest now. I just had to wait.

I walked over to the hut and pushed open the door. It was a bit bigger than it looked from the outside. Inside were a couple of chairs, a small table, some blankets on the floor and a wood burner in the corner with a pile of logs, some kindling and a box of matches. On the table were a candle, a tin cup, a tin plate and a knife. There was no window. Very comfy, I thought. A bit lonely, though.

It was about midday now. I decided to make a small tour of the locality.

There was little evidence outside of this hut being occupied. No trampled undergrowth and no clear path. Behind the hut the land climbed quite steeply and, through the trees, I could see the rocky mountain peaks beyond. Below, there was thick forest, but between the trees, some two hundred metres from my position, I could just make out parts of a road running through the valley. No sign of any traffic. My position was totally obscured from the road below. No one would know this place existed.

I decided to settle in. I took a chair from inside and positioned it just outside by the door. I sat myself down on my new terrace looking into the trees. Then I remembered the sack given to me by Collette. I popped back into the shed and returned to my terrace. Reaching in, I drew out a bottle of water. Then a paper bundle which turned out to be half a loaf of bread with a thick layer of jam running through the middle; a roll of toilet paper and something wrapped in a cloth of some sort. As I drew it out of the bag it became obvious. It was a gun! I had not handled a gun since my time in the Somme. I didn't have a pistol back then either. We were all given the standard issue Lee Enfield rifles and trained to take good care of our weapons as they were susceptible to jamming if grit or dirt got into the firing mechanism. Most of us wrapped cloth around the firing mechanism to keep it clean whilst in the trenches. The Lee Enfield had a ten-bullet magazine and we were expected to be able to fire off the ten bullets, reload a new magazine and fire a further two shots in one minute. It was a great rifle, although I rarely needed to use it. I never had my own pistol, but our Commanding Officer carried one in a holster attached to his shiny brown leather belt. Occasionally, he needed to clean and check all was operational, so he showed me and the other infantrymen how it worked. It was a Webley Mk 4. It looked much the same as a cowboy handgun, with a revolving six-round cylinder. This pistol was very similar. Also in the bag I found two boxes of twelve cartridges. I did not expect to go out and fight a war – just get back to England. Perhaps Collette thought I might need to be armed. I played with the gun a little, spinning the cylinder and aiming into the trees, then faking a shot being fired. This was real, I thought. I needed to be ready, just in case.

I spent the rest of the day pacing around outside the hut until the sun began to disappear behind the trees. It grew darker as dusk fell over the mountains. I retreated into the hut and lit the candle. It was not cold enough to light the wood burner. I also did not want to attract any attention. As darkness fell, I could hear the sound of trucks approaching along the road. I went outside to see if I could see anything. It was quite dark and I could only make out the headlights flickering as they moved past the trees. Two trucks moving quite quickly. Soon they had passed and disappeared into the distance. I retreated back into the hut and made ready for a night's sleep. I wondered if the trucks were driven by Frenchmen or Germans. I would need to get a closer look next time.

I was woken by the sound of a vehicle engine approaching, twigs snapping under the wheels as it neared my hideaway. I peered through the crack in the door to see the grey van pulling up alongside the hut. The large Frenchman levered himself out of the van, followed by his black dog. He lumbered over towards me. I opened the door.

'Bonjour, Monsieur,' he bellowed. 'OK?' he quizzed. He knew my French was limited and tried to keep communication simple.

'OK,' I replied.

'You stay one more day,' he said. 'I come again tomorrow. I have food.' He held out a paper bag.

'Merci,' I said, trying to make an effort. He smiled, turned away and, within a few moments, was gone.

That was brief, I thought. I supposed I was here to stay. Where else could I go? I returned into the hut and opened the bag of food. More bread and some saucisson. The knife was sharp, so it was easy to slice the saucisson into manageable morsels.

By midday I was bored, so I decided to venture a little deeper into the forest. With the gun pushed into my trouser belt, I moved downhill towards the road along which I had seen the trucks pass by the previous night. The slope was steep and it was slippery underfoot. I needed to be careful I did not find myself tumbling down through the undergrowth. I moved carefully between the trees, using them to prevent myself falling. Perhaps I should have taken a route traversing the slope, instead of straight down hill. Fifteen minutes or so later I was fifty metres from the road. I could see it clearly now and the undergrowth thinned as the gap between the trees created a gash through the valley. As I approached the road, slipping between the tall grey trees, I heard the sound of a diesel engine in the distance. The sound grew louder and I thought I had better take cover. The slope was too steep to climb back up quickly, so I needed to find some thick bush or shrubbery to hide behind. The chance of being seen by a passing vehicle was almost zero, so I was not too concerned as I crouched behind a bush.

As the vehicle turned a gentle corner, it came into view about eighty yards to my left. A German truck with canvas tarpaulin. The gears ground as it changed up and gathered speed. I had a good view from my hideout. As it approached my position the truck disappeared from view, obscured by the branches and leaves of the bush. I crouched in silence, looking through the greenery, trying to get a clear view. As the truck neared, it slowed and came to a stop almost alongside my position. 'Oh shit,' I thought. Maybe I had been spotted. If I had been seen I was in deep trouble. I squatted in silence, waiting to see what was to happen next.

The truck had pulled up on the edge of the road, the passenger-side wheels just off the tarmac road on the dirt. Whilst the engine idled, the passenger door opened and a German soldier climbed out. I drew the pistol from my belt and held it before me, pointing at the oncoming soldier.

'Hey, Otto. Schnell, huh!' the driver shouted from the cab.

'Ja, ja, Hans!' the soldier replied.

He walked quickly, directly towards me. As he approached he began to reach down to his trousers and grappled with the buttons. He was going to have a piss. Oh my God! He came closer and closer, then stopped right in front of me. The only thing between me and the German was the bush. I gripped the handle of the pistol tighter, my hands beginning to sweat. If he came any closer he would be pissing on me.

Releasing the buttons, his flaccid penis fell out of his trousers and almost simultaneously the urine began to pour out. He was just a few feet away from me. I glared through the branches and leaves at his face. A tall man, strong and compact, his army cap just perched on the side of his head. His hair blond and cut close to the skin, piercing blue eyes, blond eyebrows and eyelashes. His sharp jawline had a day's growth of bristle – difficult to see due to his blond colouring. I would have no chance in a struggle. I squatted in absolute silence, the pistol pointed directly at his chest. Adrenaline ran through my body. I could feel my face warming and my finger tightening on the trigger. The slightest move could spell my end. He looked down towards the direction of the urine which flowed into the branches. I felt the odd splash of urine land on my hands. He must spot me at any moment. I would have to shoot him. How many more soldiers might there be in the back of that truck, I wondered. Perhaps there was only him and the driver? I might have a chance. If I did end up shooting them both, though, it would not be long before a search party would be sent out. I had no idea where I was and no way of contacting Jean-Pierre. The urine continued to flow. The soldier looked up to the sky and let out a long sigh.

'Ahhh. Das ist gut!' he groaned.

'Schnell, Otto!' came another call from the truck.

'Ja. Ja. Ich komme!' he replied.

He stood arched slightly, with his penis protruding out of his trousers. His hands hung freely by his side. His head tilted backwards, looking up into the sky. If he looks directly forward he will see me, I thought, of that I am sure. He does not have a gun, so I have the advantage. For God's sake, man, finish your piss and get back in that bloody truck, I pleaded in silence to myself.

Finally, the power of the stream slowed. He looked directly forward into the bush behind which I was crouched. Surely he must have seen me. He was looking directly at me. Perhaps he had seen me and decided not to react. Perhaps he saw my pistol pointing directly at his chest. He was unarmed. He did nothing to make me think he had spotted me, just glared directly towards me. As the flow of urine tailed off, his head dropped and looked down. With his right hand he took hold of his penis and shook it up and down. A few droplets flew off, one striking me on the cheek. As he pushed the flaccid tube back into his trousers he turned and walked towards the truck, grappling with the buttons as he went. Would he return with his gun and fellow soldier? I would have to wait.

He climbed into the cab, slammed the door shut and with a roar the truck moved off back onto the road. I was still paralysed with fear. It took several moments for my body to loosen up enough to stand. My knees and thighs had frozen and it was a struggle to straighten my legs. The immediate danger had gone, but had that soldier seen me? Was he going to return with more men and guns? My curiosity and boredom had got me into this mess and I had damned nearly ended up in the shit. I needed to get back to my hut. It was a close-run thing, but I was alive.

CHAPTER SIXTEEN
PAUL

Morning came, daylight began to fill the train and the occupants of our compartment started to stir. It had been a long day the day before and most of us had slept through the night. Anxiety and confusion had taken their toll and we had needed the rest.

The sky was overcast and grey. Heavy cloud, but no sign of rain. Jeanne stood and reached up for her suitcase. She lowered it carefully on to her lap, flicked open the catches and lifted the lid, exposing an assortment of wrapped packages, including various types of fruit and two large bottles. From a paper bag she picked out three pastry buns and handed one each to Monique, Stephen and me. Pain au raisin was one of my favourites. It was a little dry but the nourishment was welcome. Jeanne returned to the suitcase for two small bread rolls, wrapped in white paper. She handed one to Albert and took a bite out of the other.

The train continued on as we tucked into our breakfast. Once I had finished, I felt that I needed to visit the toilet. I asked Jeanne where I should go and she stood and said she would accompany me.

As I got up, Albert leaned over and pulled open the sliding door to let us out. We entered the corridor, turned left and made our way towards the end of the carriage where two soldiers stood smoking and chatting. They looked at me curiously. The door marked "Toilettes" was heavy. I had to put all my weight into pushing it open, revealing a small confined space with metal toilet and hand basin. I turned and looked at Jeanne, who smiled and said, 'In you go.'

As we made our way back along the corridor, we were followed by our guard. I peered into the other compartments as we passed, which were full with people of all ages, squeezed together as we were.

In the compartment next to ours was a family of six. They wore hats and shawls and, heads tilted forward; they were rocking back and forth. I paused to look. They were praying.

'N'arrêtez pas! Continuez!' the soldier called out. 'Juden! Verboten!'

As I moved on, I could see the yellow stars sewn on to their coats. We returned to our compartment and as I sat down next to Albert, I asked:

'Why do the people next door wear yellow stars on their coats?'

'Because they are Jews,' replied Albert. 'The Germans demand that all Jews wear the Star of David, so that they can identify them. They will all be taken to camps to work.'

I felt sorry for the family next door who wore the yellow stars.

The train gradually began losing speed. Before long we were travelling at only a snail's pace. Then there was a lurch to the right as the train left the main track for a siding. After a few minutes, there was a jolt as we came to a halt. Out of our window we could see the main track running alongside.

While we waited, we struck up a conversation with our fellow occupants. They were French and being repatriated to Amiens in northeast France. They had run from their home to escape the fighting and travelled west across the country to cousins who lived in Quimper in the southwest of Brittany. The Germans had arrived in Quimper some days before they had reached Port Navalo. Our fellow passengers, too, had been identified and instructed to return home.

After about an hour there was a sudden roar from the main track as a black steam engine thundered by. The roar of passing carriages rumbled through our compartment as we watched trailer after trailer of German tanks travel past. Every three trailers were separated by a wagon, a German soldier sitting aloft with goggles and the customary machine gun. The train had many carriages – after the tanks came trucks, and then smaller vehicles. The roar continued until the last carriage passed and then rapidly diminished to silence as the train disappeared into the distance.

We remained in this siding for most of the day as more and more military trains passed by. More tanks, troop carriers, wagons and then finally a French passenger train like the one we were on. Late in the afternoon, we shunted back into life and moved slowly backwards on to the main track, where we paused briefly once more before moving gently forwards and then gradually picking up speed.

Our next stop was Angers, where we waited again for several hours, before moving on to Le Mans, where we arrived early the following morning. By now we had begun to circulate among our fellow passengers, listening to their stories. Most of them were French, from the northeastern part of the country, but there were also a few Belgians. Our German guards had relaxed a little now and allowed us to stand in the corridor chatting to each other. No one was allowed to communicate in any way with the passengers in the compartment next to ours, however, and those poor unfortunates were not permitted to leave, other than under armed guard for visits to the toilet.

At Le Mans station, the train took on food supplies, our first nutrition since we had left Vannes. It was bread rolls and bottled water – not much, but particularly welcome among those who had not brought any food with them. We took our allocation and Jeanne quietly packed the rolls into her suitcase. We did not know what we might face later, so replenishment of our stock was more important than consumption now.

The train shunted into life again and we moved on towards Chartres and Paris.

An hour or so after departing Angers, we were once again redirected into a siding, where we remained for much of that day. Once more, the familiar trains, filled with guns, troops, supplies and vehicles, passed us by, heading towards the east coast and Bordeaux. Monique, Stephen and I would jump up and run to the window to watch them, and we even tried to count the number of carriages if we could.

We passed through Chartres late at night but, as dawn broke, the train slowed again as we began to wind through the suburbs of Paris. Then, looking out of our window, we caught a glimpse of the Eiffel Tower, projecting up against the horizon. We would shortly be arriving at Paris Gare du Nord. Our guard walked down the corridor, banging on the doors and calling out:

'Paris bientôt. Préparez-vous à quitter le train! Quinze minutes!' (Paris soon. Prepare to leave the train! Fifteen minutes.)

He repeated this over and over as he moved down the length of the carriage. We gathered together our various items of clothing, put on our shoes and coats and prepared for departure. We were weary but excited. I had not been to Paris before!

The guard told us to remain in our compartment until we were directed to leave. Pulling into Gare du Nord, we saw that here, too, the platform was dotted with German uniformed soldiers, standing facing us, every ten metres or so. The tall, iron-girder structure holding up the glass roof towered high above us.

I wondered what was happening to our neighbours in the next compartment. They had been taken out and pushed down the corridor towards the exit at gunpoint. They climbed down from the train onto the platform to join the other passengers who wore yellow stars. Guards encircled them and corralled them into larger groups, which were moved down the platform away from the main entrance and concourse. They were pushed and cajoled by the Germans as they disappeared from sight. Again I felt sorry for these people who wore the yellow stars.

A few minutes later, our guard moved down the carriage, calling out:

'Allez-y maintenant! Sortez le train! Schnell!' (Go now! Leave the train! Quickly!)

Our fellow passengers in the compartment left first as Albert reached up to pass down our suitcases. Then we moved along the corridor towards the exit and, following Jeanne, climbed down from the train.

The platform was soon crowded with refugees, standing with their luggage, awaiting instructions of where to go next. Soon the mass of people began to move as one towards the main concourse. There at the gates stood several more German soldiers in long, dark, shiny coats, demanding 'Papiers!'

The crowds filtered through the gates, as their documents were scrutinised. Some were directed left, some right and others straight on. We moved slowly forwards until it was our turn to hand over papers and be directed. We were sent off to the left and instructed to go to platform five. The crowd had thinned as we made our way towards the gate. We were met there by another uniformed official demanding 'Papiers!' After a brief inspection, we were guided through on to the platform and told to go to carriage number three.

This time our carriage did not have compartments, but a central gangway with wood-slatted benches facing one another on each side. The carriage was already half-full with passengers loading their baggage onto the racks above the seats. We moved along the gangway until we found some free seats. Once more, Albert placed our suitcases on the racks and we sat ourselves down.

The carriage was filled with the noise of people chattering and suitcases being stowed away. The wooden seating was hard and uncomfortable. The next stage of our journey was beginning.

The train was full and the platform empty now, except for the few German soldiers who stood looking at the compartments, heads swivelling to left and right. A whistle shrilled. Doors slammed and then there was a shunt as the train began to move. The station signs, tall steel columns and the uniformed soldiers all passed our window as we began to gather pace. And then we were out into the bright daylight beyond the station roofing and through a myriad of tracks that criss-crossed the shiny, steel lines, merging and dividing as our carriage wheels crackled over the connecting rails and junctions.

Our speed was gentle as we slid from one track to another, before ultimately finding the one that was to lead us north and east towards Brussels. As we moved slowly between the buildings of Paris, I could see that the streets were filled with grey uniforms, military vehicles of all shapes and sizes, mounted horses, jeeps and trucks. People seemed to be just standing on the roadsides, watching with a sense of bewilderment. Some walked with their heads bowed, hiding beneath the rims of their hats and not making eye contact with the new visitors.

The train gathered speed as we passed through the suburbs and then into the surrounding countryside. It was not long before the random crackling beneath our carriage became that regular clickety-clack. We travelled parallel with one of the main roads into and out of Paris for several kilometres. There was almost a solid traffic jam of German military vehicles travelling towards the capital. Heading out of it, the road was moving freely, with the traffic consisting mainly of private cars and commercial trucks, interspersed with the odd German troop carrier.

As we travelled north, whenever we ran alongside a main road, the story was the same; jammed solid with military vehicles heading south, and just the odd car or van heading north. Further into the countryside, we began to see more and more people walking beside the roads, carrying bags and pushing carts loaded with all kinds of household items, some accompanied by animals, from dogs to donkeys. It reminded me of the journey from Brussels up to the north coast. The scenes were similar. A tear trickled down my cheek as I remembered Dad sitting in the driver's seat. It seemed such a long time ago. Where was he now?

By late afternoon, we had reached the suburbs of Brussels and soon pulled into Gare de Bruxelles, just to the south of the city, in Saint Gilles, near to where we had been living.

Once more, Albert lifted our luggage from the overhead racks. When all our bags were on ground level and allocated appropriately, he gathered up Monique in his arms and carried her towards the door. Jeanne took Stephen's hand and, whilst pulling him along the passageway behind her, motioned me forwards. We descended down the carriage step onto the platform and made our way towards the main entrance hall.

There were no guards or men in long coats demanding 'Papiers!' here. We moved towards the front entrance and, as we left the foyer, were confronted by a barrage of grey uniforms once more. The concourse was filled with German soldiers – walking along the pavements in groups, sitting in the cafés and filling almost every vehicle we could see. The occupying forces were here in huge numbers. While we had been away, they had moved in *en masse.*

Albert moved us along towards the old taxi rank at the far end of the station. A couple of cabs were lined up and he approached the one at the front of the queue. A few words were exchanged and we climbed in, bags and all. We were soon driving through the streets and looking through the windows at the crowds of uniformed soldiers, who outnumbered the plain-clothed public by two to one.

Some fifteen minutes or so later, we turned into the driveway of 20 Avenue de la Sapinière – right next to the house from where we had left with Dad in his Studebaker just a few weeks ago.

As we drove into the driveway, the front door burst open and Madame Dejong came running out towards us. Albert had climbed out of the taxi, helping Monique out from the back door. Before Monique had taken a step, Madame Dejong had swept her up into her arms, crying out:

'Mon Dieu! Ma petite chérie. Mon Dieu. Ma belle petite fille!' (My Lord! My little darling. My Lord. My beautiful little girl!)

As Stephen and I moved around the back of the cab, she crouched down, holding out her free arm and pulling us close into her embrace. Jeanne stood beside Albert, watching this emotional moment, a gentle smile across her face.

The cab driver was paid and together we moved as one towards the front door. After all that had happened, we were back where we started.

Over the next few days, we were reunited with Yvonne and arrangements were made for us to reoccupy number 22. The house had been empty whilst we had been away, although Yvonne had visited once a week to do a little dusting and cleaning. She had been staying with friends nearby and had not found any work during this time as the Germans had swarmed through Belgium, pushing the Allied forces north. The streets had been filled with trucks and tanks and thousands of people had fled from the capital, leaving everything behind. The situation had become very unstable and most people who had stayed did not leave their homes unless absolutely necessary.

During the following weeks, we tried our best to settle back into a routine. It was mid-summer, so there was no school to attend. We spent our days with the Dejong family, with occasional outings to the nearby park and sometimes a little further afield, to visit friends and family of the Dejongs. During these outings we noticed that many houses had been abandoned. Gardens had become overgrown, windows and doors were shuttered up and there were no signs of life. Many shops were closed and those that were open had thinly stocked shelves, and queues formed on the pavement outside. It had changed quite a bit since we had left just a few weeks ago.

It was strange not having Dad about. To me his absence now was more noticeable than his presence when he had been here. There had always been something missing: he had never been one to actively participate in our daily lives and had not taken us to school or come to see us take part in school activities. He had always been a little remote from us. Seeing him sitting in his chair in the front room reading the paper, had been reassuring, even though I sometimes wondered if he noticed we were there.

Now that he was not there, and the chair was always empty, it left a blank space in my life. There was a subconscious emptiness, too. I didn't really understand it, but it was an emotion I often experienced.

I wondered where he might be. I had a clear recollection of him sailing away on that fishing boat as we stood and watched him go. Stephen's gentle sobbing had made it difficult to stop my eyes filling with tears. I was confused and did not really understand why he had left us there. I knew something was wrong and he had to go, but why did he have to leave us behind? Now we were back in our home without him. The same house, garden, front room, dining room and bedroom. Everything was as before, except that Dad was not here. It was an uncomfortable mystery. I lay in bed at night wondering if I would ever see him again. Would he ever come back? I had no mother and now no father, either. It was lonely, thinking that I had no parents. Jeanne and Yvonne were so wonderful to us.

They had picked up from where they had left off before our sudden journey, but they were neither Mum nor Dad. I was parent-less. Both my little brother and I were parent-less.

For the next couple of months, almost every day, we would hear the deep rumbling of aircraft engines, look up and watch the dots moving across the sky in groups. It became a regular pattern and as the days passed the numbers in the groups increased. Some hours later, we would see them pass over again, flying in the opposite direction this time. Sometimes the soldiers around us would cheer and wave as they passed overhead. This continued on throughout September and October as the Battle of Britain raged. We often wondered where they were going.

CHAPTER SEVENTEEN
HARRY

It took a good half hour to climb back up the hillside. It was much steeper than I had thought and I had to traverse the slope several times to reach my hideout. My head was still spinning with the thought of what had just happened. Would the soldiers return? I would simply have to wait and pray. Not that I am a believer, but I didn't think it could do any harm if I did say a short prayer. Or perhaps I would wait and see how things developed before I took to praying.

All remained quiet for the rest of the day and, as dusk fell the birds took over, filling the forest with whistles and squawks. No vehicles passed by on the road and darkness filled the valley. The terrifying experience earlier in the day had taken its toll and it did not take long before I was in a deep sleep.

The noise of the birds woke me at dawn. A dull grey sky hung overhead, with a fine shower of light rain falling on the forest. It was damp but not cold. I decided to remain in the hut. I had not eaten the previous evening and was hungry, so took the opportunity to consume a few slices of bread accompanied by saucisson. Just as I finished this simple breakfast I heard the sound of breaking twigs from outside. I peered through the cracks in the wooden door. The grey van of Jean-Pierre was approaching. I opened the door and moved outside to greet him. His window opened and he leaned out, gesturing to me to approach. He looked hurried.

'Venez! Vite! We go!' he said.

'Now?' I quizzed.

'Oui. Maintenant!' he replied.

I quickly returned to the hut and rammed my few belongings into my sack. I grabbed the pistol and shoved it into my coat pocket, slung the sack over my shoulder and exited the hut, closing the door behind me. I walked quickly over to the rear of the van and climbed in. I was glad to be leaving this place. I was still worried that the German pissing machine might be back with his pals. The van moved off. I did not know where I was going to next; I was just glad I was not staying here any longer.

We moved slowly through the forest and then on to a dirt track. The stones flew up, bouncing off the undercarriage of the van as we sped along the track. A few minutes passed and we turned on to a tarmac road. We were on this road just a minute or so when the van suddenly pulled over into a lay-by. Jean-Pierre climbed out of the van and opened the rear doors. He stood before me with his dog beside him. I was crouched in the back, looking out. He beckoned me to exit. I climbed out. A Citroën was parked in the lay-by, with Claude sitting in the driver's seat.

'Come!' he called out to me.

I hurried round to the passenger side, opened the door and climbed in.

'You go to Espagne by boat. Today!' he said.

'By boat?' I asked, looking somewhat confused.

'Oui. By boat. I have arranged it. We must go to the port now.'

'OK.'

We soon arrived in the harbour and pulled up alongside the market, which was still busy with traders carrying trays of fish and loading small trucks. The smell of fish was pungent. We disappeared through a small doorway leading into an office behind a warehouse. There we were met by a tall, dark-haired, Spanish-looking fisherman who sported a thin moustache. I stood beside Claude whilst a conversation took place. The fisherman looked over at me and then back at Claude. All I could distinguish from the hurried conversation was, 'OK.' Claude turned to me and said:

'You go with Mario. You go now.'

'But I have to say thank you...'

'No time,' Claude interrupted me. 'You go now. Bon chance!'

Shaking my hand, he reached into his pocket and drew out some bank notes.

'You take these,' he said. 'When you get to Espagne you take train to Lisbon. You can get a boat to England from there. Go now, my friend. Bon chance,' he repeated. Before I could respond, he was gone.

Mario reached out and took my forearm. His grip was firm and strong.

'Come,' he said, and pulled me towards another doorway.

After we had passed along a short corridor, a final door led us out on to the quay. Mario looked to left and right and then pulled me out into the light rain. I had no idea what was happening – I was just being swept along. We walked briskly along the dock and then suddenly turned onto a wobbly, wooden walkway between the dockside and a fishing boat. Within seconds, I was aboard and being hurried through the bridge. Then we went down a short flight of stairs into a cabin where there was a bed on each side and a fold-down table pinned to the wall. Mario turned to me, and said:

'You stay here. No move.'

I looked back at him, somewhat bewildered. I might be being kidnapped by gangsters! I had no idea who this man was. All I could do was trust the people who had brought me here. With that, the door closed, Mario was gone and I was alone in the cabin.

Within minutes, the engines started up and I could see through the porthole that we were moving away from the quay.

As the boat chugged out of the harbour into the grey mist of rain, the engine's pitch increased. The bow tipped upwards as we accelerated away from Saint Jean-de-Luz into the calm, open seas. I could hear the wash bouncing back off the hull as we lurched forward, cutting a path through the water. The constant groan from the engine vibrated through the boat.

Soon the coastline disappeared into the haze of rain, and I knew that, to anyone on the shore, we would also now be effectively invisible.

About half an hour passed. Then the door suddenly opened and Mario peered down into my watery cell.

'OK, English?' he asked and I managed a 'Si!' in response. He stood at the top of the stairs, grinning. 'Soon we arrive in España,' he said. I smiled back.

In mid-morning the engines slowed. I was up on the bridge, watching our approach into the small bay which sheltered San Sebastian harbour. Freedom! I thought – although my journey was by no means over.

Once we were secured alongside a pontoon, Mario helped me climb over the fishing boat railing and on to the floating raft. From there, we climbed some steep steps on to the main quay.

The railway station was only a short walk from the port. Carrying my black sack over my shoulder, I walked the couple of hundred metres along the beach until I reached the famous Hotel de Londres, which dominated the frontage overlooking the bay.

This magnificent building had been here since 1865 and was previously know as Hotel Inglés, before it changed its name in 1902. What an irony that my first reference point after escaping France had the same name as my so-desperately-sought destination. Was it a sign that I was going to make it?

As instructed by Mario, I looked for a street named Easo Kalea, which ran past the hotel into town and towards the station. It was only about eight hundred metres from the beach front to the station. As I walked down Easo Kalea and came closer to my destination, I could make out increasing numbers of people gathered together. The streets were full of people of all ages, milling about and pushing and shoving towards the main entrance. It was much the same scene as when I had arrived at Bordeaux station. San Sebastian had become a focal point for refugees escaping from south west France. Most had come by sea under cover of darkness from various ports dotted along the western coast. Bigger ships, packed full of refugees and soldiers, had come from as far north as Brest and others from Bordeaux and Bayonne. There were thousands of people here, all trying to get aboard trains to take them away to safety in various parts of Spain and beyond.

I fought my way through the crowds into the station to find some form of map which would give me a route to Lisbon. I had never been to Spain before and was unfamiliar with the geography of the country. It was difficult enough trying to push through the crowds, let alone find a map. I decided that the best option was to get a ticket to Madrid. From there I could work out a route to Lisbon. The main thing was to get out of here – the situation was pretty chaotic and was only going to get worse.

Several hours later, after much pushing and shoving, I had a ticket and climbed aboard a train destined for Madrid via Burgos. The carriages, just like the station, were packed full of people. Children sat on the laps of family members and the gangways and aisles were clogged with standing passengers. Bags, suitcases, packages and boxes were everywhere. People sat, stood and kneeled on their few belongings. How this train was going to move at all was beyond me. It was hot and stuffy and smelled of stale sweat. No one seemed to be complaining, though – they were glad just to have got on board. There was plenty of conversation and the carriage buzzed with the chatter of voices. Suddenly there was a jolt and the mass of people moved in unison, with a sea of heads swaying together. There was nowhere to fall; we just leaned into one another as the train began to move. This was going to be a long and uncomfortable journey.

At nine o'clock in the evening we finally pulled into Madrid station. I had been standing for six hours as the train had meandered its way through the northern hills of Spain to Burgos, and then across the flatter terrain towards Madrid.

People pushed and bumped their way out of the carriage on to the platform. Bodies filled the available area as we all headed towards the main concourse.

Having reached there, though, it was immediately apparent that Madrid Station was much less crowded than those I had visited in the last week. You could almost walk in a straight line without having to step over or move round someone else. I wandered about, looking for a sign indicating a ticket office.

Finally, I came across a row of glass windows – but their shutters were all down.

It seemed that I was going to be spending another night on the floor of a railway station. I was beginning to understand what it might be like to be a homeless soul or a drunk. Although uncomfortable, these public buildings were an ideal place to seek overnight refuge. They had twenty-four-hour access and it was easy to find a corner to lay a weary head. I strolled around the station looking for a suitable spot to bed down. A rock-hard floor was not my preferred option. I remembered that, after descending from the train onto the platform and walking towards the main concourse, I had negotiated my way past several benches that split the platform into two. A bench would be perfect. It was warm in the station and, now that we were several hundred miles further south, the ambient temperature was bound to allow for a little outdoor sleeping. I walked to the furthest platform and made my way along its length. I was relieved to see that there were several benches available, all in pairs, backing onto one another. I lay my black bag at the end of one, sat down in the middle and lowered my head onto the bag. I pulled my feet up onto the wooden slats. It was good to take the weight off them. I felt the pressure being released from my shins and the tightness of my shoes slackening. I leaned forward and undid my laces. I laid back and shut my eyes. Sleep came quickly.

I was woken by the sound of a train pulling into my platform – the screeching of steel on steel as it drew to a stop. I sat up and pulled my bag to my side, presenting myself as if I had just arrived at that bench and was waiting for a train. People clambered out of the carriages, completely ignoring my presence. They walked on by as if I was not there, all busy, all with somewhere to go. As the platform filled, I got to my feet and, lifting my bag over my shoulder, joined the procession towards the main concourse. A ticket to Lisbon was my objective.

The queues were short at the line of glass windows. When my turn came, I asked in my best Spanish:

'Lisbon, por favor.'

The cashier looked at me with bewilderment.

'Que?' she responded.

'English,' I said, pointing at myself. 'I go to Lisbon.'

'Ah! Inglés,' she said. 'Lisboa. You go Internacional.'

She pointed to her right.

'Internacional,' she repeated, leaning forward and pointing again. I looked across to my right and caught sight of a sign displaying just that word above a window a few metres down.

'Thank you,' I said, and moved away in the direction she had pointed.

There was no one queuing at this kiosk, so I stepped forward, placing my bag at my feet as I leaned towards the glass. Behind the window sat a darkly tanned elderly man with jet-black hair.

'Lisbon por favor,' I said.

He looked at me and said simply, 'Pasaporte?'

I riffled through the breast pocket of my coat and pulled out a wad of papers. Sifting through them, I found my passport and slid it under the gap between the glass and the shiny steel plate of the counter. A few minutes later, I walked away with a priceless, small, rectangular ticket in one hand and my bag in the other.

The next train to Lisbon did not leave platform one until eight in the evening – an overnight train. I had some time to kill. The first thing was to find something to eat.

Walking out of the main entrance, I crossed the street and made my way down a side road in search of a café. It was not long before I was sitting outside a small bar with a cup of coffee and a bread roll alongside a wedge of cheese. The small bundle of folded notes given to me by Claude had proved to be the most valuable gift I had ever received. I had not even had the chance to thank him.

I would sit here for a couple of hours, watching the world pass by. There seemed to be no sign of war here.

When I returned to the station, I found another bench and sat down again until my train arrived.

At eight o'clock precisely, the train pulled out of Madrid station. Destination Lisbon.

At six thirty in the morning, the train filled with refugees collected at the various stops made during the night pulled into Lisbon Station. Once more, I saw a station that was packed full of people fleeing the Germans. Lisbon had become a focal point of escape. I pushed my way through the crowds to the main entrance. Outside, it was a sea of escapees. As I moved among the throngs, I could hear my mother tongue being spoken, but I decided not to engage in conversation with my compatriots. I was not in the mood for long stories of escape. And they were all here for the same reason I was: to get back to England. I had rather hoped that getting aboard a ship back to England was going to be a simple process, but it was not to be. I decided to make my own way to the port and find out what was happening there.

It was quite a walk from the station to the harbour. The passenger terminal was, again, awash with people. I pushed my way through and, as I arrived at the entrance, was stopped by a uniformed policeman. I did not understand what he said, but he was not going to let me pass. When I said I was English, the policeman just said, 'Embassy!' I moved away, trying to see a route back by peering above the hordes of people pushing towards the entrance. I had been one of them just a few moments ago. This was crazy. I decided to take the advice of the policeman and find my way to the British Embassy. I had no idea where it might be, but some of those gathered here had probably already been there. I changed my decision about not speaking to my fellow countrymen and began asking anyone who I overheard speaking English whether they knew the whereabouts of the embassy and what its procedure was. Before long, I had the information I needed.

I had to go to the embassy and register my arrival. I would then be added to the list and allocated a departure date. I made my way there.

I was to remain in Lisbon for three weeks before I was finally aboard a ship back to England.

I arrived in Portsmouth in mid-July 1940. My journey from Port Navalo to England had taken almost five weeks.

When I walked through the front door of Tangier Lodge, I must have been looking somewhat weathered. Before me stood Beatrice, who had taken over as the principal housekeeper since mother had passed away ten years earlier.

'Oh my God!' she said. 'Harry! We have all been so worried. We had no idea what had happened to you. It was only a few days ago that we heard from Mister Dejong that you had left Port Navalo alone. We had no idea whether you were alive or dead.'

'You have heard from Monsieur Dejong?'

'Why, yes, Harry. About a week ago, through the Red Cross.'

'And the boys. Where are the boys? Are they safe?'

'Yes. They were all repatriated to Brussels. They are back in Saint Gilles.'

'Oh, thank God.'

For the first time since Abbi passed away, my eyes filled and I began to sob.

CHAPTER EIGHTEEN
PAUL

One year later.

As summer drew to an end, we returned to school. More than half the class was missing. Several teachers were too, but attending three days a week still brought a level of normality back into our lives. As we made the journey from home to school, we would frequently see groups of German soldiers marching along the road, singing. It was puzzling to me why they seemed so happy when most of our friends seemed so sad.

As autumn arrived, Monsieur Dejong spent more days at home than at work. His plumbing business had slowed significantly as there were fewer and fewer customers able to pay for his services. Many customers had left before the Germans arrived and those that had remained were suffering from lack of trade and so had no money to spend. Cash had become scarce and the rationing, which had been introduced shortly after the Germans arrived, was beginning to bite. There was less and less food available from the shops, prices were soaring and the black market was becoming the only way to get any form of meat or fresh produce.

I could not really understand why Dad had not come back. Madame Dejong sat with me one day and tried to explain that it was because of the war. I didn't understand why there was a war. Why was everyone fighting? Where had my friends gone? Why were all these soldiers here in our town? She tried her best to explain. It did not make sense to me, but she assured me that one day soon we would be together with Dad once more. In the meantime, we would have to stay where we were.

The International Red Cross had been in touch with the Dejongs and, once a month, Dad was able to send some money, accompanied by a short letter. This was our only communication with him. We looked forward to receiving his letters and spent some time on writing back, even though we were only permitted to write twenty-five words. The money took a little pressure off Monsieur Dejong now that his financial resources had reduced significantly and feeding all of us had become increasingly difficult.

Every Saturday, Stephen and I would accompany Monsieur Dejong and Monique by car to the market in town. It was a treat, a little time away from the routine of school and homework.

One chilly October day, wrapped up in our coats and with long scarves, we arrived in the gravel-covered car-park area that was surrounded by a row of large trees shedding their leaves. We climbed out and made our way towards the market, kicking through the ochre piles left by the wind, each wanting to be the first to scatter them.

As we approached the market, we noticed that several shops now had signs in the windows in German, Dutch and French, stating that they were "Jewish Enterprises". I asked Monsieur Dejong why these shops had the signs. He told me that the Germans had told the shopkeepers that they must display them. I remembered the family in the compartment on the train when we travelled from Port Navalo. I had felt sad for those people with the stars on their jackets. Was this coming to my hometown now?

There were more soldiers on the streets now, and I noticed that some of the locals seemed weary of them and their guns, and walked sheepishly, their heads bowed beneath their hats. Many of these townspeople were dressed in heavy, dark, knee-length coats and stood with arms folded across their chests, not looking around but focussed on the ground in front of them. It was a strange sight. They remained in the background, rather than mingling in the crowds. It felt as though they were afraid to be seen.

We walked on between the tables of vegetables and various items of clothing, but there was little colour or variety there – it was just basic produce, with very limited choice. Although things were obviously getting tough, we enjoyed the outing. Monsieur Dejong treated us to some sweets and we chatted to friends among the crowds in the fresh autumnal air. We returned home with rosy-coloured cheeks.

Christmas came and went with little celebration, although Madame Dejong did prepare a Christmas lunch. Chicken had become a rare treat, but Monsieur Dejong had somehow managed to secure one. We all sat around their dining table and enjoyed a veritable feast. There were homemade paper hats and streamers, but no crackers, tangerines, gingerbread or chocolate this year. Our Christmas presents were hand-knitted clothing. A woolly hat for me and a pair of knee-length socks for Stephen.

By the end of 1941 things had become a lot worse. Shops had run out of produce and there were serious shortages of food. Rationing became more and more severe. Luckily, earlier in the year, we had made plans to grow our own produce and during the spring we had dug up the lawn and planted potatoes. The fruit trees in the garden became important for making jam and we bred rabbits to eat and made gloves for us all from their skins.

Money and letters continued to arrive from Dad every month and, although things had become increasingly difficult, we survived the year quite well. It looked as though 1942 would be even tougher but then, on 7th December 1941, the news broke that Japan had attacked and seriously damaged the American fleet at Pearl Harbour. America immediately declared war on Japan. Four days later, Hitler and Mussolini declared war on the United States. This was to change everything for us.

CHAPTER NINETEEN
HARRY

Being back in Tangier Lodge was strange. Although I had lived in this house for most of my life before I had emigrated to Belgium with Abbi ten years ago, I felt like a fish out of water. I knew every crevice and corner, but the place was foreign to me. I was constantly restless and unsettled. I would walk about the house from room to room, unable to rationalise my thoughts. I had been in touch with the Red Cross and, through them, had heard from Monsieur Dejong and the boys. They were safe and back at school, but this knowledge was not enough for me. I felt helpless and guilty. My thoughts constantly turned to the boys. Had I made the right decision? Could I have done things differently? How could I get them back and away from the terrible developments of war? Whatever direction my thoughts took, I just came up against a brick wall. Could I travel to Belgium? No. Could Monsieur Dejong get the boys to the coast? No. Was there any military action that might be able to rescue them? No. Was there any resistance organisation which could smuggle them out? No.

What could I do? Nothing. I could only send a short note each month and then wait for a reply. It was a desperate situation.

I had only been back a few weeks when I received a letter from Toni, our nearby neighbour in Brussels, who, having escaped Belgium, had moved in with her sister in Wales. It was good to hear from her. She was the only person who seemed to understand my situation, the only one I could relate to. I would call her as often as possible and we would talk for ages. We would discuss the times we had shared together in Brussels and the trips we had taken to the holiday house in Mimizan. She would reassure me that the boys were going to be fine and that they would be well cared for by the Dejong family. It was good to chat to someone who knew so much of what I was talking about. She knew our friends, neighbours and the locality. It was soon apparent that she was feeling somewhat unsettled in Wales with her sister and her husband. It was a difficult situation for both of us.

The Battle of Britain had been dominating the news and things were not looking good for our country. Our airfields had been taking a battering for several weeks and there was a deep fear that before long the Germans would stage a major military landing on our shores. We would listen every day to the radio for reports and updates.

On 7th September 1940, the Luftwaffe began its assault on London. The attacks continued night after night and it became apparent that every able-bodied person was needed to help. I decided, at the ripe old age of forty-eight, that it was time to step forward and do what I could. Three days after the first aerial attack, I made my way down to the ARP recruitment centre that had opened up in a local shop.

There was a queue of about twenty men on the pavement outside. I joined the line and, within half an hour, stood before a small trestle table where two men in blue uniforms sat, with tin helmets bearing the letter 'W' placed in front of them. I was asked my name and address and then told to attend a training day near Marylebone Station the next morning at 9 a.m. They said I should come in old clothes, as no uniforms were available. I would be issued with a helmet in due course. With that, I moved away and the next man took my place in front of the officials.

It had all been done in a few moments. I had expected there to be more to it than this, but the role of warden was not, of course, official, but purely voluntary, so perhaps it was understandable.

I made my way back to Tangier Lodge and told Beatrice how I had got on. Next I called Toni and spent over an hour telling her all about my decision to join the ARP. Signing up reminded me of when I joined up in the First World War. There had been many joining the queues back then. It had been a kind of camaraderie where everyone joined in. You felt very much like an outsider if you didn't. And that feeling would become much worse as the war went on, with friends and neighbours all asking why you were not away fighting. I recall the pressure, too, of youngsters wanting to be older. It was as if there was nothing else to do but fight. You had to join up, and, if you didn't, there was something wrong with you. People would give you peculiar glances and sneers. It must have been very disconcerting.

And now here I was, twenty-five years later, signing up again because I felt that sense of camaraderie once more. I had to be involved somehow. At forty-eight years old, the army was not interested in me, but I did not feel forty-eight. I felt strong and full of energy. I had been feeling a little disengaged since my return to England, having spent the past ten years in Belgium, and being so distanced from the mood of my country, but it did not take long to develop the sense of needing to be involved. I did not even think about the risks. I did not believe that I was going to get hurt – no one ever did. You just got on with it, because this is what you wanted to do. You knew you were part of a team and did not want to let your fellow team-mates down. I was not a keen sportsman in any sense, but this desire to be a part of my country's defence was irresistible. Toni listened to what I was saying and told me that she, too, wanted to do something to help. She was a compassionate woman and knew her mind. How could she contribute?

The following morning, I was on my way to Marylebone, dressed in some old farm overalls and carrying a small bag containing sandwiches and a bottle of water.

I took the bus from Barnes to Paddington Station, and then another for the remaining mile or so to Baker Street underground station. All the way, the air was strong with the smell of burning timber. London had been the recipient of another night of Luftwaffe bombing and smoke from the smouldering buildings drifted across the city.

Arriving at Baker Street tube, I left the bus and walked down Chiltern Street towards Crawford Street, where I had been instructed to meet a couple of ARP wardens. They would run through the basic training techniques for a group of us new recruits. As I turned into Crawford Street, the air was filled with smoke and dust. I covered my mouth and reached into my pocket for a handkerchief. My eyes began to water and I hunched my shoulders as I peered ahead into the smoke-filled street.

A group of people were standing around a gaping hole in the row of terraced buildings. Rubble lay strewn across the street. Men in blue overalls were climbing in amongst it. Blackened timbers still smouldered, lying like pick-up-sticks between the remaining brick walls of adjacent houses. Items of clothing and furniture were scattered among the piles of bricks and glass.

I hurried towards the scene. A man in blue, his tin hat bearing the letter "W", stopped me.

'Who are you, sir?' he asked.

'I am Harry Barker reporting for duty, sir,' I replied. It was an automatic response, one that I had carried with me since 1918. I did not even know if this man would be aware that a training session had been arranged for new recruits.

'Right, Harry,' he said. 'See that fellow over there with the swagger stick under his arm. Report to him. Go, go, go!' he shouted at me.

I hurried towards the man with the swagger stick. As I arrived at his side, I stood to attention and saluted.

'Harry Barker reporting for training, sir,' I said.

'Ah, yes,' he replied. 'I am Captain Jones. I'll be in charge of your training. You are going to be thrown in at the deep end, I'm afraid, Harry. A bomb hit this site last night. Fortunately, no one was in the building, but it's in a right mess. It'll be a good opportunity for you to see what the job's like first hand, old man. Get yourself over there to Smithy and he will find you a helmet and gloves. Report back here as soon as you have them.'

Equipped with helmet and gloves, I spent the morning and afternoon clearing rubble from the street and becoming acquainted with the six other recruits who were also beginning their training that day.

By mid-afternoon I was covered in soot and dust, and tired and weary. I was not used to this level of exercise. It reminded me of how I had felt after a day or two cycling through the Landes Forest. Exhausted! But the time had passed quickly and I now felt I was involved. I felt a huge sense of satisfaction about being able to contribute. This abrupt initiation had been unexpected, but had probably been the best way to discover what kind of work I would be expected to do as an ARP warden. I made my way home looking more like a coal miner than a new trainee.

During the following weeks, I was issued with a basic uniform consisting of a set of overalls, a pair of Wellington boots, an armlet, a black steel helmet and a small silver-coloured badge. Being a warden was the most rewarding job I had ever had. Helping the community and making friends made me feel relevant again, despite the continuing pain of wondering where my boys were and what kind of life they were leading. My thoughts were being diverted in a positive way. There was little I could do about the boys, but it was good to feel that I was involved and making a difference, however small.

My relationship with Toni had begun to get serious. With my new responsibilities, though, it was nigh on impossible for me to take time out to visit her in Wales. My duties as an ARP were demanding, particularly during the Blitz, and I was expected to be available at all times. After a few months, she decided to move to London. It was something we had talked about for a while. She was not happy living with her sister and she was keen to find a way to get positively involved in the war. As a result, she had decided to apply to become an ambulance driver. She had received some training as a nurse and, although it did not qualify her to work directly in medicine, the idea of charging around London in an ambulance was exciting and challenging.

In London, she would often come to Tangier Lodge to visit. It was difficult, though, for me to find the time to see her and she would sit around for long periods here, waiting for me to return from duties. This became quite a pressure for us. We increasingly enjoyed each other's company and it was frustrating not to be able to spend time together.

The Luftwaffe raids stopped by the summer of 1941 and London slowly began to return to some level of normality, although there was much rebuilding to be done. Food was rationed as we increasingly relied on supplies from the United States. Children were evacuated to the countryside and there was little work or money in the capital.

Britain's focus now was on survival and manufacturing arms and munitions for our limited defences and fleeting incursions into Germany. Being a thorn in the side of the enemy was the best we could muster at this time. We had won the Battle of Britain and the threat of an impending invasion had reduced, but we had by no means won the war. Britain was still exposed, vulnerable and on the edge. Churchill was in charge and we put our trust in him.

Our family were working at full capacity to produce foodstuffs for the civilian population. More and more people, women and men, were hired to work in the fields. I myself had given up working the land when I left for Belgium with Abbi. Another twelve years had passed since then and many things had changed in the world of agriculture. I had left the job of farming to my brothers, who were much better informed and up-to-speed with developments than I was.

At the end of 1941, I lost touch with the boys completely. When the Americans joined the war, my communications through the Red Cross were severed. There was now no way I could find out what was happening to them and I could only assume that they were being cared for by the Dejong family. Whether Jeanne and Yvonne were still helping, I had no idea.

I was relatively confident that they would not have been taken into care by the Germans. There was no reason for them to do that – unless you were Jewish, they were not interested. Many children had been taken into care by friends and neighbours as their parents fled for a variety of reasons. Some had gone to France or come to England to join the forces fighting the Nazis. All I could do was simply hope that Paul and Stephen were alive and well somewhere in Belgium.

CHAPTER TWENTY
PAUL

After Pearl Harbour, the Red Cross letters and money from Dad stopped.

During the early months of 1942, rationing became more severe and we were glad to have the supplies from our own gardening efforts. We got used to eating dandelion salad and cakes made from carrot flour. With no money coming from Dad, we were no longer able to enjoy any treats and the table rarely produced any fresh meat or vegetables. Potatoes and cabbage dominated our daily diet. Attending school was what made things bearable. It took our attention away from the continuous struggle and the worry of where the next meal was coming from.

On visits to town, we witnessed more and more people wearing the yellow star badge. We would occasionally see small groups and families being ushered down the streets by German soldiers and loaded on to waiting trucks. Jeanne would tell me that they were being taken to holiday camps in Germany. I was not convinced, but I did not know enough to question her further.

One weekend in April, Jeanne decided to visit some friends of hers in Halle, a small town just south of Brussels and a short train journey from St Gilles. She asked me to accompany her. Monsieur Dejong drove us to the station. It was the first time I had been on a train since our return from Port Navalo. I was excited at the prospect of a day away from the humdrum routine of school and home.

During the past eighteen months, it had become virtually impossible to travel and visit friends. There were German soldiers everywhere and many of our friends had now left Brussels and were far away. Belgians had been offered the opportunity of work and good pay in Germany and, with no work available here, many had opted to take the offer. This had resulted in even more people moving away. Several of the houses in our neighbourhood now stood empty and our class size had reduced from nineteen to twelve. The opportunity to go and visit some friends for the day filled me with excitement.

Climbing onto the train with Jeanne holding my hand reminded me of our journey from Port Navalo, but that thought was soon diverted by the excitement of the day. I sat by the window, with Jeanne beside me, looking out at all the activity on the platform. Soon the train bumped into motion as we moved along the track towards Halle. There were several stops along the way and the landscape changed from residential to rural. It was good to see the open countryside again.

We soon arrived at Halle and descended the train onto the platform. Waiting to greet us were Jeanne's friends, Monsieur and Madame Deville. I had met them once before, although I didn't remember them very well. They immediately recognised me and keenly pointed out how I had grown. They had been friends of Jeanne for several years, knowing her from Spa, where Mother had died when I was only four years old.

They ran a smallholding where they had a stable and kept horses. The Devilles had become involved with horses at the end of the First World War when thousands of the animals had been left behind by the armies fighting on the Western Front.

Monsieur Deville explained to me that horses were gathered by the Allies from across the world during the Great

War – from as far away as South America, New Zealand and China, as well as from Spain, Portugal and England. He said that towards the end of 1917 the British Remount departments had 93,000 horses and 36,000 mules in training, all of which went to the Western Front.

I spent the day being shown around the stables and looking up admiringly at these enormous creatures. I had not had any experience of being around or even near horses, other than occasionally seeing them being ridden by military men around town. These were truly magnificent beasts.

The day passed quickly and we were soon on our way back to the station.

The train this time was made up of five carriages and we climbed into the third. There were quite a few more people for our return journey and most of the seating had been taken. I was lucky, though, again, to find a seat by a window. I enjoyed watching the people milling about on the platform at each station and the scenic views of the countryside. I was happy, although a little tired after my day out.

The third stop from Halle was Ruisbroek. As we drew into the station, I noticed that there was a heavy military presence on the platform. At previous stations there had been few, if any, soldiers present. As we came to a stop, we saw a platform lined with grey-helmeted soldiers, their familiar machine guns pointing towards the train. No sooner had the train come to a halt than several important-looking uniformed men wearing knee-length black-leather coats, shiny black boots and black officer hats marched along the platform in pairs. A few others wore the black uniforms with baggy jodhpur trousers and the red armband displaying the swastika symbol. I knew they were the Gestapo. As they moved along towards us, an officer disappeared into each carriage that was passed. When they reached our carriage, one of the officers, accompanied by two soldiers, suddenly appeared at the doorway, paused and scrutinised the passengers filling the carriage. He was a fierce-looking man with round-rimmed spectacles beneath the peak of his hat. A soldier stood behind him, gun pointing ahead.

Then a loud tannoy message came from the platform:

'Everyone to remain in their place for an inspection. Do not move from your seat. Remain in your place and prepare to present your papers.'

Jeanne began to riffle through her bag for the tickets and our identity papers as the officer began to move slowly down the aisle, holding out his gloved hand and demanding papers. After a careful stare at the paperwork and a glance at the passenger, the papers were handed back and he moved on to the next person. He was soon by our side, holding out his hand to Jeanne. He took a look at me and glanced back at the papers. 'Danke,' he said. Then he handed the papers back to Jeanne and moved on down the carriage, followed by the machine-gun-brandishing soldiers. I did not quite know what to do or feel. I was almost paralysed with fear, but also fascinated by the black uniform and aggressive efficiency of the officer.

I twisted my neck round as far as it would go to look over the back of my seat as the two Germans moved off down the corridor.

Suddenly there was frenzied activity on the platform as soldiers ran towards the carriage adjoining ours. Loud voices rang out from there and I could just see, through the windows of the doors separating us, a German officer grappling with someone. The two Germans who had inspected our papers abandoned their inspection and rushed back down the carriage towards the door, hurling it open and sending it crashing into the wooden panelling. They disappeared into the next carriage and I got up to see what was happening. Everyone was now leaning and stretching to get a view. The Germans had apprehended someone and were dragging him along, jostling and pushing their way towards the exit, shouting as they went. I could not quite make out whom they had grabbed. I looked out of my window to see him being shoved onto the platform. He was a young boy, no older than me. He fell to his knees among the soldiers. Struggling back to his feet, he stumbled and staggered along, nudged from behind and dragged by his collar towards the waiting group of three coat-clad officers. They stood in a line with the brick wall of the waiting room behind them. The boy was wearing grey shorts, socks around his ankles, brown shoes, a dark blue shirt and a brown satchel, just like the one we all wore to school. He was pushed back on to his knees in front of the officers.

All the searching officers and soldiers had now returned from the carriages and were gathered together on either side of their superiors. The most senior-looking officer pulled the boy to his feet and turned him to face the train, gripping him with a hand on each shoulder. The boy was quivering with fear and his face was white. Head bowed, he was sobbing uncontrollably, his hands twitching as they hung by his side. The officer lifted the flap of the boy's satchel and, in full view of all the passengers, pulled out a pistol. It was dark grey, with a square handle. He lifted it into the air above the boy's head and called out:

'Whoever has placed this gun in this boy's satchel will come forward now!'

There was silence on the platform and the train. Trembling, I looked around our carriage to see if anyone would respond. There was nothing. Not a word.

A few moments passed and then the silence was broken by the German officer, who began again.

'I repeat,' he said, 'whoever has placed this gun in this boy's satchel will come forward now. Otherwise the boy will be shot!'

I looked at Jeanne, bewildered.

'Will he shoot that boy?' I asked quietly.

'I don't know,' she whispered.

The boy continued to sob.

A minute passed. Soldiers and officers looked up and down the platform for any movement. The whole station was silent, waiting for some sound. I gazed at the boy in silence. I could feel the blood drain from my face.

Once more, the silence was broken by the officer holding the gun above the boy's head.

'Last time. Whoever placed this gun has ten seconds to come forward or the boy will be shot!'

Silence.

The German handed the pistol to another officer and took hold of the boy by the arm. Turning to his left, he lifted him up by his armpit on to his toes and tilted to his side, marching along the platform. The boy stumbled and tripped as he tried to keep pace with the officer.

The German walked the length of the train and stopped. Again he called out:

'Who knows this boy? Come forward or the boy will be shot!'

Again there was no response. Then he walked the boy the full length of the five carriages back to the other end, where he stopped and repeated his demand. There was still no reaction. Returning him to the centre of the platform, he stopped directly in front of my window. The boy, still being held up by the officer, looked limp and paralysed. He continued to sob.

'No one knows this boy?' the officer bellowed. 'Last chance!'

Still there was silence.

Turning the boy around, he took him to the edge of the platform, facing the empty track. The officer unbuttoned his black coat and pulled it around his waist, revealing his uniform. He raised his right hand to his holster. Unclipping the fastener, he drew out his pistol. He pushed the boy forward. Raising the pistol to the back of the boy's head, he squeezed the trigger. A loud crack rang out across the station. The boy slumped off the platform and fell on to the track below. My whole body turned cold.

The officer replaced the pistol in his holster, turned and, rebuttoning his coat, marched off down the platform towards the exit. The uniformed soldiers followed.

I could not believe what I had just witnessed. I was numb. Jeanne embraced me, squeezing me tight. A few minutes later, the train once more bumped into motion and we continued on towards St Gilles.

As rationing became increasingly tough, with little food or provisions of any kind available now, our resentment towards the occupying Germans grew. They looked down on us and seemed not to care about our living circumstances. They segregated themselves from the locals – whilst insisting that they wanted to integrate. They paraded themselves about in groups and tried to appear friendly, but whenever they did not get what they wanted, they turned nasty. They treated some of us with huge disrespect, for no reason. When they were performing what they called their duties, their behaviour was appalling. They were threatening and vulgar and swore and cursed. It was all very uncomfortable for me as I had always been told to be respectful and courteous to everyone, in particular my elders. The incident at the railway station with the boy had shocked me to the core and had instantly alienated me from them. I feared them, but I had no respect for them. I never knew how they might react to a situation and frequently witnessed them turn to the rule of terror when it suited them. Strutting around in their dark trench coats with their guns, they felt they could do whatever they wanted, regardless of whether it was right or reasonable. They sat outside the cafés during the day, enjoying coffee and beer, gesticulating at passers-by and demanding service from the waiters.

No matter how they tried, on occasions, to massage and cajole us, beneath the surface we had no trust or faith in whatever they said or did. Rumours had begun to circulate, too, that the rounding-up of Jews had a sinister purpose. Families who had their friends taken away never heard from them again, despite promises that they were going to a better place.

The resistance movement had gathered pace and become more organised. We would hear of incidents where the Germans would round up locals and interrogate them over how a truck was blown up, or part of the railway track had been sabotaged. Men who had been questioned would come home with cuts and bruises to their faces. They had no idea who was organising such activities – those involved did not show themselves. It was better not to know who the resistance were – that way you would be in no danger.

In our adolescent naivety, we thought the German soldiers were completely stupid. My school friends and I made our contribution to the war effort by putting sugar in the fuel tanks of military vehicles we found unguarded. This would cause the engine to stop after a short distance and necessitated a complete cleaning of the fuel-tank system. We considered this a good lark and were unaware of the potential consequences which would certainly include arrest, if not the same punishment as had been meted out to the boy on the train.

Finally, a bit of good fortune came our way as Albert somehow secured work as a plumber for the Japanese Embassy. This was a huge benefit for us, as through his work he managed to locate all sorts of unobtainable food and thus appeared on our table unheard-of luxuries such as whole hams and other forgotten delights. Our diets improved significantly. Monsieur Dejong would secretly distribute some of his ill-gotten gains among close friends, and he drilled it into us that we were not to tell a soul about the illicit meals we were lucky enough to enjoy once a week. There was no wisdom in sharing good news. Suspicion was everywhere and you did well to keep such matters close to your chest. We only trusted those who were closest to us.

We had been living in the same house since our return from France and Jeanne and Yvonne had become our parents to all intents and purposes. Stephen and I had accepted that this was now the way we were to live and without them our future would have been very bleak. There was no word from Dad and no likelihood of having him back in our lives in the near future.

We did not know whether he was alive or dead and he, presumably, knew nothing about our fate.

The big house became increasingly difficult to manage. It was not long before we had to leave the villa and move into a small flat nearby. Jeanne managed to keep us on as little money as possible and she and Yvonne continued to live-in full-time. Our school life continued, despite being just three days a week.

The deportation of the Jews had begun in earnest now and almost every day we would hear the ominous rumble of trucks passing through the streets on their way to load up families. The sound was repeated as they moved off again, but this time mixed with the harrowing cries of the passengers inside.

Before long, they declared that all Belgians over the age of eighteen were to go to labour camps. This process was voluntary, but for most people it was almost impossible to say no, as for them it was the only way to ensure that they had enough to eat. Albert managed to avoid the call-up as he was considered to be essential labour for the Japanese Embassy. How he managed to persuade the authorities on that, I have no idea. The Japanese seemed to like him and, as they were allies of the Germans, they had influence.

The summer passed. The shortages and fears brought by the war and the absence of Dad were difficult to bear. My thirteenth birthday approached. For me things were about to change.

CHAPTER TWENTY-ONE
HARRY

Once the Red Cross communication channels with the boys had been terminated by Hitler it became increasingly difficult to live at Tangier Lodge. Paul and Stephen were constantly brought up in conversation. I could understand that my sister and brothers had the best intentions, but constant reminding was not helpful. Discussions always ended with, 'Well, there's nothing you can do.' This in no way made me feel better. If anything, it made matters worse. What could I do? It was unbearable. I would retire to my bedroom early each evening and lay on the bed staring up at the ceiling for hours. The pistol, which had travelled with me from southern France all the way back to England, lived in the top drawer of the chest in my bedroom, hidden beneath my socks. I had taken it out occasionally and pondered about ending it all. One shot would be all it would take. An instant and it would all be over. I needed to do something to take away the thoughts. There was nothing I could do. I was trapped. There was no solution. No knowing and no way of knowing. Torturing myself would not resolve this issue. I had no choice but to wait it out. Just hope that they were OK and survived this war. There were no signs that it was going to end soon. I had to find a way to stop thinking and talking about Paul and Stephen.

In early 1942, an opportunity arose for me to buy a property in Park Road, just off Marylebone Road and close to Baker Street Station. The main reasons for selecting this part of London were that I would be close to my ARP station, I was now reasonably familiar with the area and I liked the idea of being close to an open space, namely Regents Park. As it turned out, I was presented with the opportunity to buy three properties next to one another. One had suffered some bomb damage and sadly the owners of the second had been killed in the air raids.

In the summer of 1942, I moved out of Tangier Lodge into 107 Park Road.

The actual process of shifting the contents from one house into the other was fairly straightforward. I had few personal possessions. Having left Brussels at the drop of a hat, there had been little chance to take anything but basic clothing and, by the time I arrived back in England, I literally had nothing but the shirt on my back! All my other possessions had been left in Brussels, so I had no need to hire a truck for my move.

Naturally, the family had sorted out some basic furnishings and domestic equipment that anyone would need when moving into a new home. The rest of the furnishings I would have to find for myself, either new or from one of the second-hand furniture shops that, for obvious reasons, had popped up over the city during the past few years.

Toni travelled from her sister's place in Wales and moved in with me. As two single people who would be cohabiting, it was a decision we had needed to think hard about. To live together before being married was seen as unacceptable among some. I, however, was now a senior citizen and Toni, although a few years younger than me, had never been married. I was not concerned about the acceptability of the union. It just made sense for both of us. Times were difficult enough without getting caught up in the politics of acceptability. There were many women who had found themselves alone, some temporarily while their husbands were away fighting and some permanently, having lost their partners to the war. There were also some men who were on their own, having lost wives to bombings in the Blitz. No one resented any of them finding new relationships and security. Toni and I needed to be together and help one another. The old-fashioned stigma about people living together before marriage was changing and even in myself I had felt the stuffy attitude relaxing. People were increasingly doing what was practical and sensible, and that was what Toni and I decided to do.

Moving into Park Road was a new and exciting project for us. The past few years had been filled with disappointment, uncertainty and worry. Laying foundations for a new beginning and a future was refreshing and inspiring. Over the next few months, we spent our free time seeking out furniture and fabrics to make our new house into our home. I had to believe that one day I would be reunited here with the boys, a family once again.

I continued to work in the ARP and Toni secured her position as an ambulance driver. Both positions were voluntary, so we lived on the money coming in from my investments and savings. Money was not a serious issue for us. I was fortunate enough to have several properties which generated income in the form of rent, as well as the farm at Worplesdon, which I had got back in 1934 and re-let, and which was still doing very well. Toni came from a wealthy family, too. All in all, even during this time of war, we did not need income from paid work.

Together, we set about refurbishing and redecorating. The electrics were in a poor state, as was the plumbing. Back in Brussels, I had not been keen on central heating, which had been all the rage there. Albert Dejong had constantly tried to convince me of its benefits and how the latest boilers and radiators were so wonderful, but I had refused to listen. In fact, I had arranged for the existing system there to be removed. I preferred an open fire in the lounge and the Aga in the kitchen. Sleeping in a cool, fresh bedroom was what I liked. I even insisted that the windows remain open throughout the year – there was something almost primitive about it. Those panels circulating hot water just made the whole house stuffy.

The refurbishment of these three houses would, however, include full, up-to-date central heating, running hot water and inside toilets. Times had moved on and I wanted to move with them. I was approaching my twilight years and now I wanted to live in relative comfort. There was enough hardship all around and if I could bring a little comfort to those who would rent the other two houses, then that was fair enough.

Getting the work done was not difficult. Despite many men going off to war, there were plenty of tradesmen looking for work and businesses were happy for the custom.

During the next few months, if I was not carrying out my duties as an ARP and Toni was not charging around London in an ambulance, we were supervising the renovation of the houses or out ordering kitchens, bathrooms and furnishings. It was fun and kept us both busy.

As I became more experienced as a warden, my responsibilities increased. Instead of rushing from one bombsite to another, I found myself investigating and assessing the installation of prefabricated Anderson and Morrison shelters.

The Anderson shelters were designed for six people and their construction was reasonably simple. The main part was formed from six corrugated-steel panels, onto which flat corrugated-steel panels were bolted to form the sides and end panels, one of which contained the door. The shelters were 1.4m wide by 2m long and 1.8m high. Once constructed, they were buried in the ground and then covered with a thick layer of soil and turf. The Anderson shelter was free to those with an annual income of less than £250. For those who didn't fall into this category, the price was £7.

The Morrison was a simpler shelter. It came as a kit that could be bolted together in the home and was 2m in length, 1.2m wide and 75cm tall. It was designed to be slept under at night and used as a table for the rest of the time. It had a steel, table-like top and wire-mesh sides, one of which could be lifted open and used as a door.

The Morrison was not designed to survive a direct hit from a bomb, but it was very effective at protecting people from the effects of a bomb blast. Many thousands of these were made and given free to any household which earned less than £350 a year. My job was to assess the feasibility of supply and installation and the financial status of the household, recommending whether the unit be provided free or at the cost price. It was a responsible job and sometimes it was not easy to break the news to a family that they were just above the threshold for a free shelter. Shelters were delivered and installed all over London and the job kept me pretty busy.

By the end of 1942 the works in Park Road were complete and the two houses on either side of us had been rented out. It was good to have my own home again, although this one was different to what I had come from in so many ways.

I was back in London and with a new companion, but I was without my children. There was an inner pain constantly nagging away at me. I could not put it out of my mind. What kind of life were my children living? Where were they now? What were they doing? It was a constant ache. I felt guilty and immensely frustrated by the fact that there was nothing I could do. Where were my children? No word, no news. Were they alive? Were they safe? Were they separated or together? These questions remained unanswered in my mind.

Toni and I settled in to our new house. It was warm, comfortable and homely. On the weekends, we took strolls through Regents Park and watched the passers-by from one of the many benches that lined the paths running through the park. I would watch kids playing and we would talk about the boys.

We spent Christmas and the New Year at Tangier Lodge. We had not yet met many people close to our new home in Park Road and so chose to spend these special times with family. Beatrice knew how to put on a spread and we enjoyed the most fabulous meals over the festive season. We were the lucky ones, of course, and many were not so fortunate. The Barkers, as food growers, had always been able to provide a feast on occasions like this. It had been the case during the First World War and it was still the case now. There was much less that was fancy or ornate now, but the food was in abundance and was absolutely amazing.

On 30th December, Paul became a teenager, celebrating his thirteenth birthday somewhere in Belgium – I did not know where, or with whom. On this highly personal and significant day, I got carried away with emotion and asked Toni if she would be my bride. It was a strange thing to do at my age, but it felt right. I did not wish to spend any more time alone. The deep sadness of not having my children around seemed to highlight my feelings of loneliness. It was wonderful to be able to share my life with someone else – I had never really managed to get past losing Abbi. Although perhaps the boys had helped to fill the void created after I had lost the love of my life. Certainly, I had never felt the need to move on. I had the boys and they had been my life. The outbreak of war, which had led to that moment on the quayside at Port Navalo, had brought a profound change in my life. I had not gone through all that effort to find my way back to London for nothing. I had been motivated by the need to get home and then find my children. To get them to safety and carry out my responsibilities as a father. And to make a home for both the boys and me, one where we would be able to live once we had been reunited. I could not be alone now and think morbidly of what might have been. I had to have a life and to be able to share it with someone. Toni had brought me love and friendship, which was very special. That was a good enough reason but, as well as that, when I got the boys back, they would have a mother again. It was the right thing to do. Arrangements were made for our wedding to take place in March.

CHAPTER TWENTY-TWO
PAUL

Autumn 1942

Both Stephen and I had begun school again. Still only for three days a week. Jeanne had been sure to keep us up to speed with our studies. Her English was quite good, so she gave us English lessons on one of the weekdays we did not attend school. Stephen struggled, but I had become quite good. I had begun my learning of English when Dad was still here. She felt it was important so that when this war was over we would be able to communicate with Dad, although we had not heard from him for many months.

On our first day back at school it was apparent that another couple of kids from my class were missing – Christian, whose parents were German, and Claudette. They were not my closest friends, but I was disappointed that they were not there. I asked our teacher why they were not at school.

'Claudette has moved back to be with her grandparents,' the teacher explained.

'But why her grandparents?' I asked.

'Her parents have moved to Germany for work,' she said. 'Claudette has gone to Hasselt to stay with her grandparents. She won't be coming to school any more.'

'What about Christian?' I asked.

'Ah. Well, Christian turned thirteen in July and has had to attend the summer Hitler Youth camp in Antwerp. He should be back later in the week.'

'What is the Hitler Youth?' I asked.

'It is a military training programme for young boys and girls, organised by the Germans. It is called the "Jungvolk" and all German children must enlist.'

'But I am to turn thirteen in December. Must I attend this programme?' I asked.

'Oh. I don't know, Paul. You must ask at home.'

As soon as I got back home I told Jeanne about Christian. I could see her eyes light up with concern.

'We must go and see Monsieur Dejong immediately,' she said.

We hurried round to their house and Jeanne told Monsieur Dejong the story.

'Right, Paul,' he said, crouching down before me. 'You must not go back to school for the time being. Jeanne will explain that you have gone down with a fever. I need to make some enquiries and decide what must be done.'

Neither Stephen nor I attended school for the rest of the week. We stayed indoors and waited to hear what was to happen. On the weekend, Monsieur Dejong came round and explained.

'Paul, we need to get you away from here. The Germans have been making enquiries at all the schools about boys approaching the age of thirteen. We are not sure exactly why, but the fact that your friend Christian has been away to a youth camp is worrying. You are Belgian by birth, so perhaps they will not require you to attend the camps, but we can't take the chance. We have made arrangements for you to attend a different school away from here. Jeanne will take care of Stephen and I will take you to your new school in a few days.'

At six o'clock in the morning of 21st September 1942, I was woken by Jeanne.

'Up you get now, Paul. We must be ready by eight for Monsieur Dejong.'

I was all packed with the same suitcase I had when Dad left in the fishing boat in Port Navalo. This suitcase had seen some tough times with me and, once more, we were to journey away together from those I loved and who were effectively my family. The beginning of yet another adventure at the ripe old age of twelve. But this time I was alone, sad and scared. As we drove through the streets and out into the countryside, tears rolled silently down my cheeks.

I sat alone in the back seat of Monsieur Dejong's car. Jeanne, who had been a mother to me ever since I could remember, sat beside Albert in the front. She had no idea that I had begun to cry. I sat in silence as sadness filled my heart. Where was Dad now? What was going to happen to Stephen? We had become so close and the thought of not being with him every day was unbearable. He himself did not seem too bothered, though – he had not even got up out of bed to see me off. I knew that he would miss me, and, by golly, I was going to miss him. We had not been separated at any time in our lives before. Even at school we would spend break times together. We were attached at the hip. I had always been so protective of him. If he was ever threatened or got into any tangles, I would be there, protecting and reassuring him. He was my only real family and I had taken it upon myself to take care of him. But now I could not do that any longer. Jeanne would take up the reins, I knew that. She regarded Stephen as her own and would let nothing harm him, but it was not the same as being there myself to keep an eye out at those times when Jeanne was not able to.

I sat alone, looking out of the window as the trees passed by. And then I began watching the telegraph poles as they came and went, and before I knew it I was counting them down, one by one. Another and another. Closer and closer. I was scared.

By 1 p.m., we were deep in the Ardennes Forest, following a winding road and climbing higher and higher. Surrounded by tall green trees, we slowed to take a sharp right. We crossed a small bridge and then we were travelling uphill again, deeper into the forest. After a kilometre or two, we negotiated a tight bend and then, on the right, passed a wooden building the size of a small house. A hundred metres or so ahead, a grey stone wall stretched from left to right, with an arched gateway through which we would enter the grounds of the school. Monsieur Dejong slowed as we approached and Jeanne turned around and said:

'We are here, Paul. This looks like a magnificent school!'

As we drove slowly through the archway, the landscape opened up into a courtyard with a lawned centre and a gravel drive circling around it. A cloister ran the full length of the inner side of the grey wall, with arches opening into the courtyard. Two tall spires reached high into the sky, with a huge, arched, wooden door dividing them. I guessed that this was the entrance to the abbey. Adjoining the church on the right, the building extended onwards for some distance, fronted by a row of trees bordering a gravel path. To the left, the two-storey, grey walls continued around the edge of the quadrangle. In the corner between the church and its attached buildings were two wooden doors, one in the centre, facing the quadrangle. Standing by that door was a man in a black, full-length gown with a rope belt and his hands cupped together in front of him.

We drove around the gravel driveway and stopped beside the man, who began to move towards us as we came to a stop. My face was pressed up against the window as I tried in vain to see the tops of the buildings, which were obscured by the roof of the car. My eyes moved from left to right, trying to take in the place where I was going to be living for the foreseeable future.

Monsieur Dejong and Jeanne climbed out of the car and moved towards the monk. There were no handshakes, just a bow of heads between the host and the new arrivals.

'Bonjour, Monsieur et Madame. I am Père Marc Mélot and will be Paul's tutor while he is here with us. He will be in my care.'

A few moments passed while Albert and Jeanne chatted with the monk. Then Jeanne turned and walked back towards the car, opened the door and beckoned me out. I got out with great trepidation, looking all around me. I was surrounded by tall, grey buildings which reached high into the sky, and a grey wall with cloisters. Albert had moved to the boot of the car. There was a click and a squeak as the boot was opened. He picked out my suitcase and followed Jeanne and I, who were being guided by the monk through the great wooden door.

As we entered the lobby, the monk turned towards me and said:

'Welcome to Maredsous School, Paul. I am sure you will be very happy here. Now you wait here while I show Madame and Monsieur out. Do not move. I shall return very soon.'

He turned and took the suitcase from Monsieur Dejong and then, gesturing forward, guided the two of them back towards the door through which we had entered. As Jeanne and Albert were guided out, they called out:

'Bye-bye, Paul. We shall see you in the holidays.'

And before I knew it they were gone. No drawn out farewell. No hugs or reassurance. Ushered away as quickly as possible. I was alone again.

That night, I lay awake in my bed in a dormitory of eight, thinking of where Dad might be now. Why was he not here to rescue me? Here I was in a prison, all alone. I knew no one.

Maredsous was a Benedictine monastery founded in the mid-19th century by monks who followed the rule of St Benedict. The abbey was made up of four main parts. The school had about 150 pupils, all boys, most of whom came from very privileged backgrounds. They were the children of senior politicians, royalty and successful businessmen. I did not know how or why I was here. My family was neither rich nor famous – certainly not in Belgium. The schooling side was split into two sections. The academic side focused on the study of Latin and Greek, with the aim of forming a logical approach in the mind. Mathematics, other languages, history and the arts were of secondary importance.

The second part of the school's approach was all about practical learning – working with your hands and using tools. The buildings where these skills were taught were located about two hundred metres away from the cloisters and were separate from the main buildings. The pupils here did not learn about plumbing or building, though, but about making high-quality jewellery and fine art, sculpture and joinery. I think I might have preferred to study in this side of the school, but my time at Maredsous was destined to be taken up with studying Latin and Greek.

The cloisters, where the monks lived and prayed, were attached directly to the church. We were seldom permitted to enter the cloisters. Only consultation with the head monk offered any possibility of a visit here. Important guests were sometimes seen disappearing through its wooden doorway, and I was also to see German soldiers push their way in; but, in the main, no one other than the brothers had access here.

Finally, the church itself. This was a magnificent, huge building fronted by three peaked spires, the two taller outer spires housing the bells. The left-hand spire, viewed from the outside, housed the main bell and the right, five smaller bells. The centre section was fronted by an arched porch sheltering two wooden entrance doors and above by three tall, arched, leaded windows that poured light into the entrance of the church.

Services were held every day and were attended in force by the local community on weekends. Running down the left-hand side of the church from the altar at the far end were six alcoves dedicated to particular saints and brothers. I was to spend a considerable amount of time in this building.

My part of the school, though, was a rectangular building on the other side of the cloisters, with a central quadrangle covered by a steel-framed glass roof. It provided shelter from the weather, but was extremely cold during the winter. This was our central meeting place. Every day we would line up in the quadrangle before we went on anywhere else – before eating, attending class, going to church, sports, outings or going to bed. The quadrangle also served as the point of public humiliation and punishment. Surrounding it were the classrooms, dormitories, showers, dining room and individual tutor studies. Everything we needed was within the surrounding buildings. Doorways led to the entrance courtyard, the gravel-covered sports courts, the path to the grassed playing fields and finally, the most used, into the church.

Maredsous was a real shock to me. The discipline there was fierce and cruel and punishments very severe. We did physical training outside at seven every morning in all weathers, summer and winter. Punishments included kneeling on the metal grille in the centre of the quadrangle for periods of between thirty and sixty minutes. Beatings were carried out using the cat-of-nine-tails. Other punishments included being confined in the cell beneath the main bell tower with bread, water and Latin translation. The bells rang out every half-hour, so there was no possibility of sleep. I was to do twenty-four hours of this once. There were weekly reports, and depending on your termly total, you might be held back from going home for periods of a half-day to two or three days. During this time you would be locked in a classroom with more Latin translations. It did not really matter to me as I had no family to stay with during term time nor for short holidays. My only escape from this prison was at Christmas for a week and a couple of weeks during the summer. For the rest of the time, I was a permanent resident.

Religion was of paramount importance in the school and was really pumped into us. We attended mass in the church every morning and complines every evening. On Sundays we spent the whole day there: low mass, terse, high mass (sung), afternoon vespers and complines.

As the months went by, I became quite religious and was eventually re-baptised as a Catholic (although no one knew if I had actually been baptised before).

I was desperately unhappy at Maredsous and I really missed my mother. I was convinced that she was in heaven and that, if I prayed to her, she would help me. In fact, I did often feel that she was helping me. I had always missed her, but this was the time I did so the most.

The dining room was beneath the chapel and we would line up to enter it every mealtime. The room was made up of long tables with a single chair at the head of each and we sat on benches. A table captain would be appointed each week to ensure that all the condiments and cutlery, et cetera, were present and correct before we entered the room. He was also in charge of our behaviour at the table and, if anyone needed to communicate anything during the meal, it would be done via him.

We all squeezed into what was a relatively small room for 150 pupils and the few brothers who also supervised. On two sides, windows looked out on to a small courtyard where provisions were delivered to the kitchen beneath. At the far end of the room was a wooden, seated pulpit. Here a monk would read from the scriptures throughout the meal. Otherwise, there was silence in the room. No talking was allowed between us. We were served by other pupils wearing white cloth gloves, the dishes placed gently before us so as to make no noise. If you dared to break the silence or, worse still, spill your drink or drop a plate, punishments were administered. Serious breaches would result in time on the grille, but lesser offences would be punished by a rap across the fingers with the blunt side of a table knife. At the end of the meal, we stood and said a prayer of thanks before quietly leaving, led by our table captains. I recalled that Dad was quite strict about table manners and not leaving food: no elbows, eat all you get or it will reappear at the next mealtime, and sit properly. No slouching and behave. Dining at Maredsous was on another level!

For the first few weeks I struggled terribly with homesickness. I felt very alone and lost. I was the only new boy in my class as all the others had joined the year before and knew one another well. They all seemed different to me, coming from wealthy and important families. They did not seem to know what going without a meal was. Describing how we had survived on dandelion salad and made gloves from rabbit skins was completely alien to them. Shocking, in fact. They liked hearing my stories and were fascinated, even bewildered, as to why we did what we did to survive. The story of my attempted escape with Dad and return to Brussels was listened to with great intrigue. They asked lots of questions about the Germans and the Jews, many of which I could not answer. They did not seem to even be aware that there was a war going on out there. It did break the ice a little, but after the stories they huddled together in their groups and giggled. I was not one of them.

In amongst the boys in my class I eventually found a friend in André van Rolleghem. He was the same age as me and we increasingly spent as much time as we could together. He was from Watermael, a commune close to St Gilles, where I had lived with Dad. We had quite a bit in common and he was the only person who seemed able to relate to me. The fact that he was familiar with where I had lived made me feel a little more at home at the school. Most pupils came from a different world to me, and André was something of a saviour. His family had been diplomats of some sort. I did not understand it really, nor did I get the feeling that he quite knew what his father did or where he was, as he had not seen him since the war had broken out. He had simply been sent away to this school. It didn't matter anyway. We just clicked and became good friends. We would spend almost all our free time together and were beside one another at every activity and ceremony. We lined up together, sat beside one another in church, sang in the choir together and even managed to secure sitting together at mealtimes, although we were not permitted to speak, of course.

Maredsous school positively encouraged sports and whilst playing or taking part in some sporting event either on the gravel-covered sports courts or the playing fields, we would often see Lancaster bombers passing overhead, returning from raids on Germany. Some flew quite low, with smoke pouring from an engine or two as they struggled to keep airborne. We often wondered if they made it to wherever they were going. We all knew that airmen had been received at the abbey. I had seen them myself a couple of times. Two or three plain-clothed men with rifles over their shoulders entered the abbey by the rear doorway accompanied by uniformed air crew, and then left without them. It made me think of Dad, and I occasionally hoped that they might take me with them back to England. Once the airmen had disappeared into the cloisters we never saw them again, and we were told to never mention having seen anything.

It was shortly after the arrival and then disappearance of a group of airmen that we would most likely receive a visit from the Germans. They would force their way into the cloisters, but always left empty-handed. On one occasion, certain that the crew of a downed bomber had survived the crash, the Germans were convinced that they were being hidden by the monks at Maredsous. We were visited by two officials in black uniforms, the Gestapo we assumed, who were not going to leave empty-handed this time. They arrived in a jeep accompanied by a truck containing ten soldiers. They marched straight through the church entrance and bashed loudly on the cloisters door. A monk greeted them with a bow. They barged past and headed directly for the office of the abbot – an office they knew well. A couple of minutes later they marched out of his office, back through the cloister, through the church entrance into the courtyard and ordered the soldiers out of the truck.

'Suchen die Gebäude!' (Search the building!) one of the officers yelled out.

The ten men ran into the main entrance of the church. We heard doors being slammed and boots running through the corridors. The two Gestapo officers remained in the courtyard, slapping their jodhpurs with their sticks whilst pacing back and forth and occasionally exchanging a few words between one another. We stayed in our dormitories looking out the windows, which overlooked the courtyard. Suddenly, our dormitory door banged against the wall as it was flung open. A soldier rushed in, looking beneath our beds and in the cupboards. He went about his search as if we were not there. A minute later he had gone, on to the next dorm. This went on for at least an hour. Finally, the soldiers reconvened in the courtyard, lined up and stood to attention.

'Nichts!' (Nothing!) one of them called out.

The two officers re-entered the church and disappeared down through the cloisters to the office of the abbot. Twenty minutes later they reappeared, this time accompanied by six monks walking in a line, their heads bowed and hands in the praying position. This was to replace the six airmen that the Germans knew had been taken into hiding somewhere in the area. The brothers crossed the courtyard, climbed into the waiting truck and were driven away.

(Only two monks taken that day survived incarceration and, after the war, returned to the monastery.)

Towards the end of February 1943 we saw more Allied aircraft flying overhead. They passed over almost every day, sometimes during the day and sometimes we heard their groaning engines as they flew over the abbey late at night. Groups of twenty, thirty or more would fly south and then a few hours later we would see or hear them returning. Sometimes fewer than had passed by earlier and sometimes with smoke trailing from a wing. The noise from the engines was unmistakable. We would hear them coming in the distance, look up and, sure enough, after a few minutes, they would appear as dots in the sky, growing larger as they approached. Their route was sometimes directly over the school. We could almost see the faces of the men sitting at the guns protruding from the glass bubbles in the front and rear of the aircraft. We would wave and jump up and down as they passed by, but never knew if they saw us or not.

As the warmer weather arrived in early April, André and I occasionally had the opportunity to spend a few precious hours away from the school in the nearby fields. We would wander through the forest and lie in the field, looking up at the blue skies, trying to conjure up images from shapes in the clouds to get away from the regime and procedure of school life in the abbey. It was like being free. No one ordering you to do anything or be anywhere. Just wandering along the path between the trees and across fields. We had done this many times and had various favourite spots where we would stop to take in the peace and quiet.

As we wandered across the field picking the yellow dandelion flowers, which appeared all over at this time of year, I recalled that this was a main source of food for me only a year or so ago. I wondered how Stephen might be. Where he might be. I hoped he was safe and being well looked after by Jeanne and Monsieur Dejong. I was lucky now. I had good food and plenty of it. Once more the familiar groan of Rolls-Royce Merlin engines sounded in the distance. They grew louder as the aircraft, a group of about twenty, appeared from the south. They were high in the sky, occasionally disappearing behind the odd drifting fluffy cloud. As usual, we stood to watch as they flew nearer. As they were high this time we couldn't make out any figures. Suddenly, there was a loud roar as one flew over our field, much lower than the others. Heavy black smoke left a trail in the sky as it flew over. Just as it passed by, to our amazement, five men jettisoned from the side door and fell tumbling towards the ground. Almost instantly their white rounded parachutes popped open and their fall was stunted. They swung from side to side as they drifted towards earth, disappearing behind a row of trees at the end of our field. We both stood gazing in shock. We looked at one another and just knew that we wanted to run over to see the airmen.

We ran as fast as we could across the green grass and through the dandelion flowers, our arms flailing and our legs almost giving way beneath us, stumbling as we ran across the field and into the shallow woods. We stopped at the edge of the field beyond, searching to see if the airmen were there. Sure enough, all five were there, two still kneeling in the field, frantically gathering up their parachutes into their chests. They had grouped together and looked weary and lost. We ran out into the field to greet them. As we approached they crouched down on their knees, held out an arm and pointed their pistols at us. We stopped immediately and stood quite still, side by side. Our eyes widened as we stared at the five men in British RAF uniform. One had blood running down the side of his face. Another was cradling his arm. They looked as frightened as us.

'Speaky English?' one of the men asked.

We just stood in silence. I understood him but was too scared to respond.

'Français?' he asked again.

'Oui,' I replied.

'Hey, Philippe. You speak French, don't you? Talk to these kids,' he said, turning to another man crouched just behind him.

'Bonjour,' he said. 'Nous sommes Anglais.'

We moved closer. The men lowered their guns and stood up. For a moment we all stood in silence then Phillipe broke the silence.

'André?' he quizzed, looking directly at André who stood beside me. 'C'est toi? André?' he asked again more feverishly.

'Oui,' André said quietly, looking rather confused.

'C'est moi, André. Papa!' he said, moving towards us.

André looked closer and almost as if a sudden recognition overcame him, he called out, 'Papa! Papa!' and ran towards the stranger.

'Oh my God!' exclaimed one of the airmen. 'It's his bloody son! Can you believe that! Phillipe's bloody son! It must be a bloody miracle!'

After an emotional reunion, we led the crew back to the monastery. We were greeted by Père Mélot, who ushered the men into the abbey via the back door into the cloisters. I never saw them again.

(After being hit by flak on a sortie to Germany, the father of my best friend at school, whilst flying with the free Belgian Air Force in England, had bailed out of a Lancaster bomber and landed in a field in Belgium only to be reunited with his son. It was hard to believe that the descent of André's father from the sky, into the arms of his son, was anything but a miracle. All the airmen we found that day, including André's father, were successfully returned to England to fly once more. By 1943, there were more Belgian pilots in the Royal Air Force than there had been in the Belgian air force in 1940.)

It was June 1943. The trees, which surrounded the school, were full of rich green leaves. Hot summer days were on the way. I was looking forward to the summer holidays, although I was unsure where I might go. I had not heard from or seen Monsieur Dejong or Jeanne let alone Stephen. I had no idea where any of them were. I had given up on ever being reunited with Dad. Père Mélot was my dad now, or so they kept telling me. I had managed to come to terms with the fact that this was where I was now. I had increasingly put my faith in God. I had begun to get comfort from those hours spent in church. The life of a monk seemed untroubled and safe. Secured within the monastery. After all, I had no home. No father or mother. I had been separated from my brother. Who was there? No family. No love. A life alone. I didn't know whether any of those who had been my family were even alive. I knew my mother was dead. Perhaps my life was to take another route. I began to attend mass, terse, vespers and complines with deeper sincerity. Contemplation and prayer became a source of peace, away from the fear and loneliness. I had begun to find a new home and family.

On a warm early summer's day in 1943, the abbot received a visit from the German commandant in charge of affairs in the principality and was told that the bells in the tower were needed by the Wehrmacht for the production of weapons in the fight against the Soviets. He was informed that a team of soldiers, accompanied by engineers with specialist knowledge of church bell towers, would be arriving within a few days to remove the bells.

This was a matter of great concern to the monks. The bells had been in the abbey since it was founded in 1872. Their impending removal came as a huge shock. The issue of what might be done to protect them became an immediate priority for the abbot. There was little he and the monks could do, but they did have good connections with the local resistance groups. Perhaps they could help in some way.

A few days later, several trucks with soldiers, official-looking engineers and workmen arrived in the courtyard of the abbey. Pushing the monks aside, the men clambered up the stairwells to the tops of the towers and began to assemble pulleys and ropes to lower the bells. Before long, the great bell was being lowered to the ground, to the place where we gathered every day before entering the church. Here it occupied most of the floor. Proceedings came to an abrupt halt when it was noticed that the large bell was too large to fit through the door.

Much discussion ensued and it was finally decided that the bell was to be broken up and removed in pieces. This would cause some delay, as equipment was needed. The soldiers and workmen left, advising that they would return the next day with the necessary equipment to break up the great bell and remove the others.

The following day, workmen returned with the necessary equipment. They were not accompanied by soldiers this time, just two uniformed officials who were to supervise the removal. Their instructions were to smash the great bell into manageable fragments and load it, along with all the smaller bells, on to the waiting trucks.

By mid-afternoon, the great bell was in pieces and, bit by bit, they carried it out to the courtyard. The remaining bells, with their headstocks intact, had been lowered from their bearings, through the belfry to the ground and carried out to the three waiting trucks. By 4 p.m. the convoy, fully loaded, was on its way out of the courtyard and heading off towards Chateau de Montaigle.

The route took the convoy along Rue des Abbayes and on towards Sosoye. As it approached the small village, the convoy was forced to stop when a fallen telegraph pole lay across the road. The uniformed men in the lead truck climbed out and walked to the back of the convoy. Instructions were given for the workmen to move the obstruction from the road. They began to climb out of the last truck and make their way up the road towards the obstruction. As they walked towards the front of the convoy, seven resistance fighters, armed with machine guns, appeared from the woods.

'Hände hoch!' they shouted at the uniformed officers. The workmen looked around at one another, completely stunned by the appearance of the resistance fighters. The two officials began frantically grappling to unclip the holsters containing their Luger pistols.

The sound of ack-ack-ack-ack-ack filled the silence in the wooded scene as three machine guns fired at the two uniformed officials, their bodies twisting and writhing as the bullets tore through their uniforms. Moments later they lay still, blood seeping on to the road from the shredded clothing. The remaining men stood paralysed by fear with their hands stretching as high as possible above their heads.

'Ici!' (Here!) one of the fighters called out, pointing with his machine gun towards the edge of the road that he wanted the workmen to move to. They moved together, with their arms pointing skywards, towards the side of the road.

'Ne bougez pas!' (Don't move!) he shouted at them, knowing that they were most likely to be French workmen.

The fighters spread out down the line of trucks, telling the drivers to get out and join the others on the roadside. They then climbed into the cabs and the three hijacked trucks rumbled off down the road, leaving behind them eight workmen, standing in a line on the roadside, and two dead, crumpled and twisted torsos beside them.

Shortly after, having passed through the small village of Sosoye, the trucks turned off the main road on to a narrow dirt track which led them through the trees towards the banks of the River Meuse. They were met by about twenty men, all wearing heavy coats, muddied boots, baggy trousers held up by thick dark leather belts and, to a man, berets. Each had a rifle hanging over his shoulder. Within moments the trucks were surrounded by men moving quickly. The bells were lifted out of the trucks and lined up beside a small wooden jetty, beside which a barge was tethered. One by one, the bells were loaded onto the barge, which was paddled out to the middle of the river and the bells were pushed off the edge into the water. One by one, the bells disappeared into the depths of the River Meuse. Half an hour later, the job was done and the three trucks were driven several miles further along the main road, into the woods and abandoned. The Germans had no idea where the bells had gone.

(At the end of the war, the monks guided a retrieval party to the site of the discarded bells, which were recovered from the river and returned to their tower, from where they still ring out today.)

CHAPTER TWENTY-THREE
STEPHEN

A few months before Paul left to go to boarding school, it became apparent that the house was too big for just the three of us. Yvonne had recently left. I did not know where she had gone, but we three were alone in the big house with Jeanne. We spent a great deal of time with the Dejong family and usually, when I was not at school, I was with Monique. As a girl, she was not always keen to play my sort of games. Engines and cars were not her thing and dolls and prams were not really mine.

The garden was too large for us to manage on our own and food was becoming ever more scarce. We only occupied a few rooms on the ground floor and it was a struggle to keep them warm when winter came. We had few resources in the way of fuel or wood to burn and we had no money of our own. It was decided that we would need to move to somewhere smaller.

Monsieur Dejong had some friends who knew of a small flat nearby which had been vacated by its occupants some months earlier. Rumour had it that they had fled to the countryside and just abandoned the place. The front door had been left ajar and the windows open. It was only because the neighbours had noticed the curtains blowing in the wind that they had ventured in to check. The occupants must have left in a hurry as there was still food in the cupboards and the furniture was all still in its place. No one knew where they had gone. The neighbours had shut the windows and door and left it as they had found it.

It was just right for us – we would be warm and safe there and I could walk to school. Monsieur Dejong would keep an eye on us, calling in every day on his way back from work at the Japanese Embassy. He would bring food and stay a short while every evening to check that everything was all right.

So we took our few possessions and moved into the flat. We left everything in the way of furniture and fittings, none of which we needed, in the big house and shut it up. Perhaps we would return some time in the future to pick them up and take them wherever we might go. The future, though, was very uncertain and the priority for now was to be somewhere where we could just survive. Chairs, furniture and pictures had little value to us. We felt safe in the flat, but I was soon to be alone with Jeanne when Paul left for boarding school in September.

The winter of 1942/3 was long and cold. I spent most days cooped up in the front room, playing with the few toys we had brought with us. Jeanne would read to me and we would often sit at the table doing school work. She was not going to let that lapse and on days when it was not possible to get to school, we would have lessons at home.

We looked forward to Monsieur Dejong coming, as this was sometimes the only contact with the outside world we would have during the day. Occasionally, he did not come because the weather prevented anyone venturing out. Deep snow would cover the gardens and roads. There were no trucks clearing the way and the only vehicles we would see were driven by the Germans.

Somehow, Jeanne and I survived the winter and, as spring arrived, we were able to get out and about. There were more days spent with the Dejong family and some walks into town.

School was more regular now and I was grateful for the opportunity to go to friends' houses and play outside.

After we moved to the flat, we began to attend church on a more regular basis. Jeanne was a Catholic, as was my mother's family. Dad, however, had not been interested in religion, although he was a stickler for routine and tradition. I discovered that Jeanne's faith was central to her life, although she had never talked about it with us, almost as if she had been keeping it secret. Now that we were alone together, though, she had to take me with her every time she attended church.

I had no idea that she went to church so frequently. She must have been going there outside her normal work hours, maybe early in the morning or late in the evening.

We would go every Sunday and once during the week. St Gilles Catholic Church was a short walk and, as it held a market almost every day in the square which it fronted, it doubled-up as a place to both pray and shop. The square was known as Parvis de Saint-Gilles and many local farmers would go there to sell their produce. There were not many in attendance at the moment, though, and supplies were sparse, but it was still the cheapest place to buy food.

Our days were a struggle to find food and warmth, but there was a need for inner warmth, too, and Jeanne got both that and the strength to carry on from her faith. At a time when we had little to cheer about and no idea what the future held, her relationship with the church brought reassurance and the will to continue. It made her feel that she was not struggling alone.

It was through the church that Jeanne was told about a Jesuit school nearby that arranged for young boys to spend a few days in the country during the summer. It gave them an opportunity to get away from the humdrum routine of life in the city, out into the fresh air and to enjoy the countryside. It also gave the parents and carers a break.

In the summer of 1943, Jeanne arranged for me to go and stay at a holiday farm in a small village called Hachy in the Ardennes, a stone's throw from the Luxembourg border. A Jesuit family had set up a children's adventure camp there where accommodation and board were free, but the guests had to help out around the farm. It was a kind of working holiday for children and I was really looking forward to going. Being stuck in the flat day after day had become very boring. The idea of a week away in the countryside was fantastic. I couldn't wait.

The day soon arrived and, with my small bag all packed up, I was walked down to the church, where all the kids had gathered. There were about twenty of us and I knew a couple of them from school. We were all so excited. The bus was waiting in the square and, once we were all ticked off, we clambered aboard with not so much as a wave goodbye to the onlooking parents and guardians. I was not the only kid with a guardian as opposed to a parent – it was by no means uncommon. Some children had lost their parents in the fighting, some had been abandoned with neighbours, perhaps for similar reasons to mine, and others had simply been found wandering the streets. We did not care how our new friends had ended up here. We were all just kids, going on holiday.

There was a lot of noise on the bus, with everyone talking over one another to be heard. We did not even hear the engine fire up, nor notice the gentle movement as we set off. We were much too busy talking and making new friends. I turned back just as we left the square and saw Jeanne walking towards the open doors of the church.

Before we knew it, we were heading south towards the forests of the Ardennes.

A couple of hours later, our pace slowed as the road became increasingly twisty. The open countryside had been replaced by forest and woods. This was of little interest to us, though, as the furore of noise continued unabated. The four responsible adults, sitting in the front seats, seemed totally unconcerned and chatted continuously with each other. There was a wonderful atmosphere and a great feeling of freedom.

Soon we turned into a narrow drive, which led up to a large stone farmhouse with a collection of small wooden buildings alongside. The woods had given way now to fenced fields and corrugated roof sheds. The ground was puckered with tractor-tyre indentations, small potholes and plenty of hoof markings. This was a real farm, with real live animals, including cows, pigs, goats, ducks, chickens and a couple of dogs that were lounging on the terrace of the farmhouse. The air was strong with the smell of dust and dung.

All of us had our noses firmly pressed against the windows of the bus as we entered the courtyard of the farm. The bus bumped to a halt and we all moved forward in unison.

One of the adults stood up to face us and called out:

'OK, children. We are here. Welcome to Hachy holiday farm. Everybody out. No pushing, please!'

Ignoring the instruction, we all pushed and shoved our way out onto the dusty forecourt, where we waited to collect our bags from the driver, who was busy unloading them from the rear of the coach. This was going to be fun.

Jeanne spent twenty minutes or so in the church, and then made her way out into the bright sunlight of the market square. She stopped for a brief moment and looked around. It was unusually quiet. Normally there were many stalls and people busy buying and inspecting produce, but the square was nearly empty. Just a few soldiers milling about and the odd local going somewhere in a hurry. It seemed that everybody was in a hurry when outside in the open – then life would slow almost to a stop when you got indoors. As she moved across the square and headed off down the street towards the flat, she suddenly felt very alone.

The flat had seemed empty. Although she had frequently walked to and from it alone and had spent many hours on her own there when I was at school, she suddenly felt very lonely.

That night she had trouble sleeping – worrying about me and whether I was all right. What if something had happened to me, she thought? If I had fallen or been attacked by one of the animals, it would have been her fault for sending me there. And she had promised to take care of me.

By morning she had decided to follow me to Hachy and to spend the rest of the week there. I was her responsibility, she thought, and she had to look after me.

At four the next afternoon she disembarked at the tiny rural station of Hachy and made the two kilometre walk to the farm. She walked into the forecourt at 5.30 p.m. with her bag in her hand.

'Who are you?' quizzed one of the farm hands.

'I am Jeanne Briffaud, responsible for Stephen Barker, who is staying here with a group from Brussels. Where can I find the proprietor?' she said.

It was agreed that Jeanne could stay while I was on holiday on the farm.

Over those few days, she became good friends with the proprietor, Madame Villaine. They had a common interest in that Madame Villaine's husband had fled to England at the beginning of the war and joined the Free Belgian Forces to fight alongside the Allies. The fact that I was English and we had been left in Belgium by our father struck a chord with our hostess and, by the end of my five-day stay, arrangements had been made for Jeanne and I to stay on the farm permanently. There was little reason for us to remain in Brussels. There would be food enough on the farm for us and Jeanne could help out with its running.

A deal was struck and, after a brief return to Brussels at the end of my holiday to explain to Monsieur Dejong and collect our few possessions, we moved to Hachy.

Life on the farm was much more fun than in Brussels. Jeanne continued my tuition personally and I would have lessons on weekdays from nine in the morning until twelve-thirty. Homework was also set and I spent one hour every evening on it, with my teacher. During the afternoons, I would be out and about on the farm, helping where I could. My favourite job was feeding the pigs. They made such a din when I arrived with my metal buckets of grain. They snorted, grunted and charged around the pen with excitement, almost knocking me off my feet. It was quite a job to keep upright and dodge these manic beasts which were desperately trying to raid my buckets. By comparison, feeding the chickens was a breeze. They never seemed in much of a hurry. They just meandered casually towards me as I entered their coop and sometimes I would even need to bang on the bucket to attract their attention – and even then they did not all respond. I would scatter the grain around and they would wander about, pecking at the floor.

At harvest-time we would go into Arlon to buy food supplies for the animals. These would be used to stock up the sheds for the winter months, as the farm did not produce any crops. We were a small-scale farm and not geared up for full commercial production, but we did breed and eat our own animals. Chicken and pork were a real treat for most at this time and I got used to the fact that we had to kill some animals to obtain them.

Once a month we went into Arlon to buy food for ourselves and trade some animals and meat at the Saturday market. On one occasion, the Germans were in town, collecting produce for their soldiers. Various vehicles were being loaded in the market square. One truck had been piled high with potatoes and, as it set off up the hill leading out of the square, a young boy jumped up on to the back and released the bolt on the tailgate. As the truck continued up the hill, the potatoes poured out of the back and rolled down the street. Children and adults alike rushed on to the road, picking up as many potatoes as they could, stuffing them into their pockets and under their jumpers and coats. It was a sight to behold. The truck did not stop – the driver was probably unaware of what was going on behind him. He was in for a big surprise when he arrived at his destination, I thought.

As Christmas approached, we prepared for the festive season and, with there being a strong religious presence at the farm, a large number of decorations and nativity pieces appeared from the loft. The farmhouse was furnished with various colours of tinsel, and a wonderful tree filled the front room, laden with homemade decorations. It had been a while since I had enjoyed a Christmas with friends and family – and a family was what we had become at Hachy. But my biggest surprise was still to come.

CHAPTER TWENTY-FOUR
PAUL

By the autumn of 1943, there had been significant advances by the Allies on almost all fronts. The British had landed in Italy, having pushed the Germans out of North Africa. In November, the Red Army liberated the city of Kiev. The Americans were winning the fight against the Japanese, with major advances in the Pacific. The tide had turned and the Germans had upped the pace of their murderous deportation of the Jews, and recruitment of more soldiers into their armies. All men in occupied Europe over the age of eighteen were being deported to Germany to work in the factories. Inside Germany, a recruitment drive had begun, drawing principally on seventeen-year-old volunteers, but boys of sixteen and some who were even younger eagerly joined. During July and August 1943, some 10,000 recruits arrived at a training camp in Beverloo in Belgium.

During the months running up to Christmas, we had an increasing number of visits at the school from German officials looking for enemy airmen and enquiring after the ages and nationalities of the pupils. The reason why I had been sent to Maredsous seemed to have followed me here. So far, the monks had managed to resist their enquiries, but the matter was becoming one of increasing concern. It was decided that any pupil who did not have clear Belgian nationality should leave the school and either be reunited with their parents or sent into hiding. The possibility of forced recruitment into the German military or internment in an "Enemy of the Reich" camp had become a serious one. That my father was British put me on the list of pupils who would have to disappear. Monsieur Dejong was duly summoned.

My tutor, Père Marc Mélot, took me into his study and explained that I was to leave the school at Christmas. Discussions with the local resistance had taken place and I was to go into hiding. Monsieur Dejong would come to collect me when the school broke up for the Christmas holidays and take me to my new home. I was instructed to ensure that I had all my belongings and was ready to leave.

On 18th December 1943, at 9.30 a.m., I stood in the lobby of the school into which I had been led by my tutor fifteen months earlier. I had said my goodbyes to my fellow pupils, as well as to my close friend André. I was going to miss him. I recalled the moments when Monsieur Dejong and Jeanne had bade me farewell and left me here in this lobby. Here I was again, alone and scared once more, with my trusty suitcase which had accompanied me through a host of moves. Where was I going this time? On every occasion in recent years, when I had been all packed up and ready to go somewhere, I had known nothing about where I was going or what was going to happen when I got there. Once more I stood beside my suitcase, ready to go into the unknown.

A few moments passed and then, as the great wooden door opened, a gust of cold air rushed into the lobby, dragging with it a few leaves from the courtyard. The trees out there were almost bare, their great, crooked branches reaching high into the sky. There was no trace left of their summer plumpness and greenness; now they were just grey and skeletal.

Père Marc Mélot stood before me, with Monsieur Dejong just behind him. Père Mélot gestured me to move outside.

'Come, Paul. Don't forget your suitcase, boy.'

I leaned down and gripped the bag firmly. It was quite heavy – everything I owned was inside, plus a few books on Latin, which I did not really want to take. I lifted the suitcase and sighed as I moved out into the courtyard, swaying from side to side and towards the waiting car. I had hoped Jeanne might be there too.

Père Mélot remained at the doorway watching, his black tunic billowing in the wind. I climbed into the passenger seat and Monsieur Dejong pushed the door shut behind me. Père Mélot raised his right hand and offered a gentle wave.

'Adieu, Paul,' he mouthed soundlessly.

The engine fired up and we moved slowly towards the large, arched entrance that I had come through when I arrived. Despite the uncertainty about where I was going, I was pleased to be leaving. Driving through those gates was like leaving a prison. I had been very unhappy here but, nevertheless, I wondered whether I would really be safer in hiding. I trusted Monsieur Dejong completely, but I wanted to know what it was that I was going to be hiding from. What was going on out there that I needed such protection? I was soon to be fifteen – all grown up. I could take care of myself. People had been pushing me from pillar to post ever since Dad left me on the quayside in Port Navalo. Shoved into the back of a truck, stuck on a train for days, sent to a big, empty, cold house and finally to what had near enough been a prison. I had had about enough of being told what to do and where to go. And the thing I wanted more than anything was to find Dad and get back together with him, but I had no knowledge that he was even alive.

The car weaved its way through the forest of frost-covered branches, heading south. Monsieur Dejong stared directly ahead. I glanced over towards him and he turned briefly to look back. He smiled and said:

'It will be OK, Paul. You don't need to worry.'

And with that, he turned back to focus on the road ahead, still wearing his gentle smile.

I knew Monsieur Dejong reasonably well. He had, to all intents and purposes, been a kind of father since that moment on the quayside when Dad had said to him, "To you I leave Paul". I liked him, but we had never really become close. He had made sure I was safe and cared for, but had never been hands-on. Dad had always been in the background until the Red Cross parcels and letters stopped. I assumed my being sent to Maredsous was his decision, but I still did not know why I had been sent there. Anyway, whenever things changed in my life, he turned up.

A couple of hours later, we turned off the main road on to a narrow track leading up to a farm courtyard. The track was covered in a thin film of frost. As we entered the courtyard, the potholes had frozen, shiny windows reflecting the clear blue sky above. As we drew to a halt by the front door of the main house, out stepped Jeanne, followed by Stephen! I couldn't believe it! I looked at Monsieur Dejong and a huge smile appeared across his face.

'A surprise for you, Paul. You are to stay here with your brother and Jeanne for now.'

I still couldn't believe it. I climbed out of the car and, as I stood beside the open door, Stephen ran towards me with arms outstretched, calling my name, over and over.

Jeanne came towards me with a huge smile. I could not remember the last time I had seen them. I stood there in my grey trousers, tie peeking out from the top of the coat that hung just below my knees. With my short, trim hair and shiny shoes, I must have looked a proper gent. Stephen was in tatty trousers with holes in the knees, worn boots and a baggy jumper. Positively agricultural, I thought. It was good to be together again.

We all went into the main house and I was introduced to Madame Villaine. The adults sat around the kitchen table while Stephen took me through to the annexe to show me around my new home.

An hour or so later, after a light lunch, Monsieur Dejong departed, waving goodbye and promising to come back and visit soon. His car disappeared down the track, bumping through the potholes as it went.

That evening, after a hearty stew, we sat around the fire. From the door came three loud thumps. Madame Villaine stood up from her armchair and went to see who it was.

She opened the door, and before her stood three men.

'Ah, Jacques,' she said. 'Entrez,' and she moved to one side to let them enter.

They made their way into the lounge and on into the kitchen. The wooden chairs scraped against the stone floor as they took their seats around the heavily worn wooden table. Madame Villaine took four glasses from the sideboard and, a finger in each, carried them over to the table. A bottle of red wine was produced from behind the curtain that concealed the larder. The four sat down and Jacques poured the wine.

The men wore heavy, dark coats, thick, sack-like trousers and leather boots. All had black berets, which they removed and placed on the table. Two of them were completely bald, but Jacques had a thin covering of grey hair, which stood upright after he removed his beret. He swept his hand across his head to flatten the unruly wisps. All the men had heavy, dark-grey moustaches that hid their upper lips. They and Madame Villaine sat and talked for a few minutes, while Stephen, Jeanne and I remained in the lounge in front of the fire.

I wondered what was going on in there, but then Jacques poked his head round the corner and called out to me, in French:

'Paul. Come in here, please. We want to talk to you.'

I looked up in surprise when I heard my name. I did not know these men. I made my way into the kitchen.

'Sit down,' said Jacques, pointing to a vacant chair at the head of the table. 'My name is Jacques, this is Bernard and over here is Degaré. We are friends of Madame Villaine and we work with the French Resistance in the Ardennes. I don't know how aware you are of the course of the war, but we know you have been at Maredsous School. We have friends there who told us about you.'

'I don't know anything about you,' I said.

'Ah, but you do know about the Resistance!' said Jacques.

'Yes, I do know a little. That you fight the Germans and looked after the British airmen who came to Maredsous. I don't know any more than that,' I said.

'That is right, Paul. We do fight the Germans and we do look after the British airmen who find themselves lost in Belgium. We are Belgian soldiers fighting against the Germans from inside Belgium. You may be aware that the war has changed and that we must do what we can to help the Allies to win. Very simply, we do things to make it more difficult for the Germans to be here. But there is something you can do to help us.'

'Oh! What's that?'

'Well, Paul, we know that you speak pretty good English. Is that right?'

'Yes I do. I used to speak it with my father, who is in England.'

'We know that your father is in England, Paul. And that you are stuck here in Belgium. Monsieur Dejong has asked us to look after you and keep you safe from the Germans. That is why you have been brought here. We shall protect you, but there is something you can do to help us. Would you like to help us, Paul?'

'How can I help you?'

'That is good, Paul. I want you to understand that we are here to help and protect you. We will not hurt you or your little brother. No harm will come to you, but you must try to stay here on the farm at all times and, if you see any Germans, you must hide. We will make a safe hiding place for you in the barn. It is important that you stay out of sight. Do you understand?'

'Why must we hide?'

'The war is changing, Paul. We believe that the British are preparing an invasion force and we must help. The Germans are very worried about these stories and, if they find you, they might send you away. We will not be able to protect you if they find you and take you away. Do you understand?'

'I think so. What do you want me to do?'

'It is very simple, Paul. We want you to listen to the English radio, called the BBC, and translate for us what is being said. That is all. Can you do that?'

'Yes, I can do that. When do you want me to do this?'

'We will give Madame Villaine a timetable for you to follow. One of us will come here every few days to collect your translations. It is very important work, Paul, and nobody must know that you do this. It would be very dangerous for you if anyone knows. You must not tell anyone. Is that absolutely clear?'

'I understand,' I said.

'OK, Paul. We will talk to Madame Villaine now and make arrangements. You can go back into the lounge.'

With that, I returned to the company of Jeanne and Stephen. Twenty minutes or so later, the three men left.

Eleven days later, on 29th December, I celebrated my fifteenth birthday in Hachy with Stephen, Jeanne and Madame Villaine.

Before we knew it, Christmas had come and gone and 1944 had arrived. What was this new year to bring? We stayed indoors in the warm, venturing out only to feed the animals and check that all was well. The days were short and cold – it was dark when we got up and dark again by late afternoon.

I had been given my timetable, so I knew when I needed to listen to the BBC news broadcasts. The listening and translating took up about two hours each day. Stephen had no understanding of English and so was not in the slightest bit interested or even curious about what I was doing. It became a routine for me, but not a word about it was mentioned to anyone.

We began to notice an increasing presence of German soldiers moving around the countryside. We had been reminded to make ourselves scarce if they were seen in the neighbourhood so, whenever they did appear, Stephen and I would run and hide in the barn, deep within a stack of hay bales. A hiding place had been made there specifically for us, so that if any Germans did look around it would be almost impossible for us to be discovered. For Stephen, rushing into the barn like this was fun, but he was not really aware of the danger. To him it was a great game.

For the moment, though, we were relatively untouched by the war. I would sometimes hear Jeanne and Madame Villaine talking about it and, as I listened and translated the BBC news reports, I began to acquire a good understanding of what was going on. The tide had turned, I knew, and the Germans were now under pressure on both the eastern and western fronts. We ourselves had plenty in the way of food, but I was aware that there were severe shortages among the local villagers.

As the weather warmed in spring, we were able to spend most of our time outside in the fields. We would watch the bombers flying overhead almost every day. They came in droves and then, a few hours later, we would see them flying back again. The groan of their engines overhead became a regular feature of our lives and did not deter us from playing and running in the fields.

During my time at Maredsous, I had matured enormously. I now had considerable awareness and understanding of what was going on, both in my life and in the world outside. The last communication I had with Dad was over two years ago. He was unlikely to know that I had been at Maredsous, and probably knew nothing about Stephen's whereabouts or situation. There was nothing, though, that I could do about any of this. Stephen and I would have to continue to live with the fact that we were to remain apart from our father for the foreseeable future. No-one knew how long this war would go on – or if we would ever be reunited with Dad, or if Dad was even alive. We had to focus on today. We were alive, that was the main thing. And we had food – and people who cared about us.

As the summer approached, there was talk among the locals that an invasion was imminent. No one, though, knew where or when it would begin. There was an even more heightened presence of German military now, both in the numbers of soldiers and the activity of vehicles in and around our neighbourhood and Arlon. We were close to what used to be the border with Luxembourg and we saw more and more trucks going back and forth. They came filled with soldiers and returned filled with food.

On 6th June, Stephen, Jeanne and I took the train to Arlon for our weekly shopping trip. As we came over the level crossing on the main road, the gatekeeper called out, 'The Allies have landed!' and everyone on the train cheered.

It was six in the evening when the BBC announced that a huge landing had been launched on the beaches of northern France. The British were coming! The newsreader asked that everyone who supported the Allies unite against the Germans, increase the Resistance attacks and do everything they could to make life difficult for the occupiers.

We all leapt to our feet and cheered, our arms in the air. Jeanne hugged Stephen, crying out that the war would soon be over. Madame Villaine was very subdued, by comparison. She stood in silence, but with a smile on her face. I guessed that she hoped she would soon be reunited with her husband. Stephen joined in the celebrations.

My translations continued and the visits from Jacques and his friends became a daily event. It was a few days before we found out that D-Day had been a success and that the troops had managed to secure their landing. There continued to be a sense of celebration among the locals, but we noticed an increasing unease or even panic among the German soldiers. Some rushed from place to place without really seeming to know where to go or what to do. Others sat around in groups, waiting for orders, tense and nervous.

The BBC news reported on the progress made each day by the advancing forces and told us to build shelters, which we could use when the battle reached us. We dug one for ourselves, well hidden, a short distance from the farm.

As the weeks went by, my involvement with the Resistance increased. Jacques insisted that we stay out of sight of the Germans which, with their ever-growing presence, meant that we were increasingly barn-bound. My translations made me very aware of what was being asked of the Resistance fighters. Things were hotting up in Belgium as the Allied forces advanced through France and resistance efforts were being stepped up all the time.

As communications between the Allies and our Resistance group intensified, my translation services were called for more and more.

One evening, as darkness fell, I was collected by Jacques in his Citroën van and driven off into the forest, about five kilometres away from the farmhouse. We crept along a narrow track between the trees, the engine barely more than idling, branches and twigs cracking beneath the tyres. The dimmed lights of the van faintly lit the way until, a couple of hundred metres in, we came to a clearing with a small hunting hut hidden amongst the trees. Already there were two other vehicles hidden beneath a makeshift lean-to. Jacques turned off the engine, leaned over to me and said quietly:

'Follow me, Paul, but don't slam your door. Close it gently. As little noise as possible.'

I could see light coming from the small window of the cabin. We approached the wooden door and Jacques pushed it open. Inside were four men, gathered around a table. I recognised two of those who had visited us at the farmhouse. They wore heavy, dark coats and woollen hats, pulled down over their ears. On the table were a map, an ashtray and some small glasses. The air was filled with smoke. A paraffin lamp hung from the ceiling, casting a yellow light across the room. Jacques joined the others around the table and, leaning forwards, they talked quietly to each other. I sat in a chair in the corner of the cabin, watching.

Half an hour or so passed. Then Jacques turned to me and said:

'OK. We go now.'

One of the men went over to a wooden trunk beneath the window. He dragged it into the middle of the room and knelt down in the space it had left. Reaching into his pocket, he took out a knife. He squeezed a button on the handle and, with a click, a shiny blade appeared. Leaning forward, he pushed the knife between the floorboards and dislodged a plank. He pulled it up and leaned it against the wall. Another three planks followed and were piled up against the first. He dipped down into the void again and I heard the clanking of metal on metal. A small machine gun appeared and was thrown over to one of the men, who caught it with a slapping sound. Another gun was retrieved, then a third, fourth and fifth, the last being passed to Jacques. The man was still leaning into the dark hole, though, and, last of all, he drew out three well-worn and tatty leather satchels, each about the size of a small suitcase. He tossed them into the arms of the nearest men. The planks were replaced and the trunk pushed back.

Jacques looked round at me.

'Right, Paul. Let's go,' he said, and made his way towards the door.

We walked over to his van, followed by the four other fighters. I climbed into the cab with Jacques, as the others went round to the rear. Jacques leaned over and said quietly:

'You must do exactly as I say, OK? Keep absolutely quiet at all times.'

'Yes,' I replied. 'Where are we going?'

'We are going to set a surprise for the Germans up on the rail track.'

'Oh. OK.'

'What I want you to do is keep an eye out for us while we set the explosives. I will drop you off at the end of the lane. We will be just twenty metres ahead. If you see anyone or hear anything, just walk towards us. Do not shout or make any noise. Just walk towards us. We will know that someone is coming. And, if that happens, just follow us away, OK? Do you understand?'

'Yes,' I said.

Adrenaline began to pump into my veins. I was full of excitement.

'Once we have set the explosives, we will come back to you at the end of the lane and all make our getaway. OK?'

'OK.' I shivered with anticipation.

We soon arrived at a lay-by in the lane that led up to the railway tracks. Jacques turned off the lights, opened the door and stepped out. The van swayed from side to side as the men climbed quietly from the back. I got out too and moved around to meet Jacques.

Three men each took a satchel from the van, which they slung over their shoulders. We walked in a group towards the narrow lane. As we arrived at the turning, Jacques stopped me with a gentle tug on my arm.

'OK, Paul. You wait here. Keep an eye out in both directions. If you see or hear anyone coming, just walk up the lane towards us. Do not run. Just walk. We will see you and then you just follow us. Clear?'

'Got it,' I replied.

The five men moved slowly away up the lane, disappearing into the darkness. I stood alone, looking feverishly to left and right. But there was nothing there. And no sound. Total silence.

It felt like a lifetime, and I had begun to shiver with cold rather than fear, when the five men finally reappeared out of the darkness.

'All OK, Paul?' came the voice of Jacques.

'Yes. Nothing to report,' I said.

'OK. Let's go.'

We walked back towards the van and climbed in. The engine started and we moved gently away. We had just left the forest track for the main road when a loud "BOOM!" suddenly filled the air. Jacques looked at me and smiled.

'A good job done!' he said.

By the road that led back towards the cabin, the van stopped and the four men jumped out.

'Adieu, Jacques. Be in touch, eh?' one said, and they disappeared into the darkness.

Ten minutes later, Jacques dropped me off at the farmhouse. Our mission was complete.

This was the first of many actions in which I became involved with the Belgian Resistance Movement over the next few months. It was exciting and, after a while, I lost my fear and considered it to be great fun. I had the attitude that the Germans were too stupid to catch us. This was far from true, though, and it was only a few weeks after my first excursion that the unit next to ours was caught and all thirty-five members shot. It was a chilling reminder of the reality of what we were doing. I wondered what Dad would have thought if he could have seen me now.

At the end of August, we started hearing guns in the distance. The Allies were advancing and the fighting was getting closer. There were a few air raids nearby and, during one, Hachy Railway Station was blown to bits. The Germans were now in full retreat, and heading for Germany with everything they could carry, including furniture and possessions from the farmhouses that they had occupied in recent weeks.

On 1st September, Allied troops crossed into Belgium from France. The next day, resistance fighters successfully sabotaged a convoy of 1,500 political prisoners who had been rounded up by the Germans and were due to depart Brussels Midi Station that day. They were all freed and disappeared into the streets of the city. The day after, the British Army under General Sir Miles Dempsey, arrived on the outskirts of Brussels and, in the afternoon, the 2nd Armoured Division entered the capital along Avenue de Tervuren.

The last Germans had already left, but, before their departure, they had set fire to the Law Courts in an attempt to destroy the documents that were kept there. The people of Brussels gathered in their hundreds in an effort to put out the blaze, but were unable to prevent the collapse of the building's impressive brass dome. In the cellars, they found enormous quantities of food and luxury items that had been stored there by the Germans.

The following day, a group of Belgian fighters known as the Piron Brigade and led by Colonel Jean Piron, entered Brussels. The Liberation Front immediately began to search out collaborators, who were dragged through the streets. Some were hanged, some had their heads shaved and many were publicly beaten. On Thursday 7th September, General Montgomery was officially welcomed at the City Hall of Brussels by Mayor Vande Meulebroeck.

As the news spread about the liberation of Brussels, our Resistance unit joined up with neighbouring ones and came out into the open to fight. I was with them every day as we were now in hourly contact with the Americans.

The Americans were led by General Patton and his Third Armoured Division. The Germans were no match for this force but, even so, there were some 300 tanks facing us and the Americans told us to take cover and hide in any shelters we could find.

On 8th September, a number of Germans turned up in Hachy, calling themselves the 136th Regrouped Company of Infantry. They were a ragtag crew made up of soldiers, sailors and airmen. Between about 150 men they had one anti-tank gun and almost no ammunition. They seemed lost, but they took the farm as their headquarters. Stephen and I had hidden in the hay barn, and, as night fell, Jeanne and Madame Villaine headed off to the shelter.

That evening, a barrage of shelling began. It went on all night, getting nearer all the time.

At daylight, the shelling stopped and, as we peered out from our hiding place in the barn, we saw a Tiger Moth aircraft circling above, guiding artillery fire towards nearby buildings.

During the morning, there were three raids by planes carrying machine guns and cannons. We decided to make a run for it from the barn and head for the shelter. When we got there, we rushed down the ramp, only to find it full of German soldiers! They looked at us, and then just gestured towards the back. There was no sign of Jeanne or Madame Villaine – they must have returned to the farmhouse. It was too dangerous for us to leave now, though. We had no choice but to stay. The soldiers had more important things to worry about, and ignored us as we huddled in the corner.

The shelling continued for another three hours. The sheltering soldiers finally realised that things were looking very bad for them and decided to evacuate the shelter. The last to go was a sergeant, who turned to us and said:

'We will be back at Christmas!'

As it turned out, they nearly were, when they advanced again in the Battle of the Bulge in December and were within ten kilometres of here.

Once the soldiers had gone and the gunfire had finally ceased, Stephen and I climbed out of the shelter and walked to the main road, which was about three kilometres from the farm.

And there they were! American tanks and jeeps, flanked on each side by hundreds of soldiers, marching in their green uniforms. We were finally liberated! It was 1.30 p.m. on Saturday 9th September 1944.

CHAPTER TWENTY-FIVE
PAUL

Stephen and I walked towards the main road to greet the Yanks. As we approached, a soldier stopped and asked in English:

'Hey, kids. Where are you guys goin'?'

'We live here,' I replied, 'but our father is in England.'

'Hey, guys!' he shouted out. 'These kids are Poms! Where's the sarge?'

I had no idea what he was talking about. Poms? What are Poms, I thought? Within a few minutes we had been taken to meet the sergeant.

'Hi, kids. What are your names and where are you from?' he enquired.

'I am Paul Barker and this is my brother Stephen. We are staying with friends on a farm just down the road. Our mother is dead and our father is in England,' I explained.

'OK. You'd best come with me,' he said.

We followed him towards a group of Americans, who were trying to pursue a conversation across the language barrier with the mayor of the town. I offered to help translate. The mayor wanted to know whether the soldiers would go into town to remove any remaining Germans. An American officer replied that he could send a jeep with four soldiers, and he called out to the occupants of one nearby:

'Take a ride into town, will ya? Check to see if there are any Krauts still hangin' about.'

'Yes, sir!' came the response and the soldiers drove off down the road.

We were then taken off to meet an American colonel, who was in charge of an engineer unit. Our brief story was repeated.

'I will need details about you two youngsters before I can make any enquiries about your father,' said the colonel. 'Once I have the necessary information, I can pass it on to command HQ, who will relay it to the Brits, and we will see what happens.'

Turning to the sergeant, he said:

'Take these two kids home and find out about their father. Get their names and places of birth and get the information back to me pronto!'

'Yes, sir! Come on fellas, we got work to do!'

We were led away and, before we knew it, had been lifted into the back of a jeep and were zooming along the road back to the farm.

Jeanne and Madame Villaine were waiting for us in the courtyard. As the jeep drew up beside the house, they both ran over to us, calling out.

'Thank God! You are safe. Where have you been? We thought you had been lost or taken by the Germans.'

'We are OK,' I reassured them. 'We hid in the shelter and, when the Americans came, we went to meet them. We are fine, honestly. The American colonel told us he's going to contact Dad and let him know that we have been found. Isn't that fantastic?'

'Er... bonjour,' said the sergeant, who had joined us. 'Speak English?' he asked.

'Yes, I speak a little English,' said Jeanne.

'Ah, great,' he replied.

'We'll go inside and you can tell us what we need to do,' said Jeanne.

The five of us made our way into the house, where we sat around the worn table, just as the resistance men had done. This time, though, I was part of the group.

Over the next fifteen minutes, Jeanne presented our passports and the various documentation she had for us, and gave the sergeant all the information she had about Dad. Our last communication stated that he was at Tangier Lodge in Barnes and she had all the relevant information about his birthplace and family.

Having noted everything down, the sergeant gathered together his notes and made his way out to the jeep.

'See ya later, fellas. I'll be back as soon as we have any information for ya.'

The next day, he and an American officer arrived at the farm in a jeep similar to the one which had brought us here the previous day. The two men climbed out of the vehicle and came to the door. Neither could speak any French, so I did the translating.

'Well, young man,' the officer began. 'We have been in touch with the British authorities and told them about you two guys. They will be making enquiries about the whereabouts of your father. Once they have tracked him down, they will notify him that you have been found and we can begin to make arrangements for you to be transported to England. It may take a while, I'm afraid, as there is still a war on, but hopefully, not too long. For now, you must stay here. Either I or someone else will be back to let you know what is happening.'

He rummaged in his briefcase and pulled out a paper bag.

'Here you go, guys,' he said. 'Have that and enjoy. We'll be back.'

And, with that, they turned and walked back to the jeep. As they shot off down the track, bumping from side to side through the potholes of muddy water, I wondered if they might get thrown out.

We closed the front door and went back into the kitchen to find out what was in the bag. Jeanne emptied the contents on to the kitchen table. To our absolute delight, out fell chocolate, sweets and chewing gum. We had forgotten all about these delights. The celebrations were well and truly on.

HARRY

As dusk fell, I poured myself a small whisky. Suddenly there was a loud knock at the door.

'Who could that be at this time?' called out Toni.

'I've no idea,' I replied. 'I'll go.'

I made my way from the lounge to the entrance hall and opened the door. Before me stood two policemen in full uniform, their hats tucked under their arms. The porch-light lit their heads.

'Mr Barker?' one enquired.

'Yes, that's me.'

'We have some news for you, sir.'

'You do? What about?'

'Can we first check, sir. Are you Mr Harry Barker, and do you have any children?'

'Yes, I am and I have two sons who are in Belgium.'

'Do you have a passport or any form of identification, sir?'

'Certainly,' I replied, and disappeared off to the study to get my passport.

'Who is it?' called out Toni.

'The police,' I replied.

'The police? What on earth do they want?'

'It's about the boys. I need to give them ID.'

'Oh God! Have they found them?'

'I don't know. I need to give them identification.'

I returned to the front door and presented my passport.

'Thank you, Mr Barker. We were given this address by your sister at Tangier Lodge in Barnes, but needed to verify your identity. That's how we found you. We have been contacted by the American military in Belgium and have been informed that they have found your sons.'

'Oh my God! They've found Paul and Stephen! Where?'

'I'm not exactly sure, sir, but they were found by American soldiers in southern Belgium yesterday. They are both safe and staying at a farmhouse in the area. That is all we know, sir. If you would come down to the station tomorrow, my sergeant may be able to let you have some more details. You will need to be accompanied by our sergeant when you collect them, for identification you understand, sir. We just thought we would bring you the good news, sir.'

'Well… thank you. Thank you so much. I will come down to the station tomorrow, first thing. Thank you.'

The two policemen turned and headed back down the short path.

Somewhat bewildered, I closed the door and moved back towards the hallway.

'Toni, dear,' I mumbled. 'Toni. You won't believe what I have just heard.'

PAUL

A week later, another jeep bumped its way up the track to the farmhouse. This time it was the sergeant, on his own.

'Hey, guys,' he said when we let him in. 'I got some news for you. The police in England have traced your pa and they've told him that you guys have been found! The air force are preparing a new landing zone nearby and, as soon as it's operational, we shall be flying you to England! How about that, hey! Not too sure exactly when, but most likely in the next week or so. You'd better gather your things together. Be sure to be ready, OK!'

'But what about Monsieur Dejong? He'll have to be told. We can't just disappear,' I said.

'Don't worry, young fella. We'll take care of all of that. Just be ready, OK, guys?'

Jeanne gave him all the contact details for Monsieur Dejong, and he headed back down the track.

Stephen and I couldn't believe what we had heard. We were going to England! To be reunited with Dad! It had all happened so quickly. Only a couple of days ago, we were in hiding and fearing for our lives. Now, within a couple of weeks, we would be flying to England to be with our father. We had never even been in a plane – only watched them fly overhead. We were in shock. But what about Jeanne? What about Madame Villaine? Were we just going to leave them here? They were our family, our security. Were we just going to walk away? It did not seem right.

Seven days later, at ten on a bright autumn morning, an American truck rumbled up the track. Stephen and I had our suitcases ready. Once again, they contained all we had. Jeanne and Madame Villaine stood anxiously alongside us. The truck entered the courtyard and drew to a stop. Out of the cab climbed a young soldier.

'Sorry, fellas, but you won't be going anywhere just yet.'

He walked us back into the house and sat down with Jeanne and me.

'Today we received orders that all British citizens liberated in Belgium must be transported to the British Zone. That's in the northern half of Belgium. Our orders are to arrange for transportation to Brussels for you two, in a few days' time. There you'll report to the British commander and arrangements will be made for you to be flown to England.'

'So what do we do now?' I asked.

'Sit tight, and in a couple of days we'll be back to take you to Brussels.'

'OK,' I said, looking at my feet.

'Sure. Don't worry, fellas. It's all a bit chaotic at the moment. It'll sort itself out. I'll be back to collect you myself. See you in a couple of days.'

The truck rumbled back down the track.

Sure enough, two days later, the young American soldier arrived in a smaller truck to collect us and we were off to Brussels. Jeanne insisted on coming with us, so Madame Villaine stood alone on the porch as we left the courtyard. She had been so kind to us and we would never forget her, although I had no idea if I would ever see her again.

We rumbled off down the potholed track and turned onto the main road. A kilometre later, we came to a junction and turned towards Namur and Brussels. The road was busy with military vehicles of all shapes and sizes. The difference this time was that they were all either American or British. Along the way, the young driver talked almost endlessly. When he was not talking, he was shouting and waving to others along the way:

'Get outa my way, dude! Hey, Mac, when d'you start your driving lessons! You shouldn't be allowed off your leash, pal! Hi ya, fellas – sorry, no room today!'

He seemed to have a phrase for every occasion. It was an interesting journey. We did not stop until we arrived in Brussels.

There we had to negotiate several checkpoints, and at each the soldier presented a document which always satisfied the guards, and we were waved on. We finally arrived at the Hotel de Ville in St Gilles, a building I remembered well. It had now been occupied by British forces. The German soldiers in their grey uniforms had gone, and so too, had the swastika flag that had hung above the entrance to the main doors, as well as the strangely shaped jeeps and the officers with their long, black, shiny, leather coats. British soldiers in light-brown uniforms rushed back and forth across the courtyard. The more important-looking had brown, shiny shoes, while the regular soldiers and guards wore black boots. The place was the same, but the people were completely different.

Jeanne was first out and she helped Stephen and I onto the concourse. The American driver climbed into the back and passed out our suitcases, before jumping out over the tailgate.

We followed the soldier in through the heavy doors and into the main hall, where a man sat behind a desk.

'Two refugees, sir. British kids goin' to Ol' Blighty,' said our driver.

'Take them through to registration, young man. Through that hallway and on your left.'

'Yes, sir.'

We were marched off to a huge room with high ceilings and tall windows. On the right were two wide trestle tables, behind which sat three men in uniform. There was no one else in the room. We walked up to the waiting men, our American soldier leading the way.

'Two Limey kids for repatriation,' he announced.

'Thank you, soldier,' came the reply from one of the men. 'We'll take care of them.'

The soldier turned to us and said:

'Good luck, guys. Hope you make it home safe.'

And then he turned and walked away. Jeanne, Stephen and I stood before the three men with our suitcases beside us. What was going to happen now?

'Do you have any documents?' the wide-moustached soldier in the middle asked.

'Yes, sir,' Jeanne replied, handing over the wad of papers.

'Thank you, madam.'

Turning towards me, 'Paul, is it?' he asked.

'Yes, sir, and this is my brother Stephen.'

'All right, Paul. We are going to be taking care of you for now. Your father has been contacted and he knows that you are safe. We will be making arrangements for you to be flown home as soon as possible. Where have you been staying?'

'We have been staying on a farm in Hachy since Christmas, but we have friends here in St Gilles who have been taking care of us.'

'Friends in St Gilles?'

'Yes, sir. Jeanne here, and Monsieur Dejong have been looking after us since our father left.'

'Do you have an address for Monsieur Dejong?'

'Yes, sir. He lives at 20 Avenue de la Sapinière, not far from here.'

'Ah, does he? We'll send someone round to find him. In the meantime, Corporal Roberts will take you through to the next room to get your details down. If you would all go with him now.'

We followed Corporal Roberts through, where we sat down at another desk and a lengthy interrogation began. They wanted all the details about Mum, where she had died and when, and then everything about Dad, where we had lived and how we had become abandoned in France. After that, they asked how we had found our way back to Brussels, where we had lived there and with whom. I told them about being sent to Maredsous School, and translated what Stephen said about how he ended up in Hachy. It all took quite a while.

'OK, kids,' said the interrogating officer. 'We need to get you out of here quick. Things are a little hectic, but we will fly you out first thing in the morning. Monsieur Dejong will be here soon to look after you tonight and deliver you back here at six tomorrow morning. You may only take a small suitcase each, like the ones you have here now. Do you understand?'

I nodded and we were led back into the main foyer.

The following morning, Stephen and I returned with the suitcases that we had carried when we left Brussels in June 1939 in Dad's Studebaker, and which had served us in such good stead ever since. We had left in a hurry that day, our destination unknown, but this time we knew where we were going – although we had never been there before. I had almost forgotten what Dad looked like, but finally the nightmare was going to be over.

At six the next morning, we returned to the Hotel de Ville in St Gilles to be told to follow a jeep to a temporary airfield on the outskirts of Brussels. We sped through the streets, trying to keep up with the jeep and being thrown from side to side in the back of Monsieur Dejong's old Citroën. Twenty minutes later we arrived at the small airfield, where two Lancaster bombers stood proudly, the sun glinting off their fuselages.

The airfield was busy, with airmen running here, there and everywhere. We walked together towards the temporary prefabricated buildings and were ushered inside. Monsieur Dejong handed over our papers and we were taken out on to a concourse by a British airman. We turned to wave goodbye to Jeanne and Monsieur Dejong, who stood together, side by side, tears rolling down their cheeks. Stephen had begun to cry, too, uncertain about leaving behind those who he knew and loved so well. We were going to another country, without knowing what was waiting there. I took his hand and we walked across the concrete towards a huge RAF Lancaster bomber. Shiny, steel steps led up to a hatch on the side, close to the rear of the plane, and then into the fuselage. A friendly face poked his head out, saying:

'Come on in, boys. Hurry. We don't have much time!'

We climbed up the steps and disappeared into the belly of the bomber.

'In you come,' the airman repeated, as we entered the ribbed fuselage, lined with cables that ran the length of the aircraft. With a glance to my left, I could see the windows of the rear gunner's position. Looking right, along the length of the plane, I could see more windows, spilling light down the front half of the fuselage.

'I reckon you lads would like to have a look around. What do you say?'

'Oh yes, please,' I replied, holding Stephen's hand firmly and pulling him along behind me. We moved up the body of the aircraft, past what looked like a radio desk with various dials and headphones, and then into an open desk space.

'This is where the navigator sits,' said our guide.

Further forward, and over a steel bulkhead running across the fuselage, were two sets of bulbous windows, one above the other. The top window was filled with dials and levers circling a single seat. The lower one seemed just to contain various steel beams and levers. I could see the guns protruding from beneath and to the side of the glazed cabin.

'Up top sits the pilot and down below is the front gunner,' continued the airman. 'For this trip you chaps will sit out back,' he said. 'Perhaps the skipper will let you come up front some time during the flight.'

'Yes please, sir,' I said.

We clambered back into the main fuselage and took up our seats. The airman helped buckle us in.

A few moments later, there was a loud hissing noise from the right-side propeller, followed by a bang, and then a roar, as the engine fired up. The noise grew louder as each of the other three engines burst into life. It was deafening, but hugely exciting.

The aircraft began to move forward and, before I knew it, we were accelerating across the field. The front of the plane dipped forward as the tail lifted and then, with a lurch upwards, we were airborne! It was exhilarating. As I looked down the length of the fuselage I could see the runway disappearing behind us as we rose up into the sky. The houses and roads grew smaller. This was truly amazing! Our destination: Hendon Aerodrome in north London.

Once we had reached our cruising height, I was asked if I would like to go and sit up front with the skipper. An invitation I was not to refuse. I scrambled up and over the multitude of bars and cables into the glass bubble. The co-pilot had vacated his seat and I climbed in. The engines maintained a deep groan as we flew northwards and I could see the landscape below for miles around. And then, in the distance, the grey sea of the English Channel began to appear. The weather ahead did not look good – deep, grey clouds filled the skyline now.

As we flew over the beaches of Dunkirk, I could see below me, strewn across the sands and the shallow waters, many of the abandoned vehicles, ships, boats and war machinery from that fateful event six years ago.

I felt the aircraft rising as we climbed to get above the clouds. Soon the white puffs of cotton wool were below us and we were in the clear, blue sky above. I could no longer see the ground below.

In my excitement, I had not even glanced back to see if Stephen was all right. I looked behind me now. He was sitting beside the airman who had shown us in. Stephen smiled at me. He was fine. We flew on.

'Bandits at two o'clock high! Over!' shouted out the front gunner. 'Bandits at two o'clock high, skipper! Over!' he repeated.

'Righty ho! We'll drop into the clouds below and take cover! Paul – out! Get him out of here fast!' the skipper shouted.

I unbuckled my straps. The co-pilot had reappeared from behind and lifted me straight out of his seat, passing me to the airman like a doll.

'Got him!' he called out, and, holding me just above the waist, he ran me down the fuselage to mid-aircraft and dropped me in my seat. He turned and ran back towards the front, calling out, 'Get buckled up and don't move. OK!' He didn't wait for an answer. I just did as he said and checked that Stephen was securely buckled in. Fear began to replace the excitement. There were all kinds of shouting going on. The plane suddenly tipped over to the left. I felt my weight lighten and I rose slightly from my seat as we dived towards the thick clouds below. I felt my stomach rise and began to feel sick. Blood had disappeared from my face and I turned a pale white. Saliva filled my mouth and I began to retch as the plane rapidly lost height. Stephen had also turned a pale colour and just looked at me in terror.

'What's happening, Paul?' he asked. 'Are we going to die?'

'No, no. Just sit tight. It will be OK.'

The plane continued its rapid descent and suddenly the dim light within dimmed into a semi-darkness. I looked front and back and saw that the glass bubbles had now been engulfed with a grey mist. Nothing was visible. We were in the clouds. The aircraft was bumping and jumping as we were being tossed about in the air. I was still retching, wanting to be sick, but nothing was coming up. The crew were shouting at one another.

'I think we may have lost them, skipper,' came a voice from the rear. 'I don't think they saw us. Over!'

'OK. We'll stay on this flight path for now. Hold on, fellas. It's going to be a bit bumpy for a while. Over!'

In a flood, the contents of my stomach poured out of my mouth and splattered all over the floor directly in front of me. I retched again and another portion of vomit cascaded out before me. The bitter taste of acid engulfed the taste buds in my mouth, stinging my tongue. I swept my sleeve across my mouth, sat back and hoped the vomiting was over.

HARRY

'The boys are due to land at Hendon about eleven, so I need to get a move on,' I called out. 'I've only got an hour, although Hendon is not far from here. I don't know where I need to get to, so I had best give myself a little time.'

I had been to the police station at Marylebone and they had told me that the boys were being flown in by the RAF. A Lancaster bomber would be flying them over. I was terrified that they might not make it. I don't know why I was so scared, but the thought of them in a giant bomber filled me with fear. After all that had happened in the past five years, to lose them now would have been absolutely awful. I don't think I could have borne that.

I gathered myself and tried to put the negative thoughts out of my mind. Concentrate on the good. They will be here soon. We'll be together again. I had decided to go alone. Being reunited after all this time would be traumatic enough. To present them with Toni at the same time would be too much. No need to make it even more complicated.

'I'm off now,' I called out to Toni, and opened the front door.

'Hold on, Harry. Wait just a second.'

She appeared from the hallway and met me at the door. 'Here, take these,' and presented me with a wad of tissues. 'It may be an emotional time, darling. Be careful, it is very foggy out there.'

I turned and walked out into the whiteness, having to look carefully to follow the short pathway leading to the gate.

It was very difficult to see much in this thick fog. Should I really take the car? Perhaps it would be better to go on the underground. I decided to persevere with the car. It would be a slow journey, but from Regents Park to Hendon airfield was not far. Straight up the Finchley Road to Hendon. No more than five miles and more or less a straight road.

I fired up the car and crept out of the drive, turned left onto Park Road and drove slowly north towards Hendon.

About half an hour later, in thick fog, I arrived at the gates of Hendon Aerodrome. I stopped before the red and white barrier. A soldier came out of the side building and asked the purpose of my visit. I passed him the papers I had been given by the police.

'I have come to collect my children, who are flying in from Brussels,' I said.

'No flights today, sir,' said the soldier. 'The aerodrome is closed due to the fog, but please go on to the main building on the right. They will let you know what is happening.'

I drove on past the lifted barrier and crept forward, following the white-painted rocks which lined the road. I could not see any further than about twenty yards. Out of the fog appeared a building on my right. I pulled into the small car parking area and switched off the engine. I walked over to the entrance and in through the swinging doors where I was met by the sergeant from the police station. The room was brightly lit with a glass window on the left, above which was a sign saying, "Reception". I approached and was met by a very attractive young woman, smartly dressed in her pale-blue RAF uniform.

'How may I help you, sir?' she enquired.

'Hello. Yes. Thank you,' I mumbled, slightly taken aback by her efficiency and attractiveness. 'I am Harry Barker. My children are due to be flown in today from Brussels. I am here to collect them.'

'Oh, yes. The police officer has briefed us. I'm afraid there are no flights coming in today because of the fog, sir. The aerodrome is closed. Let me have a word with the CO and see if we can find out what is happening. I won't be a minute.' She disappeared through a door within the room behind the glass.

I turned to look around the room, confused. Where could they be? Perhaps the flight was cancelled. Perhaps it has been diverted. Perhaps it had not made it. Oh my God. If something had happened I just didn't know what I would do. I still had that revolver at home. My mind was beginning to race.

PAUL

'Bad weather ahead, skipper! Over!' shouted the navigator into his mouthpiece.

'What kind of bad weather? Over!' came the response from the captain.

'Thick fog, sir. Just had a message in from Hendon, sir. Aerodrome closed, sir. Being diverted. Waiting instructions, captain! Over!'

'OK. Let me know as soon as you hear. How are we doing on fuel? Over!'

'Good for about an hour, sir. Over!'

'Thanks. We'll continue on till we hear from Hendon. Stay on this heading. Any sign of those bandits? Over!'

'Can't see a thing, sir. Over!' came the reply from front and rear gunners.

'OK. Keep your eyes peeled, fellas. Over!'

'Instructed to divert to Braintree, sir. Over!' shouted the navigator into his mask.

'Braintree did you say? Over!'

'Yes, sir. Over!'

'Where the bloody hell is Braintree? Over!'

'Looking it up now, sir. Give me a minute. Over!'

There was a brief pause.

'Skipper, sir. Braintree is just north of Chelmsford, sir. About 40 miles northeast of Hendon. In Essex, sir. Over!'

'How are we for fuel? Over!'

'Should be fine, sir,' came the response from the co-pilot. 'Only another ten to fifteen minutes flying time, sir. Assuming no fog and we can find it, we should be fine. Over!'

'Let Hendon know we are diverting. Over!'

It had been half an hour since we had dived into the clouds for cover and we began to climb again. As we flew out of the cloud and into the bright clear sky, the bumping stopped. The bomber tilted to the right and then steadied. We flew on. I sat and looked at the puke scattered across the metal floor. I could still taste the sourness.

Half an hour passed and we began our descent. We flew into some more fog and I could see nothing but white outside. The plane bumped and jumped. It seemed ages before the whiteness cleared and suddenly the green English countryside appeared below. We were flying quite low now. Then a bump shuddered through the aircraft and we hit the ground. As the tail dropped, another bump. We had finally landed in England.

The diversion of the flight to Braintree meant that there was no refugee relief team at the airfield to meet us. And no one on board knew where we were to go, or how we were to get there. Stephen and I were taken to the flight commander's office and told to wait.

An hour passed and we sat there, two lonely and confused kids, wondering what was going to happen next. And then a woman, dressed in a smart, blue uniform entered the room.

'Hello, boys,' she said with a smile. 'Welcome home. I am going to look after you from now on. We will be going by train to London later this afternoon, where we will make arrangements for your father to collect you. So, grab your cases and follow me.'

I explained to Stephen that we were to go with this lady now. We followed her out of the building, towards the waiting car. From there we were driven to a military base and taken into the canteen. It was good to eat again. I was hungry after leaving everything I had eaten earlier on the floor of the bomber.

After lunch we were led into a lounge area and told to wait.

HARRY

'Excuse me, sir! SIR!' I heard a voice call out. My subconscious speculating was abruptly interrupted.

'Mr Barker. I have been told that the flight left Brussels as scheduled. However, due to the fog, the flight had been diverted to Braintree. We are not sure as to where your children are right now, but will make enquiries. If you would like to take a seat, we will make a few calls.'

The policeman and I wandered over to the far end where several chairs were lined up against the wall I slumped into a chair. The built-up anxiety and worry bubble had burst. I was not going to see the boys just yet.

The wait seemed like forever. Finally, the attractive receptionist reappeared and waved us over.

'We have been in touch with Braintree, sir. The flight has landed safely and the boys are in the care of an RAF officer. They are due to catch a train from Braintree to Liverpool Street Station. They are due in on the twenty-past-seven train, sir. You may meet them there this evening, Mr Barker.'

'Oh. Thank God!' I said. 'Thank you so much!'

'All right, Mr Barker,' said the policeman. 'I will meet you there, sir,' he said.

With that, I left the aerodrome and headed home.

PAUL

It was late afternoon when our lady in blue appeared once again and we were taken to Braintree Station in a military car. Here we boarded a train to Liverpool Street Station in London. The journey took about an hour and, as we entered the outskirts of the city and the fog lifted, we began to see the damage caused by the Luftwaffe bombings. The train slowly made its way through the East End, stopping at Stratford, Pudding Mill Lane and Bethnal Green, before finally arriving at Liverpool Street.

It was almost dark when the train slowly pulled into the station. Dim lights lit the platform. Steam filled the air and wafted along. The engine hissed and screeched as the brakes were gently applied. We leaned out of the window to see if we could see Dad. I was not sure how he might look. Would I recognise him? Would he be there?

HARRY

I decided that I would like Toni to accompany me to Liverpool Street Station and greet the boys. The fog was beginning to lift, but driving would be tricky. We decided to travel on the underground this time. We walked down Park Road, to the junction of Marylebone Road. We descended into the underground at Baker Street. It was about eight stops to Liverpool Street.

We made our way up the stairs out of the underground, up to the main-line station and on to the concourse. The train from Braintree was due in on platform six. We had about twenty minutes to wait. I wrapped my scarf around my neck and pushed my hat on a bit tighter to protect myself from the cold and damp. We made our way to the ornate metal entrance gate of platform six.

I stood with Toni on one side of me and the police sergeant on the other, gazing down the length of the dimly lit platform. I was reminded of when I had stood on the platform at Victoria Station all those years ago, waiting for Abbi. There were so many similarities. It was a cold night. It was dusk. I was waiting for someone I loved. It was the beginning of a new life. I felt my emotions welling up inside me. Finally, this chapter was coming to an end and a new one was beginning.

The black steam engine suddenly appeared out of the haze at the end of the platform. It grew bigger and bigger as it came closer, the huge powerful beast hissing and puffing. Steam filled the platform. It came to a shunting halt. A rush of hissing and more vapour pouring from the side of the great beast. I searched into the haze, just as I had all those years ago. Where are my boys? Where are they?

PAUL

Once the train had stopped, we grabbed our small suitcases and clambered along the corridor to the exit. We were swiftly followed by our chaperone. I was so excited. Finally to be reunited with Dad.

We climbed out of the carriage on to the platform. It was dim and steam filled the air. We made our way along, weaving in amongst the other passengers, looking, searching; our hands held firmly by the chaperone as we were jostled by the crowds.

'I say, boys,' said the uniformed lady. 'What is your father's name?'

'Harry,' I said. 'Harry Barker.'

I continued searching through the crowds to see if I could spot him.

Then there, appearing from the cloud, he stood. There he was! I was shaking as I walked over towards him.

'Papa?' I asked. 'Papa?'

'Yes, son. It's me,' he replied, and he took me in his arms. It was the best day of my life.

Stephen, though, stood looking on, bewildered. He could not remember Dad at all.

It had been just over six years since we had waved goodbye on that quayside. He had been only seven years old at the time. Now here he was, thirteen, unable to speak a word of English and he did not recognise his own father. This was going to be difficult for him.

I, on the other hand, remembered Dad perfectly. He was the Dad I remembered and loved – not changed very much, just a little older. He was the Dad I had been waiting so long for.

Just behind him stood a lady. For a moment I was not sure, then suddenly I remembered. It was the lady who had lived just down the road from us at Avenue de la Sapinière.

The loneliness and suffering was over. We had survived.

'Excuse me, madam,' the sergeant interrupted, directing his question to the chaperone. 'Can you confirm the identity of these boys and that they are the children of Mister Barker here?'

'Yes, officer. This is Paul Derrick Barker and this is Victor Stephen Barker. They are indeed Harry's Boys.'

The End

How I wrote this book

It took just over five years to write this book. It was obvious from the start that the writings left by my father were not enough to create a novel. Much research would be needed to find out what was going on at the time and precisely what the places he stayed at were like. To say we lived in a house near to town was very vague. I would need to find out where this house was and, if possible, go and see it.

The book begins with a scene on a quayside in the small fishing village of Port Navalo. It seemed obvious to me that this would be one of the places I needed to visit. He also talked about their home in Spa and time he spent at a school in the Ardennes. I first needed to find out if these places were still there, and if so, arrange to visit. The idea of going to see these places filled me with excitement. It was the beginning of a fascinating journey for me.

The story really begins with Harry meeting his bride-to-be. My father said nothing about this, but I had to come up with a story. I am sorry to admit that the First World War trenches and injury are indeed fiction. I do know that he met Abbi in Belgium at the end of the war and that he did participate. I decided to try and find out where and when he participated. Unfortunately, I could find no records about Harry and his involvement in the First Great War. I was told that during the Second World War a sizeable chunk of the archives were destroyed in the Blitz. Perhaps his records were amongst those. I did not know for sure until my mother passed away and amongst her things we found the two medals given to every soldier: the British War Medal and the Victory Medal. They had been handed down to his eldest son, my father, and kept safely by my mother after Dad died. From these I was able to find his service number T2/10616 and his regiment, which is inscribed around the rim of every medal. From that information, I discovered that he served in the Army Service Corps as a "Driver". Finally, confirmation that he did take part in the Great War. The medals are now in the safe keeping of Harry's great grandson, Christopher Barker.

Harry's medals.

This line of enquiry led me to find out about two other brothers of Harry who participated in the First World War. His younger brother was George Reginald, who died in France on 18th August 1918. Together with my wife, we travelled out to the Somme and spent three days visiting the amazing cemeteries and war memorials. We found my great uncle George Reginald buried in a small cemetery just outside the town of Dernancourt. He had served as a gunner in the 189th Siege Garrison Artillery. The siege batteries were equipped with heavy howitzers, sending large-calibre high-explosive shells into enemy lines. He fell just a few months before the war ended. In the heat of battle fallen soldiers were left where they lay or in shallow graves marked by fellow soldiers. George Reginald fell during the final Allied counter-offensive which began on 10th August 1918. His body was marked and left by the advancing troops. Some eighteen months later he was exhumed from a shallow grave and laid to rest in the small cemetery in Dernancourt.

The cemetery at Dernancourt.

This led me to find out about another brother, Alexander, who participated, but I am led to believe that he did not fire a single shot. He was recruited into the Army Remount Service. I had no idea what the Army Remount Service was and a call to my uncle in Australia offered no further help. In fact, Stephen did not know that one of his uncles served in the Army Remount Service. Research led me to find out that the Remount Service was responsible for the provision of all horses and mules during the war and as Alexander had considerable knowledge of horses, through his work on the Barker farms, he was recruited and promoted to corporal on the same day. He travelled to France with the Expeditionary Force at the outset of the war, being one of the first British soldiers to arrive in France. Beyond that, he spent most of his time in the UK depots. At the height of the fighting in December 1917, the remount depots were training 93,000 horses and 36,000 mules. From what I discovered, it seems Alexander did not fight but his role was hugely important.

I wanted to know about Albertine.

In my father's writings, he said: "I remember the house in Sfra, the entrance of it but not the inside." He went on: "I do not remember the actual death of my mother which occurred when I was about four years old and Stephen about eighteen months. I expect that we were kept away from the funeral etc. Mother died of tuberculosis…"

This was all I had about his mother and where they were at the time of her death. I searched for a town called Sfra in Belgium but found nothing. A call to my uncle also drew a blank. He thought his mother had been laid to rest in a cemetery in Brussels. I did not know where they were living at the time of her death, but as her family came from St Gilles, a suburb of Brussels, I decided we would start the search there. A trip was arranged and we headed for St Gilles. We decided we would also try to visit the house in Avenue de la Sapinière and possibly the Ecole Decroly, the primary school they attended, if still there.

On arrival at the Cimetiere de Saint-Gilles, we enquired in the main office and were sent across to the archives bureau.

There a very helpful member of staff attended us to and we paged through the large register. No sign of Albertine Barker. We were advised to visit another cemetery nearby and once again we found no Albertine Barker listed.

Disappointed, we headed off to visit the house at 22 Avenue de la Sapinière and the primary school, which were both still there, although the school, I expect, had changed significantly.

We returned puzzled. Still no record of Albertine.

Port Navalo

The next place to visit was Port Navalo. A long weekend was arranged and my wife and I drove down to southern Brittany, following the likely route Harry would have taken

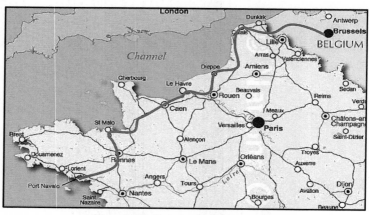

Harry's likely route to Port Navalo.

whilst trying to find a way to get across the channel back to England. We arrived in southern Brittany and the next day drove the short journey from our hotel to Port Navalo. It was a hot and sunny day. The small port was filled with tourists.

The area had been virtually desolate when Harry was there back in 1939, but now it was a thriving tourist area. Arzon had grown into a sizeable town with camping sites everywhere. The drive on through to Port Navalo took us to the port, which was almost as I had imagined. A single quayside and worn stone surfaces. I could see where they had no doubt stood on that fateful morning. It was eery. We wandered around the small port, imagining what it must have been like.

The quay at Port Navalo.

One issue which had always been a mystery was why Harry decided to leave by fishing boat. He must have had the option to travel south by car. There was a story that they had pushed the car into the harbour after Harry had departed so that it was not taken by the Germans. Another tale was that local men took it and hid it from the occupiers. Stephen had no recollection of what happened to the Studebaker. I had to choose one of the tales. This still did not answer the question as to why the fishing boat escape seemed the only option. Why? I had to ask.

It was only when Stephen sent me photocopies of a few pages of a book entitled *Commodore* written by Sir James Bissett that the mystery unravelled. In chapter thirty-two,

Bissett explains what happened on 16th June 1939 off the coast of southern Brittany. He details the arrival of two British refugee ships, the *Franconia* and the *Lancastria*, at Quiberon, which is across the bay from Port Navalo. The ships were attacked and the *Franconia* hit. The *Lancastria*, undamaged, was ordered to steam on to Saint Nazaire to rescue soldiers and refugees and would have steamed right past Port Navalo. In my father's memoirs he says: "There were British ships the other side of the bay and we could see them, but with Vannes occupied we could not get there. Dad found a fishing boat in the little harbour. The skipper had decided to flee south." Running through the time-line, the mystery was suddenly resolved. The only possible escape route at that time was by fishing boat. Follow and get aboard the British refugee ship which they had seen across the bay and which had subsequently sailed right past. The dates matched and the description of what happened matched. At about 4 p.m. the next day (17th June) while anchored just off St. Nazaire taking on refugees, the *Lancastria*, under the captaincy of Scotsman Captain Rudolf Sharp, was attacked and sunk by enemy planes. Further, it also made sense that Harry did not make it onto the *Lancastria*, which is why he had to make the long journey by foot and bicycle to Lisbon. The mystery was resolved.

It was also interesting to find out that, although several thousand souls were lost that day, Captain Sharp survived the sinking and continued to serve. However, in 1942, he was commanding another vessel, the *Laconia*, off the coast of West Africa. The *Laconia*, a converted ocean liner, was torpedoed by German submarines with the loss of an estimated 1600 victims.

The brave captain, perhaps conscious of the unfounded guilt he felt over the earlier loss of the *Lancastria*, reportedly ensured the women and children were placed in lifeboats, then walked to his cabin, locked the door and went down with the ship.

In late April 2012, Uncle Stephen was taken ill and I flew out to Australia to visit. I met up with my two brothers in Busselton. He passed away on 3rd May. My only real source of information had now gone. The only real memory he seemed to have about his family was a black and white picture of his mother which hung in his bedroom. Other than that, there was little evidence of his family in his home. He died a bachelor, so no family of his own either. I returned to England.

When I got back home I decided to post a blog on-line: "Looking for Albertine Barker, wife of Harry Alfred Barker. Died in Belgium. Approximate date of death 1934."

Seven months later, on 2nd November, I received an email from a genealogist in Belgium by the name of Georges Close. He was a retired man with a general interest in genealogy. Attached to his email was the death certificate of one Albertine Barker, wife of Harry Alfred Barker, domiciled at Worplesdon Farm, Guildford. Surrey. Angleterre. I was stunned!

Albertine had passed away in a town called Spa, well known then as a place for recuperation and well-being with a large Baths building. The town is still well known for its natural springs and health spas, as well as the venue of the Belgian Grand Prix. The next email was accompanied by a picture of the house in which they lived back in 1933, along with another showing the house today. Unbelievable!

The house in Spa in the 1930s and today.

My father's handwriting had been transcribed as Sfra instead of Spa. It was a great breakthrough, but sadly Stephen was never to know where his mother was laid. A trip to Spa was another journey to be made.

I continued to write and was now able to describe where Harry and Albertine had lived before she passed away. I knew that Harry had moved back to Brussels after Albertine had died. My father had described life in Brussels before Hitler invaded Belgium and, together with research on the build-up to the war years, I was able to describe their lifestyle with reasonable accuracy, together with some of the things they did and the people they befriended.

He went on to describe how Harry suddenly decided to make a run for it. How they were loaded up into the car at very short notice with Monique, the neighbours' daughter, and Madame Briffaud (Jeanne). How they were strafed by German fighters and the route they took along the northern French coastline, trying to get across the channel and finally ending up in Port Navalo.

He continued on to describe the momentous moment on the quayside when Harry had to make "the most difficult decision of his life…"

He wrote about their return journey to Brussels from Port Navalo and life in Brussels during the occupation by the Germans: his feelings for the people who wore the yellow star and the shooting of a young boy at the railway station.

The main entrance to Maredsous School.

My father was then sent to Maredsous. He described his time at a Benedictine Monastery in the Ardennes, how he struggled and was very unhappy. He said that it was here that he missed his mother most and how he had almost decided to become a monk. I needed to know more about this place.

I looked up Maredsous on the internet and, sure enough, there it was. A school and major visitor centre. The monastery

Maredsous Abbey.

had grown over the years and was still a school with large grounds, but now it has a sizeable visitor centre. They had become famous for their beer-making, exporting all over the world. This was not an activity in which the monastery participated when my father was there, but I was pleased to know I could go and see it.

I sent an email to the school and was referred to Father Éloi Merry, who confirmed that Paul Barker had indeed been a pupil at the school and his tutor had been Père Marc Mélot. I contacted the visitor centre and arranged a private tour. My wife and I set off once more.

The door where Paul first entered Maredsous and the quadrangle.

We were greeted by a retired teacher by the name of Christian Mattelart, who showed us round the school and grounds that Paul had attended. It was just as my father had described. We saw the metal grille upon which the pupils had been forced to kneel as punishment: the huge church, bell tower and the fields in which he had played. Christian told of how, when he arrived as a teacher for his first day, some 30 years ago, he saw two boys running around the perimeter of the snow-covered quadrangle bare-footed. This was a punishment. He said that it was time for change and from that day on such practices were forbidden.

He showed us the refectory and the wooden chair-like desk where a monk would sit and read Latin during mealtimes. He told us about how the Germans would come and search for British airmen and how on one occasion they took six monks instead. Only three returned. He also told us that at the time my father was there the school was only for pupils of senior politicians, royals and the very wealthy. I have never really found out how my father gained entry. That remains a mystery.

The wooden chair-like desk

He confirmed the story of the bells, but with a slightly different detail. The bells were taken to Hamburg and found after the war. The story of the interception by the Resistance and the bells being thrown into the River Meuse was not entirely true. It was the story my father had told and he wrote of in his memoirs. I preferred my father's story!

Paul standing to the right of tutor, Père Marc Mélot and his class of 1943.

I was also able to confirm that André van Roleglen was at the school and was his best friend. Christian was unable to verify the story about his friend's father bailing out of a British bomber. It was what my father wrote and I have no reason to doubt it. He described this incident as "The meeting of father and son must be one of the greatest coincidences of all time!"

It was a fascinating tour and I was able to get a great feeling for the place and what it must have been like. Just a few days after our return home, Christian Mattelart had been in touch with the archives at the school, who sent through several photographs taken of my father whilst he had attended the school. These are the only pictures we have of my father at this age and during these years whilst he and his brother were in Belgium.

From Maredsous we travelled across Belgium to the town of Spa. We had the address of where they had lived when